How to Prepare for the National Teacher Examinations

Revised Edition

Albertina Abrams Weinlander
Professor of Education
Wittenberg University

Barron's Educational Series, Inc.
Woodbury, New York

The author wishes to express her thanks to
the Educational Testing Service for information
on the National Teacher Examinations.
The author is grateful to Dr. Max M.
Weinlander for his encouragement and to
Cynthia Painter and Julia E. Frye who typed
the manuscript.

© Copyright 1971 by Barron's Educational Series, Inc.

Prior editions © Copyright 1968 by Barron's Educational Series, Inc.

All rights reserved.
No part of this book may be reproduced
in any form, by photostat, microfilm, xerography,
or any other means, or incorporated into any
information retrieval system, electronic or
mechanical, without the written permission
of the copyright owner.

All inquiries should be addressed to:
Barron's Educational Series, Inc.
113 Crossways Park Drive
Woodbury, New York 11797

Library of Congress Catalog Card No. 68-56408

International Standard Book No. 0-8120-0352-7

PRINTED IN THE UNITED STATES OF AMERICA
6 7 8 9 10 11 M 9 8 7 6

Contents

Introduction, 1

The National Teacher Examinations, 1
Locations Used as Test Centers, 8

Part 1

Professional Education Examination of the Common Examination, 13
Practice Test 1, 14
Practice Test 2, 48
Answers, 80
Self-Rating Practice Test Chart, 82

Part 2

General Education Examination of the Common Examination, 85
General Education Examination, 86
Practice Test 1 Social Studies, Literature, Fine Arts, 86
Practice Test 2 Social Studies, Literature, Fine Arts, 96
Practice Test 3 Social Studies, Literature, Fine Arts, 106
Practice Test 1 Science and Mathematics, 116
Practice Test 2 Science and Mathematics, 120
Practice Test 3 Science and Mathematics, 123
Practice Test 1 Written English Expression, 127
   Part I, 127
   Part II, 130
Practice Test 2 Written English Expression, 135
   Part I, 135
   Part II, 137
Answers, 143
Self-Rating Practice Test Chart, 82

Contents

Part 3

Additional Aids to Review and Study, 147
Psychological Foundations of Education, 148
Societal Foundations of Education, 151
Teaching Principles and Practices, 152
Bibliographies, 154
Famous Writers, 165
Topics in Music, 172
Topics for Review in Art, 178
English Grammar and Usage Practice 1, 181
English Grammar and Usage Practice 2, 184
Self-Rating Practice Test Chart, 82

Part 4

Teaching Area Examinations, Sample Questions, 187
Art Education, 188
Biology and General Science, 191
Business Education, 195
Chemistry, Physics, and General Science, 199
Early Childhood Education, 203
Education in the Elementary School, 206
English Language and Literature, 210
Home Economics Education, 214
Industrial Arts Education, 218
Mathematics, 221
Music Education, 225
Physical Education, 229
Social Studies, 232
Self-Rating Practice Test Chart, 82

Introduction

The National Teacher Examinations

Introduction

Since 1950, the Educational Testing Service has administered the National Teacher Examinations. In the past, the examinations have been given four times a year on Saturdays. Special arrangements are made for students whose religious convictions prevent testing on Saturday.

Preparing For the Examination

Copies of previous National Teacher Examinations are *not* available. The emphasis in the professional and area examinations is on the application of knowledge. Therefore, there is little value in cramming for this type of examination. However, a review of course notes, keeping in mind the practical application, may aid in clarifying and directing thinking. The sample Practice Tests should aid the student in becoming more self-assured with the multiple-choice type of question. Although several answers might be considered in certain specific instances as correct, the best answer must be selected on the basis of its applicability to classrooms and schools as indicated in the statement.

Care must be taken when reading the directions. Work as rapidly as you can. You will not finish the test if you spend too much time cogitating on the difficult questions. Come back to these questions later. Very few candidates finish the entire test.

This study guide, HOW TO PREPARE FOR THE NATIONAL TEACHER EXAMINATIONS was written to assist prospective teachers and teachers in the field who plan to take either the Common Examination or both the Common Examination and a Teaching Area Examination. The NTE evaluates both professional knowledge and the ability of the student to apply teaching techniques and methods in classroom situations. It is helpful to check certain ideas and concepts that are used in the Practice Tests. Such ideas and concepts are basic to professional knowledge so that you will be better able to ascertain areas of weakness in knowledge and experience. In recent years methodology has changed in the teaching of modern languages, mathematics, and the sciences. Currently, the fields of social studies and English are being changed in content and emphasis.

This guide will be helpful to you through the practice tests, self-rating check sheets, a diagnosis of weaknesses, and the planning of a study schedule based upon the selected references in the back of the study guide. Information regarding state requirements, testing centers, costs, and changes in examination content is given. Complete information can be obtained from one of the testing centers or by writing directly to: National Teacher Examinations, Educational Testing Service, Box 911, Princeton, New Jersey 08540.

Students are informed by their colleges of NTE requirements. The NTE publication, THE NATIONAL TEACHER EXAMINATIONS: SCORE USERS, lists the state and local school systems known by the Educational Testing Service to use NTE scores in teacher certification, and for the selection of grants-in-aid.

An Overview of Test Types

THE PROFESSIONAL EDUCATION TEST

The content of this test has been structured around the various roles of the elementary and secondary teacher. The candidate's knowledge and understanding of five roles is measured:

The first role concerns the teacher as an agent of the society in which he works and lives. Test questions measure basic knowledge and understanding relating to the historical and philosophical development of public education.

INTRODUCTION

The second role involves the school curriculum and the organization of instructional techniques. The learner, principles of learning, the use of educational media, and the impact of socio-cultural factors upon the learner are tested.

The third role measures the teacher as the catalyst in the social learning situation as the individual acts as a learner and group member.

In the fourth role, the teacher mediates learning and instruction and helps pupils develop concepts and intellectual skills through the application of the psychological procedures.

Last, in the fifth role, the teacher utilizes tests of various types to evaluate learning and pupil progress and to report the results through elementary statistical concepts.

Sample question

DIRECTIONS: Each of the questions or incomplete statements below is followed by five suggested answers or completions. Select the one which is best in each case.

1. The fundamental control of the public schools in the United States rests with
    (A) the parents (B) the public (C) the teachers
    (D) school administrators (E) local boards of education

    1. A ■ C D E

WRITTEN ENGLISH EXPRESSION

The Written English Expression Test stresses the application of standard written English in problems of writing. The candidate is not required to use formal terminology.

Sample question

PART 1

DIRECTIONS: In each of the sentences below four portions are underlined and lettered. Read each sentence and decide whether any of the underlined parts contains a grammatical construction, a word use, or an instance of incorrect or omitted punctuation which would be inappropriate for carefully written English. If so, note the letter printed beneath the underlined portion and blacken the corresponding space on the answer sheet.

If there are no errors in any of the underlined portions, blacken space E. No sentence has more than one error.

1. He spoke <u>curt</u> and <u>quietly</u> to <u>us</u> <u>visitors</u>. <u>No error</u>.
           A   B   C   D   E

    1. ■ B C D E

PART 2

DIRECTIONS: In each of the following sentences some part of the sentence or the entire sentence is underlined. The underlined part presents a problem in the appropriate use of language. Beneath each sentence you will find five ways of writing the underlined part. The first of these repeats the original, but the other four are all different. If you think the original sentence is better than any of the suggested changes, you should choose answer A; otherwise you should mark one of the other choices. Select the best answer and blacken the corresponding space on the answer sheet. This is a test of the correctness and effectiveness of expression. In choosing answers, follow the requirements of standard written English; that is, pay attention to acceptable usage in grammar, diction (choice of words), sentence construction, and punctuation. Choose the answer that produces the most effective sentence — clear and exact, without awkwardness or ambiguity. Do not make a choice that changes the meaning of the original sentence.

1. <u>While standing</u> at the station, the train left, and we watched it disappear around the bend.
    (A) While standing (B) Standing (C) As we were standing
    (D) While we were standing (E) During standing

    1. A B ■ D E

THE NATIONAL TEACHER EXAMINATIONS

SOCIAL STUDIES, LITERATURE, AND THE FINE ARTS

The questions in Social Studies, Literature, and the Fine Arts sample a general background in history, the social sciences, literature, and the fine arts which might be obtained from survey courses and the information presented in magazines, newspapers, and other media. Both Western and non-Western information is represented, but the majority of questions pertain to the Western world.

Social Studies: The social studies questions are drawn from the fields of American history, world history, geography, government, economics, and sociology.

Literature and the Fine Arts: The literature samples are taken from American, English, and world literature, and classical mythology.

The music questions test the candidate's knowledge of music forms, terms, and musical instruments, important composers, musical works, and performing artists. Significant music from Renaissance to current popular forms might also be on the test.

The art questions relate to the works of well-known artists of a particular period or culture which the candidate might be asked to identify. Certain concepts basic to architecture, painting, photography, and sculpture will also be represented in the questions.

SCIENCE AND MATHEMATICS

Science: The science questions will be drawn from biology, chemistry, physics, earth and space sciences.

The biology questions relate to cell biology, nutrition, photosynthesis, infection and disease, human physiology, genetics, and the properties of plants and animals.

Chemistry questions might be drawn from acids and bases, colutions, chemical bonding, the rate and yield of chemical reactions, and properties of the elements and compounds.

Concepts and principles relating to velocity, force, gravitation, wave properties, acceleration, simple machines, gases, atomic energy, forms of energy and their conversion, and electricity and magnetism are used on the physics part of the science test.

Questions about air pollution, the solar system, space exploration, the structure of the earth, erosion and weathering, rocks and minerals, and weather and climate are some of the topics from earth and space science.

Mathematics: Three types of questions are included in this test whose major content areas deal with number systems and related operations, denominate numbers and measurement, geometry and mensuration, graphs and data, formulas and their evaluation, and modern concepts and techniques.

COST OF EXAMINATIONS

Although fees are subject to change, the 1971 fees are as follows:

TEST FEES:

Common Examinations only	$10.00
Common Examinations and one Teaching Area Examination	15.00
Teaching Area Examination only	9.00

SPECIAL SERVICE FEES:

Each score report over three requested on your Registration Form	$ 1.00
Score reports requested after registering	
a) First college or school system named to receive a report of your scores	$ 2.00
b) Each additional score report requested at the same time	1.00
Test and/or center change (plus test fee if additional test is requested)	3.00
Test date transfer with or without test or center change (plus test fee if additional test is requested)	5.00
Late registration (in addition to regular registration fee)	3.00

INTRODUCTION

WHICH EXAMINATIONS SHOULD YOU TAKE?

THE COMMON EXAMINATIONS attempt to appraise the prospective teacher's background in professional and general education.

THE PROFESSIONAL EDUCATION section of the Common Examination measures the following areas: (morning session)

> Psychological Foundations of Education
> Societal Foundations of Education
> Teaching Principles and Practices

THE GENERAL EDUCATION section of the Common Examination measures the student's background in the following areas:

> Social Studies
> Literature and Fine Arts
> Science and Mathematics
> Written English Expression

THE TEACHING AREA EXAMINATIONS, each of which requires 120 minutes testing time, measure the student's knowledge of subject matter and the application of teaching methods in the following areas: (afternoon session)

> Art Education
> Audiology
> Biology and General Science
> Business Education
> Chemistry, Physics, and General Science
> Early Childhood Education (Below grade 4)
> Education in the Elementary School (Grades 1-8)*
> Education of Mentally Retarded
> Education in an Urban Setting
> English Language and Literature
> French
> German
> Home Economics Education
> Industrial Arts Education
> Mathematics
> Media Specialist — Library and Audio-Visual Services
> Men's Physical Education
> Music Education
> Reading Specialist — Elementary School
> Social Studies
> Spanish
> Speech-Communication and Theatre
> Speech Pathology
> Women's Physical Education

Those candidates who have completed special studies in the teaching of reading at the elementary level may take the *Reading Specialist — Elementary School* examination. Those who intend to teach only below the fourth grade level should take the *Early Childhood Education* examination. Those who may teach any of the first eight grades should take the *Education in the Elementary School* examination. Secondary education majors should take the area examination in their major subject.

If you are in doubt which NTE examination to take, write to the department of education, school system, graduate school or college to which you plan to send your test scores. Two states, at the present time, require the NTE for certification. If you plan to teach in Georgia or South Carolina write for information to the following addresses:

Georgia:

> Georgia Department of Education-Grants
> 230 State Office Building
> Atlanta, Georgia 30334

*See Barron's *How to Prepare for the NTE Area Examination: Education in the Elementary School (1-8).*

THE NATIONAL TEACHER EXAMINATION

Additional tests administered for certification in Georgia:

    Agriculture
    Administration and Supervision
    Guidance Counselor
    Latin
    School Psychology
    Teaching Hearing Handicapped
    Teaching Orthopedically Handicapped
    Teaching Visually Handicapped
    Trade and Industrial Education
    Visiting Teacher

South Carolina:

    Director of Teacher Examinations
    State Department of Education
    Box 11507
    Columbia, South Carolina 29211

Additional tests administered for certification in South Carolina:

    Agriculture
    Latin
    Teaching Hearing Handicapped
    Teaching Orthopedically Handicapped
    Teaching Visually Handicapped

Candidates for teaching certificates in South Carolina must take the NTE in a center in this state.

REMINDER:

Take the following items to the test center:

1) your admission ticket
2) three or four sharpened No. 2 pencils
3) an eraser that does not smudge (no pencils or erasers will be provided at the test center)
4) positive identification (your student identification card, driver's license, or social security card)
5) a watch, to pace yourself during the examinations

Do *not* take books, slide rules, protractors, rulers, or papers of any kind. You may do scratch work in the blank spaces of your test book.

Lunch facilities near the test center may be inadequate or closed on Saturday. You may wish to take your lunch as a precautionary measure.

Handicapped Candidates

Anyone with a physical handicap, such as blindness, should request special testing arrangements. Write to: Director, National Teacher Examinations, Educational Testing Service, Box 911, Princeton, New Jersey 08540. Enclose a physician's report which verifies your handicap. Specify the state department or school system to which your examination scores should be sent. If your handicap qualifies you for special testing, instructions will be provided for registering and taking the examinations.

Registration Form

Sample Registration Forms are available from the Educational Testing Service. Request the Bulletin of Information for Candidates on the National Teacher Examination. Note carefully the registration dates, late registration dates, fees, score report address, mailing Registration Form, and testing centers.

INTRODUCTION

Taking the Examination

Care must be taken when reading the directions. Work as rapidly as you can. You will not finish the test if you spend too much time cogitating on the difficult questions. Come back to these questions later. Very few candidates finish the entire test.

There are penalties for guessing on this test as the wrong answers are subtracted from the right answers. However, if you feel that you can eliminate several of the answers as wrong, answer the question, since you may be able to determine the *best* answer from the few choices left.

Allow the following time for taking the examination at the testing center to which you are assigned:
    8:30 a.m. Report to test center for Common Examinations
    12:25 p.m. Approximate end of Common Examinations
Candidates may not begin or end the examinations at any time other than the time that is scheduled.
    1:30 p.m. Teaching Area Examination
    4:15 p.m. Appromixate end of Teaching Area Examination
Be sure to check whether the time used at the testing center is standard time or daylight saving time.

The NTE Scores

There are four tests in the Common Examination battery. A scaled score for each test is obtained as well as two Weighted Subtotal Scores — one for Professional Education and another for General Education. A Weighted Common Examination Total Score is also reported. The Advisory Part Scores are reported for: a) Psychological Foundations of Education, b) Societal Foundations of Education, c) Teaching Principles and Practices, d) Social Studies, e) Literature and Fine Arts, f) Science, and g) Mathematics.

The separate tests receive the following weights:
Professional Education 3.9

General Education
    Written English Expression 1.1
    Social Studies, Literature, and Fine Arts 2.5
    Science and Mathematics 2.5

Minimum score standards may be set by state departments, colleges, or school systems, although the Educational Testing Service sets no passing or failing standards. At least six weeks usually lapses between the testing date and the reporting of examination scores which are sent to you with interpretative information.

Number of Items and Working Time for the NTE Tests

NTE Tests	Number of Items	Time
I. Common Examinations		
A. Professional Education Test	110	90 minutes
B. General Education Tests		
1. Written English Expression	45	30 minutes
2. Social Studies, Literature, and Fine Arts	65	40 minutes
3. Science and Mathematics	50	35 minutes
General Education Total	160	1 hour and 45 minutes
Common Examinations Total	270	3 hours and 15 minutes

THE NATIONAL TEACHER EXAMINATIONS

II. Teaching Area Examinations

Code	Test		
01	Education in the Elementary School	145	
02	Early Childhood Education	145	
03	Biology and General Science	160	
04	English Language and Literature	145	
05	Industrial Arts Education	145	
06	Mathematics	120	
07	Chemistry, Physics, and General Science	150	
08	Social Studies	150	
10	Business Education	160	Each Test:
11	Music Education	150	120 minutes
12	Home Economics Education	145	
13	Art Education	145	
14	Men's Physical Education	150	
15	Women's Physical Education	150	
16	Speech-Communication and Theatre	150	
30	Reading Specialist - Elementary School	145	
31	Media Specialist - Library and Audio-Visual Services	150	

Locations Used As Test Centers

Alabama

Auburn, Auburn University
Birmingham, Birmingham-Southern College
Birmingham, Miles College
Birmingham, Samford University
Florence, Florence State University
Gadsden, University of Alabama
Huntsville, University of Alabama
Jacksonville, Jacksonville State University
Livingston, Livingston University
Marion, Judson College
Mobile, Mobile College
Mobile, Spring Hill College
Mobile, University of South Alabama
Montevallo, University of Montevallo
Montgomery, Alabama State University
Montgomery, Huntingdon College
Normal, Alabama A. & M. College
St. Bernard, St. Bernard College
Troy, Troy State University
Tuscaloosa, Stillman College
Tuskegee, Tuskegee Institute
University, University of Alabama

Alaska

Anchorage, Anchorage Community College
College, University of Alaska

Arizona

Tempe, Arizona State University
Tucson, University of Arizona

Arkansas

Arkadelphia, Henderson State College
Batesville, Arkansas College
College Heights, Arkansas A. & M. College
Conway, State College of Arkansas
Fayetteville, University of Arkansas
Little Rock, Philander Smith College
Little Rock, University of Arkansas
Magnolia, Southern State College
Pine Bluff, Arkansas A. M. & N. College
Russellville, Arkansas Polytechnic College
Searcy, Harding College
State University, Arkansas State University

California

Arcata, Humboldt State College
Bakersfield, Bakersfield College
Berkeley, University of California
Calexico, San Diego State College—Imperial Valley Campus
Chico, Chico State College
Costa Mesa, Southern California College
Fresno, Fresno State College
Fullerton, California State College
Long Beach, California State College
Los Angeles, Occidental College
Los Angeles, University of California
Los Angeles, University of Southern California
Redlands, University of Redlands
Riverside, University of California
Rohnert Park, Sonoma State College
Sacramento, Sacramento State College
San Diego, San Diego State College
San Francisco, San Francisco State College
San Francisco, University of San Francisco
San Jose, San Jose State College
San Luis Obispo, California State Polytechnic College
Santa Barbara, Westmont College
Stanford, Stanford University
Stockton, University of the Pacific
Turlock, Stanislaus State College
Ukiah, Mendocino Schools

Colorado

Boulder, University of Colorado
Colorado Springs, Colorado College
Durango, Fort Lewis College

Connecticut

New Britain, Central Connecticut State College
New Haven, Southern Connecticut State College
Storrs, University of Connecticut
Woodstock, Annhurst College

Delaware

Dover, Delaware State College
Dover, Delaware State Department of Public Instruction
Newark, University of Delaware

District of Columbia

Washington, Georgetown University
Washington, George Washington University
Washington, Howard University
Washington, Trinity College

Florida

DeLand, Stetson University
Gainesville, University of Florida
Jacksonville, Samuel Wolfson High School
Lakeland, Florida Southern College
Lake Worth, Palm Beach Junior College
Miami, Allapattah Junior High School
Miami, University of Miami
Orlando, County School Administration Building

LOCATIONS USED AS TEST CENTERS

Pensacola, Pensacola Junior College
St. Augustine, St. Augustine High School
Tallahassee, Florida A. & M. University
Tallahassee, Florida State University
Tampa, University of South Florida
Tampa, University of Tampa

Georgia

Albany, Albany State College
Americus, Georgia Southwestern College
Athens, University of Georgia
Atlanta, Atlanta University
Atlanta, Clark College
Atlanta, Emory University
Atlanta, Georgia State University
Augusta, Augusta College
Augusta, Paine College
Brunswick, Brunswick Junior College
Carrollton, West Georgia College
Clarkston, DeKalb Junior College
Columbus, Columbus College
Dahlonega, North Georgia College
Demorest, Piedmont College
Douglas, South Georgia College
Fort Valley, Fort Valley State College
Gainesville, Gainesville Junior College
LaGrange, LaGrange College
Macon, Mercer University
Milledgeville, Georgia College
Mount Berry, Berry College
Rome, Shorter College
Savannah, Armstrong State College
Savannah, Savannah State College
Statesboro, Georgia Southern College
Valdosta, Valdosta State College

Hawaii

Hilo, University of Hawaii
Honolulu, University of Hawaii

Illinois

Bloomington, Illinois Wesleyan University
Carbondale, Southern Illinois University
Champaign, University of Illinois
Charleston, Eastern Illinois University
Chicago, Chicago State College
Chicago, DePaul University
Chicago, Loyola University
Chicago, Northeastern Illinois State College
Chicago, Roosevelt University
Chicago, University of Illinois at Chicago Circle
Decatur, Millikin University
DeKalb, Northern Illinois University
Evanston, Northwestern University
Galesburg, Knox College
Jacksonville, MacMurray College
Normal, Illinois State University
River Forest, Concordia Teachers College
Wheaton, Wheaton College

Indiana

Bloomington, Indiana University
Evansville, University of Evansville
Fort Wayne, Indiana University
Greencastle, DePauw University
Indianapolis, Butler University

Lafayette, Purdue University
Muncie, Ball State University
Notre Dame, University of Notre Dame
Rensselaer, Saint Joseph's College
Terre Haute, Indiana State University

Iowa

Ames, Iowa State University
Decorah, Luther College
Des Moines, Drake University
Dubuque, University of Dubuque
Iowa City, University of Iowa

Kansas

Manhattan, Kansas State University
Topeka, Washburn University
Wichita, Wichita State University

Kentucky

Berea, Berea College
Bowling Green, Western Kentucky University
Campbellsville, Campbellsville College
Georgetown, Georgetown College
Lexington, University of Kentucky
Louisville, University of Louisville
Morehead, Morehead State University
Murray, Murray State University
Owensboro, Kentucky Wesleyan College

Louisiana

Baton Rouge, Louisiana State University
Baton Rouge, Southern University
Benton, Bossier Parish School Board
Grambling, Grambling College
Hammond, Southeastern Louisiana College
Lafayette, University of Southwestern Louisiana
Lake Charles, McNeese State College
Minden, Webster Parish School
Monroe, Northeast Louisiana State College
Natchitoches, Northwestern State College of Louisiana
New Orleans, Dillard University
New Orleans, Louisiana State University
New Orleans, Loyola University
New Orleans, Saint Mary's Dominican College
New Orleans, Tulane University
New Orleans, Xavier University
Pineville, Louisiana College
Ruston, Louisiana Polytechnic Institute
Shreveport, Centenary College
Thibodaux, Nicholls State College

Maine

Gorham, Gorham State College
Houlton, Ricker College
Orono, University of Maine

Maryland

Bowie, State College
College Park, University of Maryland
Frederick, Hood College
Frostburg, State College
Salisbury, State College
Towson, Goucher College

INTRODUCTION

Towson, State College
Westminster, Western Maryland College

Massachusetts

Amherst, University of Massachusetts
Boston, Boston University
Boston, Northeastern University
Boston, Simmons College
Boston, State College
Boston, University of Massachusetts
Bridgewater, State College
Cambridge, Lesley College
Chestnut Hill, Boston College
Fall River, Fall River Public Schools
Fitchburg, State College
Framingham, State College
Lowell, State College
North Adams, State College
Pittsfield, Pittsfield Public Schools
Salem, State College
Westfield, State College
Worcester, Clark University

Michigan

Dearborn, University of Michigan
Detroit, University of Detroit
Detroit, Wayne State University
East Lansing, Michigan State University
Kalamazoo, Western Michigan University
Ypsilanti, Eastern Michigan University

Minnesota

Minneapolis, University of Minnesota
Northfield, Carelton College
Saint Paul, Concordia College
Saint Peter, Gustavus Adolphus College
Winona, College of Saint Teresa

Mississippi

Blue Mountain, Blue Mountain College
Cleveland, Delta State College
Clinton, Mississippi College
Columbus, Mississippi State College for Women
Hattiesburg, University of Southern Mississippi
Holly Springs, Rust College
Itta Bena, Mississippi Valley State College
Jackson, Belhaven College
Jackson, State College
Jackson, Millsaps College
Lorman, Alcorn A. & M. College
McComb, McComb Public Schools
Natchez, Natchez-Adams High School
State College, Mississippi State University
Tougaloo, Tougaloo College
University (Oxford), University of Mississippi

Missouri

Cape Girardeau, Southeast Missouri State College
Columbia, University of Missouri
Jefferson City, Lincoln University
Joplin, Missouri Southern College
Kansas City, University of Missouri
Kirksville, Northeast Missouri State College
Saint Louis, Harris Teachers College
Saint Louis, Saint Louis University

Saint Louis, Washington University
Springfield, Southwest Missouri State College

Montana

Bozeman, Montana Saint University

Nebraska

Lincoln, University of Nebraska
Omaha, Creighton University
Peru, Peru State College
Scottsbluff, Hiram Scott College
Seward, Concordia Teachers College
Wayne, Wayne State College

Nevada

Reno, University of Nevada

New Hampshire

Durham, University of New Hampshire
Keene, Keene State College
Manchester, Saint Anselm's College
Plymouth, State College

New Jersey

Glassboro, State College
Newark, Newark Public Schools
New Brunswick, Rutgers—The State University
Rutherford, Fairleigh Dickinson University
South Orange, Seton Hall University
Trenton, State College
Union, Newark State College
Upper Montclair, State College

New Mexico

Albuquerque, University of Albuquerque
Albuquerque, University of New Mexico
Las Cruces, New Mexico State University

New York

Albany, SUNY at Albany
Buffalo, Buffalo Public Schools
Buffalo, SUNY at Buffalo
Cortland, State University College
Dobbs Ferry, Mercy College
Hamilton, Colgate University
Hempstead, Hofstra University
Ithaca, Cornell University
New York, Fordham University
New York, N. Y. U. (Washington Square)
New York, Teachers College, Columbia University
Potsdam, State Unviersity College
Rochester, University of Rochester
Saint Bonaventure, Saint Bonaventure University
Staten Island, Wagner College
Syracuse, Syracuse University
Tarrytown, Marymount College

North Carolina

Asheville, Asheville City Schools
Boone, Appalachian State University
Buie's Creek, Campbell College
Chapel Hill, University of North Carolina

LOCATIONS USED AS TEST CENTERS

Charlotte, Charlotte–Mecklenburg Board of Education
Cullowhee, Western Carolina University
Durham, Duke University
Durham, North Carolina Central University
Elizabeth City, Elizabeth City–Pasquotank Schools
Fayetteville, Terry Sanford Senior High School
Greensboro, North Carolina A. & T. State University
Greensboro, University of North Carolina
Greenville, East Carolina University
Hickory, Lenoir Rhyne College
High Point, High Point City Schools
Mars Hill, Mars Hill College
New Bern, New Bern High School
Raleigh, William Enloe High School
Salisbury, Catawba College
Wilmington, University of North Carolina
Wilson, Wilson City Schools
Winston-Salem, Winston-Salem City Schools

North Dakota

Grand Forks, University of North Dakota
Minot, Minot State College

Ohio

Athens, Ohio University
Berea, Baldwin-Wallace College
Bowling Green, Bowling Green State University
Cincinnati, University of Cincinnati
Cleveland, John Carroll University
Columbus, Ohio State University
Dayton, University of Dayton
Kent, Kent State University
Oxford, Miami University
Springfield, Wittenberg University
Steubenville, College of Steubenville
Toledo, University of Toledo

Oklahoma

Ada, East Central State College
Chickasha, Oklahoma College of Liberal Arts
Durant, Southeastern State College
Enid, Phillips University
Goodwell, Panhandle State College
Langston, Langston University
Norman, University of Oklahoma
Oklahoma City, Oklahoma City University
Shawnee, Oklahoma Baptist University
Stillwater, Oklahoma State University
Tahlequah, Northeastern State College
Tulsa, University of Tulsa
Weatherford, Southwestern State College

Oregon

Ashland, Southern Oregon College
Portland, Portland State University

Pennsylvania

Allentown, Muhlenberg College
Beaver Falls, Geneva College
Bethlehem, Lehigh University
Bloomsburg, Bloomsburg State College
California, State College
Cheyney, State College
Clarion, State College
Dallas, College Misericordia

East Stroudsburg, State College
Edinboro, State College
Erie, Gannon College
Erie, Mercyhurst College
Erie, Villa Maria College
Gettysburg, Gettysburg College
Grove City, Grove City College
Gwynedd Valley, Gwynedd-Mercy College
Immaculata, Immaculata College
Indiana, Indiana University of Pennsylvania
Lewisburg, Bucknell University
Mansfield, State College
Millersville, State College
New Wilmington, Westminster College
Philadelphia, South Philadelphia High School
Philadelphia, Temple University
Philadelphia, University of Pennsylvania
Pittsburgh, Carnegie–Mellon University
Pittsburgh, Duquesne University
Pittsburgh, Pittsburgh Public Schools
Pittsburgh, University of Pittsburgh
Scranton, Marywood College
Scranton, Scranton Public Schools
Shippensburg, State College
Slippery Rock, State College
University Park, Pennsylvania State University
West Chester, State College
Wilkes-Barre, Wilkes College

Puerto Rico

Rio Piedras, University of Puerto Rico

Rhode Island

Barrington, Barrington College
Providence, Providence Public Schools

South Carolina

Aiken, Aiken Senior High School
Charleston, Bonds–Wilson High School
Charleston, Chicora High School
Clemson, Clemson University
Columbia, C. A. Johnson High School
Columbia, Hand Junior High School
Conway, Conway Senior High School
Dillon, Dillon Junior High School
Due West, Dixie High School
Florence, McClenaghan Senior High School
Gaffney, B. D. Lee Elementary School
Georgetown, Winyah Junior High School
Greenville, Greenville Senior High School
Greenwood, Northside Junior High School
Hartsville, Hartsville Senior High School
Kingstree, Kingstree Senior High School
Newberry, Newberry College
Orangeburg, Orangeburg High School
Rock Hill, Winthrop College
Spartanburg, Spartanburg Senior High School
Sumter, Sumter Senior High School
Walterboro, Walterboro Senior High School

South Dakota

Mitchell, Dakota Wesleyan University
Spearfish, Black Hills State College
Yankton, Mount Marty College

INTRODUCTION

Tennessee

Athens, Tennessee Wesleyan College
Chattanooga, University of Tennessee
Clarksville, Austin Peay State University
Cleveland, Lee College
Cookeville, Tennessee Technological University
Greeneville, Tusculum College
Jackson, Union University
Jefferson City, Carson-Newman College
Johnson City, East Tennessee State University
Knoxville, University of Tennessee
Martin, University of Tennessee
Maryville, Maryville College
McKenzie, Bethel College
Memphis, Le Moyne-Owen College
Memphis, Memphis State University
Memphis, Southwestern at Memphis
Milligan College, Milligan College
Murfreesboro, Middle Tennessee State University
Nashville, Fisk University
Nashville, George Peabody College
Nashville, Vanderbilt University

Texas

Abilene, Abilene Christian College
Abilene, Hardin-Simmons University
Abilene, McMurry College
Alpine, Sul Ross State University
Arlington, University of Texas
Austin, Saint Edward's University
Austin, University of Texas
Beaumont, Lamar State College
Belton, Mary Hardin-Baylor College
Big Spring, Howard County Junior College
Brownwood, Howard Payne College
Canyon, West Texas State University
College Station, Texas A&M University
Commerce, East Texas State University
Corpus Christi, Del Mar College
Corpus Christi, University of Corpus Christi
Dallas, Bishop College
Dallas, Dallas Baptist College
Dallas, Southern Methodist University
Denton, North Texas State University
Denton, Texas Woman's University
Edinburg, Pan American College
El Paso, University of Texas
Fort Worth, Texas Christian University
Fort Worth, Texas Wesleyan College
Georgetown, Southwestern University
Hawkins, Jarvis Christian College
Houston, Houston Baptist College
Houston, Rice University
Houston, Texas Southern University
Houston, University of Houston
Huntsville, Sam Houston State University
Kingsville, Texas A. & I. University
Lubbock, Texas Technical Univesity
Marshall, East Texas Baptist College
Marshall, Wiley College
Nacogdoches, Stephen F. Austin State University
Plainview, Wayland Baptist College
Prairie View, Prairie View A. & M. College
San Angelo, Angelo State University
San Antonio, Incarnate Word College
San Antonio, Our Lady of the Lake College
San Antonio, Saint Mary's University
San Antonio, Trinity University
San Marcos, Southwest Texas State University
Sequin, Texas Lutheran College
Sherman, Austin College
Stephenville, Tarleton State College
Tyler, Texas College
Victoria, Victoria College
Waco, Bayler University
Wichita Falls, Midwestern University

Utah

Salt Lake City, University of Utah

Vermont

Burlington, University of Vermont

Virginia

Blacksburg, Virginia Polytechnic Institute
Charlottesville, University of Virginia
Danville, Stratford College
Emory, Emory & Henry College
Farmville, Longwood College
Fredericksburg, Mary Washington College of the University of Virginia
Hampton, Hampton Institute
Harrisonburg, Madison College
Lawrenceville, Saint Paul's College
Lynchburg, Lynchburg College
Lynchburg, Randolph-Macon Woman's College
Norfolk, Norfolk State College
Norfolk, Old Dominion University
Petersburg, Virginia State College
Radford, Radford College
Richmond, Virginia Commonwealth University
Richmond, Virginia Union University
Salem, Roanoke County Schools
Staunton, Mary Baldwin College
Williamsburg, College of William & Mary

Washington

Pullman, Washington State University
Seattle, Seattle Pacific College

West Virginia

Athens, Concord College
Buckhannon, West Virginia Wesleyan College
Charleston, Morris Harvey College
Fairmont, State College
Glenville, State College
Huntington, Marshall University
Institute, West Virginia State College
Montgomery, West Virginia Institute of Technology
Morgantown, West Virginia University
Shepherdstown, Shepherd College
West Liberty, State College

Wisconsin

LaCrosse, Wisconsin State University
Madison, University of Wisconsin
Milwaukee, University of Wisconsin
Oshkosh, Wisconsin State University
Whitewater, Wisconsin State University

Part 1
Professional Education Examination of the Common Examination

Psychological Foundations of Education
Societal Foundations of Education
Teaching Principles and Practices

Professional Education Examination of – Common Examination

EXPLANATION: All questions are of the multiple-choice type with five possible answers from which you are to choose the *one* you believe to be the best. There are five sample answer spaces for each question. You are to blacken the lettered space for the one answer you select.

EXAMPLE:

John Dewey was a
(A) librarian
(B) college president
(C) educator
(D) politician
(E) state superintendent of instruction

SAMPLE ANSWER
[A] [B] [■] [D] [E]

Practice Test 1

DIRECTIONS: Each of the questions or incomplete statements is followed by five suggested answers or completions. Select the one which is best.

1. Mr. A had obtained his master's degree in education. Intellectually he was very competent, but he failed in teaching because:

   (A) he did not believe in lesson plans
   (B) he gave poor explanations
   (C) he could not maintain discipline
   (D) he did not understand children
   (E) he did not like the subject which he taught

   1. [A][B][C][D][E]

2. A curriculum that will best prepare students for a changing world will

   (A) place major stress on the natural sciences
   (B) emphasize modern languages
   (C) prepare students for home and family life
   (D) stress economic efficiency
   (E) stress self-realization and adaptation to the modern world

   2. [A][B][C][D][E]

3. The values of our culture seem to be

   (A) basic to the formulation of educational objectives
   (B) too nebulous to be used in educational planning
   (C) unrelated to the lives of adolescents

COMMON EXAMINATION

    (D) of little concern to educational publishers
    (E) unrelated to pupil experience

3. [A] [B] [C] [D] [E]

4. A teacher without a professional viewpoint tends to regard team teaching as

    (A) all right for some courses but not for others
    (B) so much wasted time for the outstanding teacher
    (C) an unnecessary demand upon his personal ideas
    (D) primarily for beginning teachers
    (E) something which administrators impose upon teachers

4. [A] [B] [C] [D] [E]

5. One of the main concerns in curriculum revision should be for

    (A) directed learning processes
    (B) sequence and continuity
    (C) homogeneous grouping
    (D) long-range outcomes
    (E) the qualifications of the instructors

5. [A] [B] [C] [D] [E]

6. Curriculum includes the following:

    (A) children's experiences in all the subject matter areas
    (B) only contrived experiences in the classroom
    (C) only children's vicarious experiences
    (D) only goal-directed learnings
    (E) children's learning experiences in and out of the classroom

6. [A] [B] [C] [D] [E]

7. A pupil who is graded lower than he deserves because he does not always agree with the teacher probably would

    (A) become more creative
    (B) take a greater interest in the subject
    (C) control his undesirable behavior
    (D) begin to feel insecure in this classroom
    (E) have great respect for the teacher

7. [A] [B] [C] [D] [E]

8. The values of our culture

    (A) are easily incorporated into the educational objectives
    (B) are too abstract to be effectively applied to educational goals
    (C) can be adapted to the general education objectives
    (D) are very difficult to implement
    (E) are only useful to curriculum at the secondary levels

8. [A] [B] [C] [D] [E]

9. One of the most difficult requirements of the school curriculum is to

    (A) meet the needs of individual learners
    (B) meet the needs of the gifted
    (C) meet the needs of the slow
    (D) achieve the pupil's goals
    (E) satisfy the parents

9. [A] [B] [C] [D] [E]

PART 1: PROFESSIONAL EDUCATION EXAMINATION

10. A teacher who desires to succeed must be

    (A) a creative innovator
    (B) a strict disciplinarian
    (C) permissive with some pupils
    (D) growing in self-understanding
    (E) following the dictates of educational psychologists

11. A curriculum committee should consider pupil goals and purposes as

    (A) too immature to be considered in planning
    (B) too changeable to be useful
    (C) of slight importance for long-range planning
    (D) only significant for immediate outcomes
    (E) as relevant to content and approach

12. Educators today

    (A) differ on the goals of education
    (B) differ on teaching methods
    (C) differ on both goals and methods
    (D) agree on grouping techniques
    (E) agree on evaluation techniques

13. If Miss B. is assigned to teach a class of slow learners for which she is not qualified, you would expect her to

    (A) refuse to teach the class
    (B) point out her shortcomings and seek professional help
    (C) use the same materials which she has used successfully in other classes
    (D) resign her position
    (E) resent the assignment and do as little as possible

14. The classic tradition in education assigned a

    (A) more important place to the sciences than humanities
    (B) more important place to languages than mathematics
    (C) lesser role to physical education
    (D) lesser role to music education
    (E) high role to physical education

15. The effect of the industrial revolution is demonstrated in the objectives of

    (A) humanistic education
    (B) classical education
    (C) Rousseau's *Emile*
    (D) essentialism
    (E) the seven "Cardinal Principles of Education"

16. Miss C is a junior high school teacher of English. Several of the boys in her classes show little interest in English. In an attempt to solve this problem, Miss C probably would

COMMON EXAMINATION

    (A) increase the amount of required outside reading
    (B) decrease the number of required book reports
    (C) ignore the uninterested pupils
    (D) worry about her failure as a teacher
    (E) try to find ways to interest the boys in their language development

16. The purpose of college, according to Hutchins, is to

17. The purpose of college, according to Hutchins, is to

    (A) develop an educational aristocracy
    (B) educate all who desire to attend
    (C) prepare one for vocational competence
    (D) participate in intelligent social experiences
    (E) establish naturalistic standards

18. The purpose of subject matter, according to Dewey, is to

    (A) learn to appreciate the classics
    (B) engage in knowing rather than doing
    (C) prepare one for vocational competence
    (D) have students participate in intelligent social activities
    (E) act as little adults

19. Mr. C has been assigned to serve on a curriculum committee. His work will be primarily concerned with

    (A) the *what* of teaching
    (B) the *organization* of teaching
    (C) the *who* of teaching
    (D) the *why* of teaching
    (E) the *how* of teaching

20. Teachers and pupils participate in intelligent social experiences if they develop a curriculum which emphasizes the philosophy of

    (A) essentialism   (D) reconstructionism
    (B) progressivism   (E) classicism
    (C) perennialism

21. The teacher who believes that the main purpose of the schools is to transmit our cultural heritage is an

    (A) essentialist   (D) reconstructionist
    (B) progressivist   (E) classicist
    (C) perennialist

22. Mr. B's success as a teacher is based upon his

    (A) ability to play the role
    (B) constant show of self-confidence
    (C) adaptation of teaching materials to meet pupil needs
    (D) ability to meet his daily achievement needs
    (E) concern for popular approval of his methods

PART 1: PROFESSIONAL EDUCATION EXAMINATION

23. A new social order is advocated by the

    (A) essentialist
    (B) progressivist
    (C) perennialist
    (D) reconstructionist
    (E) existentialist

24. The teaching of truth, goodness, and beauty is emphasized by a curriculum committee which is composed of

    (A) essentialist educators
    (B) progressivists
    (C) perennialists
    (D) reconstructionists
    (E) eclectics

25. Research shows that good teachers are

    (A) strict and demanding
    (B) lenient
    (C) inconsistent in assignment
    (D) rigid and autocratic
    (E) flexible and businesslike

26. Since readiness is closely related to maturation, the teacher

    (A) does not need to do anything
    (B) can assist the readiness process
    (C) should wait until the child is ready
    (D) should ignore readiness factors
    (E) should increase the number of reading periods

27. Mr. K wants to locate test questions that are too difficult, or too easy. He will use

    (A) validity studies
    (B) the test-retest technique
    (C) item analysis
    (D) correlation
    (E) a frequency polygon

28. The best way to work out a solution to a teaching-learning problem in the classroom is to

    (A) change the pupils
    (B) change yourself
    (C) change the environment
    (D) change A, B, and C
    (E) change the course of study

29. The most stable measure of central tendency is

    (A) the mean
    (B) the mode
    (C) the median
    (D) Z-scores
    (E) standard deviation

COMMON EXAMINATION

30. The significance of the difference between two means of the two tests given by Miss L to her English class could be obtained by

   (A) the two standard deviations
   (B) the null hypothesis
   (C) the critical ratio
   (D) correlation
   (E) the T-scores

31. It is generally agreed that a teacher's way of teaching depends most upon

   (A) basic motivations
   (B) professional training
   (C) constructive supervision
   (D) social interest
   (E) past experiences

32. Teachers should be cautious about giving parents a pupil's exact IQ score because

   (A) there are sharp divisions of types of persons on the normal curve
   (B) a genius is difficult to define
   (C) of the possibility of score variations
   (D) performance at different levels is very marked
   (E) the IQ is constant

33. The individual recitation method was no longer adequate in the nineteenth century school for

   (A) the reading and writing schools predominated
   (B) enrollment in the higher grades was declining
   (C) the division of labor encouraged the nongraded school organization
   (D) there was a shortage of textbooks
   (E) new subjects and larger enrollments reduced the teacher's time

34. Anything can be taught to any child in some form is a concept which can be identified with

   (A) Skinner   (D) Havighurst
   (B) Cronbach   (E) Bruner
   (C) Olson

35. Individualized instruction received a setback when the

   (A) monitorial system was introduced
   (B) boards of education purchased textbooks
   (C) workbooks were assigned for several subjects
   (D) one-room schools became popular in the Mid-west
   (E) church schools declined

36. Who is identified with the concept of organismic age?

19

PART 1: PROFESSIONAL EDUCATION EXAMINATION

(A) Anastasi
(B) Russell
(C) Olson
(D) Allport
(E) Gesell

36. [A] [B] [C] [D] [E]

37. The new graded school system of the 1830's was based on the Prussian system as recommended by

(A) McGuffey
(B) Bernard
(C) Mann
(D) Harris
(E) Dalton

37. [A] [B] [C] [D] [E]

38. The first flexible promotion system for elementary pupils was implemented in

(A) New York City
(B) Buffalo
(C) St. Louis
(D) Chicago
(E) Winnetka

38. [A] [B] [C] [D] [E]

39. A teacher who applies the concept of the importance of cultural factors in the development of the child would be referring to the work of

(A) Havighurst
(B) Ilg
(C) Spock
(D) English
(E) Horney

39. [A] [B] [C] [D] [E]

40. The teacher who practices lock-step promotion at the elementary level implies that

(A) the grade standard is the goal for all children
(B) goals must be individualized
(C) all fifth graders should read the same level material
(D) the rate and method of instruction make little difference to the learner
(E) one year is sufficient for skill mastery

40. [A] [B] [C] [D] [E]

41. The multitrack program which Baltimore had at the turn of the century

(A) had two tracks for all learners
(B) had separate tracks for slow, average, and bright pupils
(C) encouraged acceleration
(D) used mid-year promotions
(E) allowed bright pupils to complete their elementary work in six years instead of eight

41. [A] [B] [C] [D] [E]

42. Pacing the work of the child rather than forcing requirements upon him is a principle advocated by

(A) Mead
(B) Olson
(C) Rapaport
(D) Gesell
(E) Erikson

42. [A] [B] [C] [D] [E]

43. John's English teacher is using the job-contract system. This is

(A) an innovation of the 1960's
(B) a part of the Winnetka Plan
(C) similar to the Dalton Plan
(D) borrowed from British private schools
(E) ineffective for motivation

43. [A] [B] [C] [D] [E]

44. If you were asked to describe the Winnetka Plan, which one would be the most important aspect?

(A) The grade promotion plan
(B) The individual work centers for the "common essentials"
(C) Accelerated promotion techniques
(D) The emphasis on the three R's
(E) Subject laboratories for job contracts

44. [A] [B] [C] [D] [E]

45. When planning a lesson for the sixth grade in a heterogeneous group, the teacher would have to assume that

(A) about one-half of the pupils will be below the norm for that grade
(B) none of the pupils will be below the norm for that grade
(C) one-third of the pupils will be below the norm for that grade
(D) a few pupils will be above the norm for that grade
(E) a few pupils will be below the norm for that grade

45. [A] [B] [C] [D] [E]

46. Present team teaching had its origin in the 1920's in the

(A) platoon system
(B) Batavia Plan
(C) activity movement
(D) departmentalized elementary school
(E) cooperative group plan

46. [A] [B] [C] [D] [E]

47. A student teacher can make the following assumption, knowing that it will follow child development principles:

(A) Normal children can differ in both rate and pattern growth.
(B) If the child tries hard enough, he will learn.
(C) It is fair to make the child hit the average or norm for his group.
(D) Since children grow at different rates, there can be no goals for individual children.
(E) Normal children can differ in both rate and quality of growth.

47. [A] [B] [C] [D] [E]

48. Mr. D, the principal, tells his staff about many new concepts which will modify educational practices. Herbart and Dewey first recognized the positive effect of

(A) flexible classrooms
(B) departmentalized instruction
(C) the relationship between interest and pupil effort
(D) ungraded primary units
(E) educational television

48. [A] [B] [C] [D] [E]

PART 1: PROFESSIONAL EDUCATION EXAMINATION

49. The structured curriculum is in decided contrast with the child-centered curriculum which

    (A) emphasizes fundamental education
    (B) is changeable and built around student interests
    (C) is oriented to the needs of a democratic society
    (D) utilizes the theory of mental discipline
    (E) emphasizes a particular body of knowledge

50. The instructor who provides for periods of daily drill in certain subjects believes that

    (A) formal instruction produces superior performance
    (B) significant improvement is observable through daily drill
    (C) learnings will transfer easier after distributed practice
    (D) the retention rate will be higher through distributed practice
    (E) formal drill will make little difference in the performance

51. There are several ways to group children who have common needs. The *least* effective criteria for individualizing instruction is

    (A) mental age
    (B) progress in reading
    (C) intelligence quotient
    (D) interests
    (E) chronological age

52. Mr. E, the principal, attempts to arouse parents' interest in establishing an ungraded elementary school. Which one of these points would *not* be a specific advantage of this type of organization?

    (A) children's growth shows spurts periodically
    (B) continuous and sequential learning experiences can be provided
    (C) some teachers have difficulty adapting materials to ungraded standards
    (D) bright pupils are not accelerated by grades, only level work
    (E) slow pupils are not pressured to exceed their rate of learning

53. The teacher's role in formal education, in contrast to education through life experiences, involves

    (A) controlled environment
    (B) relevant stimulation
    (C) structured situations
    (D) contrived experiences
    (E) social interaction

54. Miss *E* sets up a team learning system in her fifth grade class. You would *not* find one of the following:

(A) pupils divided into two or three work teams
(B) sub-teams divided on the basis of ability
(C) discussion instead of drill
(D) team member competition
(E) team member assistance

54. A B C D E

55. Mr. *F* experimented with programmed textbooks in his general mathematics class. He found several advantages but *one* major disadvantage with programmed instructional materials:

(A) he was replaced by the teaching machine
(B) pupils may learn by memory rather than understanding
(C) the learning sequence progresses from the known to the unknown
(D) the questions reinforce learning
(E) only a small amount of material is presented at one time

55. A B C D E

56. A teacher who alternates active and inactive periods in the elementary classroom is attempting to meet the children's need for

(A) curiosity   (D) self-directed goals
(B) activity   (E) supervised play
(C) lax discipline

56. A B C D E

57. Miss *F* likes programmed instruction. She uses materials to meet individual differences in the following way:

(A) the prepared learning sequence saves her time
(B) teaching is impersonalized for some pupils
(C) some pupils need the novelty effect of the teaching machine
(D) several pupils can work alone on review or advanced materials
(E) some pupils get quick success by copying answers from texts

57. A B C D E

58. The principal tells his teachers that the success of grouping depends upon one major factor. He is probably concerned about

(A) flexibility of pupil assignment to groups
(B) the number of pupils in a group
(C) the chronological age of the pupils
(D) the evaluation techniques
(E) the special help periods

58. A B C D E

59. A student questions adult values and standards. It would be best for the teacher to

(A) reprimand the student
(B) explain adult values and standards
(C) side with the student
(D) ridicule him
(E) encourage open discussion

59. A B C D E

PART 1: PROFESSIONAL EDUCATION EXAMINATION

60. At a recent faculty meeting, Mr. D suggested the use of modular scheduling at the junior high school level to meet pupil needs. He was referring to

    (A) forty-minute periods
    (B) fifty-minute periods
    (C) block scheduling
    (D) area teaching variations
    (E) time block based upon class time required by pupils or subject

    60. [A] [B] [C] [D] [E]

61. The most effective stage for learning is established when all teachers

    (A) utilize their different backgrounds to the best advantage
    (B) subscribe to the same basic educational philosophy
    (C) recognize individual differences among pupils
    (D) stress high academic achievement
    (E) maintain good discipline

    61. [A] [B] [C] [D] [E]

62. John rejects all adult values, including *high* school achievement. Mr. *B*, the counselor, tells John's teachers that

    (A) John is overreacting to adult authority
    (B) John is projecting
    (C) John is immature
    (D) John is emotionally disturbed
    (E) John comes from a broken home

    62. [A] [B] [C] [D] [E]

63. If one were to describe the American public school system, the most accurate way to do this would be to refer to

    (A) its building and structure
    (B) the number of pupils which it enrolls
    (C) its basis on the American way of life
    (D) its local tax-support
    (E) the part the teachers play in the total process

    63. [A] [B] [C] [D] [E]

64. The schools of Puritan New England, if we look at them in the proper perspective,

    (A) were inferior to schools of our times
    (B) were inadequate for a democracy
    (C) met the needs of a people in a theocracy
    (D) offered little for a developing nation
    (E) were derived from European systems

    64. [A] [B] [C] [D] [E]

65. The average girl reaches the age of puberty at

    (A) ten   (D) thirteen
    (B) nine   (E) fifteen
    (C) twelve

    65. [A] [B] [C] [D] [E]

COMMON EXAMINATION

66. Pupils who were transferred from contemporary schools to schools of colonial times would be most disturbed by the

    (A) lack of subject matter choice
    (B) strict discipline and harsh punishment
    (C) lack of co-curricular activities
    (D) special schools for girls
    (E) austere surroundings

67. Schools in Puitan New England were similar to ours in the sense that they

    (A) attempted to prepare youth for life
    (B) emphasized the three R's
    (C) placed high value on the high achievers
    (D) encouraged good study habits
    (E) emphasized local support

68. The average boy reaches the age of puberty at

    (A) ten
    (B) eleven
    (C) thirteen
    (D) fourteen
    (E) fifteen

69. The junior high school teacher who attempts to draw every student into the discussion understands the adolescent's need

    (A) for activity
    (B) for creativity
    (C) to belong
    (D) to excel
    (E) to compete

70. The greatest contrast between the motivation for establishing schools in early times and twentieth century America arises from the

    (A) international situation
    (B) federal interference in education
    (C) militant teachers' organizations
    (D) secular nature of public education today
    (E) declining local support for education

71. Quick changes of mood are characteristic of which stage of development?

    (A) early childhood
    (B) middle childhood
    (C) pre-puberty
    (D) adolescence
    (E) early adulthood

72. The changes which took place in German schools under the Nazi regime illustrate the fact that

PART 1: PROFESSIONAL EDUCATION EXAMINATION

    (A) there is a close parallel between the public school and cultural forces
    (B) educators are easily duped by politicians
    (C) educational history reflects many mistakes
    (D) federal aid leads to federal control
    (E) schools should operate outside of the social forces   72. [A][B][C][D][E]

73. The "little red schoolhouse" disappeared mainly because of

    (A) changing educational values
    (B) changing educational theories
    (C) changing methodology
    (D) urbanization and technology
    (E) the emphsis upon secondary education   73. [A][B][C][D][E]

74. Because of growing intellectual maturity, teachers will find adolescents

    (A) easier to talk to than younger children
    (B) more acceptable to sociemetric devices
    (C) less suspicious of adult motives
    (D) more adaptable to change of attitude and value system
    (E) more concerned as to whether they are "normal"   74. [A][B][C][D][E]

75. Changes brought about by the Industrial Revolution are reflected in all *except one* of these:

    (A) increased numbers of both sexes enrolled in schools
    (B) concentration of national wealth in the cities
    (C) increased amount of time people spend in education
    (D) the lengthened school year
    (E) increased emphasis upon agriculture as a school subject   75. [A][B][C][D][E]

76. Teachers and educational leaders are expressing some concern for not all change is good, especially when

    (A) finances become the root of all educational evils in the eyes of the public
    (B) pupil drop-out rates are increasing
    (C) early marriage is interfering with secondary education
    (D) "Progessive Education" is looked upon with favor
    (E) curriculum is influenced by national problems   76. [A][B][C][D][E]

77. The teacher who understands the adolescent's need to conform will

    (A) use sarcasm as a disciplinary device
    (B) disregard unique responses in discussions and on examinations
    (C) establish a learning climate that fosters feelings of security
    (D) lecture students on their weakness of character
    (E) structure highly competitive learning situations   77. [A][B][C][D][E]

78. It has been said that the American society was ready for an educational revolution at the turn of the century. Why?

COMMON EXAMINATION

   (A) There was an affirmation of faith in the spirtual nature of man.
   (B) There was an experimentalist outlook in social and economic questions.
   (C) There was a new groping for freedom for society and the individual.
   (D) Conformity was just becoming popular.
   (E) There was a re-affirmation of faith in existing institutions.

79. If you were to select the principles which describe American education, which one of these would *not* apply?

   (A) The schools are publicly supported and controlled.
   (B) The schools are free to all.
   (C) The schools are sectarian.
   (D) The schools are compulsory.
   (E) The schools are universal.

80. Students become more proficient in using the problem-solving approach when

   (A) they are left to solve problems without help
   (B) the teacher guides and assists when needed
   (C) students select their own problems for study
   (D) the use of textbooks is kept to a minimum
   (E) the emotional and social climate of the classroom is established by the students

81. One of the most frustrating aspects of public criticism of the schools which sometimes hampers public relations is the fact that

   (A) no clear mandate has been given by the public to educators
   (B) local support varies from year to year
   (C) local interest often lags
   (D) teachers often have to lead progressive action
   (E) many parents do not attend school meetings

82. An exchange teacher asks about the American educational system. Which one of these would be an *inaccurate* statement?

   (A) The American system is government-controlled because of federal aid.
   (B) Local districts generally elect their school board members.
   (C) Each state seeks solutions for its own educational problems.
   (D) The state board of education is usually led by a professional educator.
   (E) No federal law requires a state to maintain a system of public education.

83. A teacher seeking certification in another state would need to

   (A) apply for certification through a local teacher's college
   (B) apply to the state department of education
   (C) teach a year without a state certificate
   (D) ignore local regulations as a certificate is good in all states
   (E) go to summer school prior to teaching in that state

PART 1: PROFESSIONAL EDUCATION EXAMINATION

84. The most effective use of a teaching machine is made

    (A) in a testing situation
    (B) to meet individual needs under guidance
    (C) to give the classroom teacher more free time
    (D) to teach the slow learner
    (E) as a project for the gifted learner

    84. [A] [B] [C] [D] [E]

85. One of the most important responsibilities of the state for education is its

    (A) teacher certification standards
    (B) employees retirement systems
    (C) supervision of local board activites
    (D) regulation of minimum standards in free public schools
    (E) provision for periodic school inspection

    85. [A] [B] [C] [D] [E]

86. Federal support for the establishment of schools which became the basis of state school funds was first adopted in the

    (A) Constitution
    (B) colonies
    (C) Northwest Ordinances of 1785 and 1787
    (D) requirements for statehood in the western states
    (E) the ordinances of 1805 and 1807

    86. [A] [B] [C] [D] [E]

87. The teacher who gives verbal encouragement to a pupil while engaged in a skill learning task

    (A) uses intrinsic motivation
    (B) reduces pupil error
    (C) maintains firm control over the situation
    (D) reinforces correct responses
    (E) is too directive

    87. [A] [B] [C] [D] [E]

88. The first public school funds were obtained from the township lands to the extent of

    (A) one township in each county
    (B) one square mile out of each township
    (C) thirty-six square miles in each county
    (D) the thirteenth section of each township
    (E) the uninhabitable land in each county

    88. [A] [B] [C] [D] [E]

89. The higher education institutions which were established by federal assistance and still receive some federal funds are

    (A) state universities
    (B) state teachers' colleges
    (C) small private colleges
    (D) land-grant colleges
    (E) medical schools

    89. [A] [B] [C] [D] [E]

COMMON EXAMINATION

90. The physical education teacher should regard emotional climate in her class as

    (A) of no importance to learning
    (B) under control of the students
    (C) one that must always foster competitiveness
    (D) dependent upon student mood
    (E) her responsibility for orientation to the course

91. A teacher of vocational home economics has to meet certain requirements so the local school district can obtain federal funds under the

    (A) Smith-Hughes Act
    (B) Morrill Act
    (C) George-Dean Act
    (D) George-Barden Act
    (E) Elementary-Secondary Act

92. Jerry frequently makes flippant remarks in English class. His teacher should

    (A) recognize his need for attention
    (B) send him to the principal's office
    (C) keep him in detention
    (D) give the whole class more homework
    (E) ignore him completely

93. A qualified individual could obtain college educational assistance from the federal government under Public Law 346 and Public Law 16. The general public refers to these laws as the

    (A) Barden Act
    (B) "G. I. Bill of Rights"
    (C) ROTC program
    (D) federal loans for teachers
    (E) Upward Bound Program

94. If you taught in *one* of these schools, it would be operated by an agency of the federal government. Which of these schools would it be?

    (A) American dependents abroad
    (B) public schools of Alaska
    (C) public schools of Hawaii
    (D) high schools in Viet Nam
    (E) public schools in Germany

95. Miss F's initial attempt to teach diagramming in a tenth-grade English class failed because

    (A) of lack of pupil interest
    (B) the students had already acquired this skill
    (C) they disliked her as a teacher
    (D) they saw no purpose in learning
    (E) of a combination of factors

29

PART 1: PROFESSIONAL EDUCATION EXAMINATION

96. The high school teacher who accepted the educational philosophy of Bode would believe that

   (A) self-discipline should be fully exercised
   (B) coercion is necessary for order in the classroom
   (C) the road to truth is marked out by the scientific method
   (D) the project method is essential to learning
   (E) purposeful activity leads to the reconstruction of experience

97. The structure of the school system necessary to apply Kilpatrick's democratic-character theory to curriculum development would have to be

   (A) a 6-3-3 plan
   (B) flexible for general and specialized education
   (C) a 6-2-4 plan
   (D) a 6-4-3 plan
   (E) a 6-4-4 plan

98. An eighth-grade teacher's second attempt to arouse interest in classical music was successful because

   (A) he emphasized only highly dramatic music
   (B) he began with a pupils' level of understanding
   (C) he treated them as adults
   (D) he let certain students teach the class
   (E) he used a resource person from the symphony orchestra

99. Dewey opposed a separate system of vocational schools for the reason that

   (A) education should bridge the cultural gap between classes
   (B) it is impractical
   (C) it is uneconomical
   (D) he advocated the comprehensive high school
   (E) it interferes with general education

100. Those educators who disagree with pragmatism and the omnipresence of change have come to be called perennialists. One of these concepts is *not* characteristic of perennialism.

   (A) Children should be taught certain basic subjects.
   (B) Drill and repetition is necessary.
   (C) Slow learners should learn the same basic knowledge as others.
   (D) Rationality is man's highest attribute.
   (E) Problem solving is essential for learning.

101. One of the fundamental principles of programmed learning is that

   (A) the student learns rapidly from his past mistakes
   (B) immediate feedback is very relevant to learning
   (C) errors lead to retroactive inhibition

30

(D) level of ability is unimportant
(E) attitudes change in a structured situation

102. A curriculum based upon the principles elaborated in *Emile* would emphasize

(A) quality rather than quantity of learning
(B) freedom of the child with little discipline
(C) moral freedom before intellectual freedom
(D) intellectual freedom before adolescence
(E) punishment as a necessity

103. "Psychology is a science, and teaching is an art; and sciences never generate arts directly out of themselves," is a quotation from the psychologist who wrote *Talks to Teachers*. His name is

(A) Herbart
(B) James
(C) Dewey
(D) Locke
(E) Rousseau

104. Schools which use programmed instruction most effectively hold that it

(A) is more economical than teachers
(B) will eventually replace teachers
(C) meets the pupil's needs more readily
(D) releases the teacher from teaching certain routine materials
(E) is more effective than a teacher

105. The proponents of the scientific movement in education subscribe either to behaviorism or

(A) connectionism
(B) essentialism
(C) reconstructionism
(D) perennialism
(E) classicism

106. The scope and content of Dewey's curriculum

(A) emphasizes the quantity of experiences
(B) always involves interacting, especially with the social environment
(C) are consistent with the aims of self-realization theory in a democratic society
(D) are based upon social utility and personal satisfaction
(E) emphasize the reconstruction of the family, government, and industry

107. Mr. C is a firm, autocratic type of teacher. The learning climate in his classroom probably would be described by the supervisor as

(A) competitive
(B) laissez-faire
(C) democratic
(D) purposive
(E) self-directed

PART 1: PROFESSIONAL EDUCATION EXAMINATION

108. Opposition to the movement of teachers to build a new social order through the forces of class struggle or by indoctrination was expressed by

    (A) Dewey
    (B) Thorndike
    (C) Kilpatrick
    (D) Bayles
    (E) Guthrie

    108.   A B C D E

109. A speaker made the statement that education in and of itself was neutral. He really meant that

    (A) education has no effect on the individual
    (B) education is neither positive nor negative in motivation
    (C) heredity is more important than environment
    (D) the way education is used makes the difference
    (E) human nature is unpredictable

    109.   A B C D E

110. In a group situation, such as the classroom, the factor having the greatest effect on the efficiency of learning is

    (A) the characteristics of the teacher
    (B) the material to be learned
    (C) the structure of the group
    (D) the characteristics of the learners
    (E) the characteristics of the behavioral setting

    110.   A B C D E

111. In 1958, the National Defense Education Act emphasized research on

    (A) slow learners
    (B) gifted children
    (C) the mentally retarded
    (D) educational media
    (E) aptitude testing

    111.   A B C D E

112. The Cooperative Research Program, under Public Law 531, authorized

    (A) financial aid to colleges
    (B) scholarships for veterans
    (C) school building funds
    (D) aid for home economics courses
    (E) aid for agricultural courses

    112.   A B C D E

113. The curriculum of the junior high schools shows significant trends in the direction of

    (A) self-contained classrooms
    (B) the imitation of high school subject areas
    (C) more evaluation by formal tests
    (D) accumulation of credits as preparation for college
    (E) subject-matter organization around problems and life situations

    113.   A B C D E

COMMON EXAMINATION

114. One *change* in the self-selectivity of subject-matter at the high school level shows that superior pupils often choose

    (A) college-preparatory courses
    (B) technical or vocational courses
    (C) liberal education courses
    (D) advanced mathematics courses
    (E) modern language courses

    114. [A] [B] [C] [D] [E]

115. After World War II, the "general education" movement gained much support. It

    (A) is advocated mostly for high school students
    (B) is a terminal education program for secondary students
    (C) has placed considerable emphasis upon the humanities
    (D) neglects individual development
    (E) emphasizes the practical side of education

    115. [A] [B] [C] [D] [E]

116. One of the roles of guidance is to deal with real problems of pupils. Real problems are characterized by all *except one* of these:

    (A) uniqueness for the individual pupil
    (B) emotional structuring
    (C) outcomes are nuclear to the individual
    (D) causation is simple rather than complex
    (E) outcomes offer alternatives

    116. [A] [B] [C] [D] [E]

117. The five formal steps of the "development-lesson" procedure was encouraged by

    (A) Herbart   (D) Hutchins
    (B) Dewey   (E) Kirk
    (C) Thorndike

    117. [A] [B] [C] [D] [E]

118. Effective teaching in guidance-oriented schools differs from conventional techniques in all *except one* of these aspects:

    (A) inflexibility of curricular choices
    (B) adaptation to pupil needs
    (C) different standards for evaluation
    (D) homogeneous grouping
    (E) diagnosis of learning difficulties

    118. [A] [B] [C] [D] [E]

119. One of the most typical school-community projects in the community school is the use of the school as

    (A) an art center
    (B) city school-community evening social center
    (C) a center for the "Head-Start" programs
    (D) a community library facility
    (E) a center for athletic events

    119. [A] [B] [C] [D] [E]

PART 1: PROFESSIONAL EDUCATION EXAMINATION

120. The best public relations agents for the school are the

    (A) pupils
    (B) teachers and pupils
    (C) PTA members
    (D) principals
    (E) athletic coaches

121. American Education Week is

    (A) celebrated in early September
    (B) an annual event of early November
    (C) a period when parents teach school
    (D) the scene of evening "open house" activities
    (E) seldom meaningful to parents

122. The school may reach many adults in the community through

    (A) the use of community resource persons
    (B) frequent field trips
    (C) annual "career days"
    (D) radio and television
    (E) educational television

123. In place of the report card, some elementary schools use the parent-conference. Not all teachers favor this method of reporting pupil progress because

    (A) parents and teachers gain in understanding of the child
    (B) it takes too much time
    (C) parents don't like to come to school
    (D) teachers differ in their ability to relate to parents
    (E) children do not like to have their parents talk to teachers

124. The teacher who uses a classroom newspaper should

    (A) improve upon all the children's stories for publication
    (B) permit children to use their own work
    (C) attempt to get perfect writing
    (D) use as few pupils' names as possible
    (E) not worry about public relations

125. The theory of formal discipline used in 1900 was based upon

    (A) faculty psychology
    (B) trial-and-error learning
    (C) programmed learning
    (D) patterns of behavior
    (E) problem-solving

COMMON EXAMINATION

126. A school "learning experience" is

   (A) selected by the teacher
   (B) useful only in the psychological laboratory
   (C) the result of structured stimuli
   (D) based upon insight
   (E) transferred only after drill

127. Two classes, taught by different teachers, use the same textbook, have the same assignments, are equal in intellectual ability and scores on the science pretest. Why does one class score much higher on the final achievement test?

   (A) This group had class supervised study periods.
   (B) This section had more gifted children.
   (C) The teacher explained the material in more detail.
   (D) The environmental factors were more conducive to learning.
   (E) The students disliked the subject.

128. The teacher who shows concern for the way a pupil solves a difficult arithmetic problem is giving attention to the

   (A) affective objectives of education
   (B) pupil's effective work habits
   (C) method variables
   (D) type of reinforcement
   (E) mediating processes

129. Changes take place in the learner during the learning process. The pupils in Miss A's class are more courteous during gym class in December than they were in September. This may be accounted for by

   (A) habit formation
   (B) motivation
   (C) increase in information
   (D) interest in the games
   (E) the authority of the teacher

130. Educational objectives should be

   (A) stable
   (B) always in the process of change
   (C) subject to initiation by community leaders
   (D) the primary prerogative of teachers
   (E) built only on pupil needs

131. Curriculum organization works best when it is

   (A) a coordination of teacher effort
   (B) designed by the students
   (C) out of harmony with the community

35

(D) built on variety
(E) based on immediate felt needs of pupils

132. If learning is continuous growth then all *except one* of the following violates this principle:

(A) the ladder system of grade placement
(B) the whole class as a group method
(C) reading is an elementary subject only
(D) economics should be taught in college only
(E) learning is growth of the whole child

133. In 1920 Meriam described one type of curriculum organization as *aimless* and *wasteful*. Which type of curriculum was he criticizing?

(A) correlation
(B) separate-subjects
(C) integration
(D) fusion
(E) social-functions

134. The curriculum which provides the student with the greatest integration of learnings takes the form of

(A) fusion
(B) correlation
(C) separate subjects
(D) social-functions
(E) child-centered activities

135. The main difference between the child-centered curriculum and the experience curriculum in relation to learning experiences is that the latter emphasizes the view that

(A) the needs of children can be anticipated
(B) the needs of children cannot be anticipated
(C) school subjects should be eliminated
(D) a separate period is provided for each subject
(E) centers of interest introduce learning experiences

136. Stratemeyer suggests that the curriculum be organized around

(A) activity programs
(B) persistent life situations
(C) functional experiences
(D) subject matter units
(E) life adjustment activities

137. The unified-learning philosophy first took root at

(A) Teachers College, Columbia
(B) the University of Chicago Laboratory School
(C) the University of Michigan
(D) Peabody College of Education
(E) the University of Wisconsin

COMMON EXAMINATION

138. Hildreth suggests new trends for unified teaching which include

    (A) the core curriculum
    (B) unit-work periods and time for fundamental skills
    (C) child-centered work areas
    (D) correlation of all subject areas
    (E) fusion of all subjects

    138. [A] [B] [C] [D] [E]

139. Major emphasis in recent years, regardless of curriculum organization, has been on

    (A) the use of curriculum as a panacea
    (B) readiness before teaching begins
    (C) lock-step promotion for all pupils
    (D) grouping only for elementary reading
    (E) a greater emphasis on achieving the norm

    139. [A] [B] [C] [D] [E]

140. If you established a fusion of health, safety, and science, which type of curriculum would you be advocating?

    (A) Unitary   (D) Child-centered
    (B) Integrative   (E) Modular scheduling
    (C) Broad-fields

    140. [A] [B] [C] [D] [E]

141. The principle of method which underlies all other methods of teaching is built on the foundation of

    (A) fundamental subject information
    (B) the immediate needs of the child
    (C) the child's latent creative capabilities
    (D) a well-balanced program of activities
    (E) an understanding of the whole child

    141. [A] [B] [C] [D] [E]

142. The most accurate generalization about human ability is that

    (A) it is acquired through learning
    (B) it is constant
    (C) it is stimulated or hindered by the environment
    (D) it is culturally determined
    (E) it is controlled by socio-economic factors

    142. [A] [B] [C] [D] [E]

143. The teacher can effectively increase pupil efficiency in learning facts by

    (A) delaying reinforcement or reward
    (B) punishing the learner for an incorrect response
    (C) immediately reinforcing a correct response
    (D) providing massed practice periods
    (E) reinforcing both correct and incorrect responses

    143. [A] [B] [C] [D] [E]

144. The most important task of the teacher in implementing purposeful learning is to

PART 1: PROFESSIONAL EDUCATION EXAMINATION

    (A) make all plans well in advance of the initial class meeting
    (B) make flexible plans for the group
    (C) consider pupil interest as the most important element
    (D) select appropriate audio-visual materials
    (E) help individual learners set realistic goals   144. [A][B][C][D][E]

145. The teacher who has studied educational psychology

    (A) can apply specific information to particular situations
    (B) should have a better understanding of the learner
    (C) knows that behavior is complex and often difficult to relate to causation
    (D) can motivate every learner to do his best
    (E) uses punishment as motivation for learning   145. [A][B][C][D][E]

146. Teachers with considerable experience in teaching often make errors in the interpretation of behavior. How do you explain this?

    (A) The teacher is not a good teacher.
    (B) The teacher is filled with self-doubt.
    (C) The teacher relies on the principal to solve her problems.
    (D) The teacher needs to treat each class differently.
    (E) The teacher relies on the judgment of other teachers.   146. [A][B][C][D][E]

147. A principal studying a child from "multiple viewpoints" may find conflicting comments by teachers. Why?

    (A) The child plays a different role in each classroom.
    (B) The child does not like some of his teachers.
    (C) Some teachers do not like the child.
    (D) Fatigue affects his behavior in some classes.
    (E) The child is not interested in some of his courses.   147. [A][B][C][D][E]

148. If an educational practice such as the teaching of reading were to be modified in your school system, the reading teacher would need to

    (A) duplicate the successful experiments in her classroom
    (B) structure her techniques according to the successful experiment
    (C) study the specific needs of her pupils
    (D) use identical teaching materials
    (E) work with small groups only   148. [A][B][C][D][E]

149. The measure of central tendency which will show the most often obtained score on an examination is the

    (A) crude mode   (D) mean
    (B) average deviation   (E) median
    (C) standard deviation   149. [A][B][C][D][E]

150. The use of the Initial Teaching Alphabet in the teaching of reading is based on the assumption that

(A) reading skill is based upon phonics retention
(B) the use of the word as a whole leads to poor transfer
(C) each letter of the alphabet has only one sound
(D) young children imitate sounds easily
(E) manuscript writing is similar to this alphabet   150. [A][B][C][D][E]

151. Which of the following is a *value* assumption?

(A) Girls tend to mature faster than boys.
(B) Reaility for the individual is the way he perceives his world.
(C) Students should participate in self-government to prepare for life in a democracy.
(D) Some first-graders are not ready to learn to read.
(E) Some first-graders are far-sighted.   151. [A][B][C][D][E]

152. Value assumptions are used by the teacher to

(A) measure intelligence
(B) grade pupil achievement
(C) set the course outcomes
(D) interpret pupil behavior
(E) punish delinquent acts   152. [A][B][C][D][E]

153. Psychological principles help the teacher to

(A) understand the motivation of the learner
(B) use audiovisual materials more effectively
(C) become more adaptable
(D) become more creative
(E) solve her own personal problems   153. [A][B][C][D][E]

154. One of the following is an empirical statement about education. Which one?

(A) Civic competency is a worthwhile educational goal.
(B) Fatigue reduces the effectiveness of the learner.
(C) Popular teachers are the best teachers.
(D) There is a place for vocational education in the high school track.
(E) The main purpose of education is to prepare students for life.   154. [A][B][C][D][E]

155. Which is the *least* correct statement about correlation studies?

(A) A correlational study compares the differences of performance on one variable by a group with the performance of another group on the same variable.
(B) A correlational study determines whether variable "A" causes variable "B".
(C) A correlational study shows the degree of relationship between the variables.
(D) A correlational study may show whether "A" causes "B" but not whether "B" causes "A".
(E) A study which shows a low negative correlation between two variables may be important.   155. [A][B][C][D][E]

PART 1: PROFESSIONAL EDUCATION EXAMINATION

156. A teacher who uses the case study to observe and record a pupil's responses would not be likely to

    (A) interview other teachers
    (B) consult the guidance counselor
    (C) interview the pupil's parents
    (D) interview the pupil while he was being studied
    (E) use the data obtained statistically

    156. A B C D E

157. The student of educational psychology would be *least* likely to find

    (A) specific rules for handling specific pupil problems
    (B) useful research studies
    (C) applicable information
    (D) anything worth more than common sense
    (E) an understanding of group dynamics

    157. A B C D E

158. The socialization process

    (A) is complete by school age
    (B) is the primary concern of the school
    (C) cannot be individualized
    (D) continues throughout one's life
    (E) terminates at age sixteen

    158. A B C D E

159. The objectives of the educational program are determined by

    (A) educational sociologists
    (B) educational psychologists
    (C) school administrators
    (D) the government
    (E) the public, school leaders, and the board of education

    159. A B C D E

160. Education for effective citizenship requires the school to

    (A) use authoritarian examples in the classroom
    (B) encourage student participation in democratic practices
    (C) reward the cooperative students
    (D) expel uncooperative students
    (E) discourage pupil decision-making attempts

    160. A B C D E

161. The best scholastic records are attained by pupils who

    (A) have the most mental ability
    (B) show the most growth in I.Q.
    (C) like school the most
    (D) show sustained drive
    (E) take subjects of their own choice

    161. A B C D E

162. The development of problem-solving skill is a necessary outcome of formal schooling because the pupil will

(A) have little use for facts and information
(B) become better able to solve his own problems in life
(C) be happier during his school years
(D) attain better mental health
(E) make better choices as an adult

163. Students who adopt the philosophy of the affiliation ethic will have some

(A) conflicts in relation to school achievement
(B) difficult days when making friends
(C) shallow values to sustain
(D) difficulty getting along with their parents
(E) conflict with group values

164. "Transfer of learning" is increased when

(A) much time is spent in drill of essentials
(B) pupil interest is the basis of course selection
(C) understanding underlies all learning
(D) pupils choose their own topics for study
(E) frequent examinations are given

165. A learner who finds himself in a "situation" has

(A) no choice of behavior
(B) alternative choices of behavior
(C) no use for conditioned responses
(D) more insight about his problem
(E) no precedents to follow

166. To a learner, his own goal is significant because he will

(A) give up his goal if necessary
(B) struggle to attain his goal
(C) try several other goals first
(D) use the goal to direct his actions
(E) ignore his goal until its attainment is assured

167. If a pupil's response in skill learning does not get the desired results, he will most likely

(A) give up in disgust
(B) become depressed
(C) change his goal
(D) go through a trial-and-error attempt
(E) quit trying

168. A teacher knows that learning has taken place when

(A) the pupil gives a correct response
(B) the correct response is given more often than an incorrect one

41

PART 1: PROFESSIONAL EDUCATION EXAMINATION

  (C) the pupil is satisfied with his response
  (D) the pupil practices with enthusiasm
  (E) the pupil goes on to another task

168. [A] [B] [C] [D] [E]

169. A learner is satisfied with the results of his effort when

  (A) his expectations are fulfilled
  (B) he obtains a reward
  (C) he competes successfully with others
  (D) the teacher praises him
  (E) failure is reduced

169. [A] [B] [C] [D] [E]

170. The most serious mistake which a teacher of foreign languages can make is

  (A) making pupils work hard
  (B) having class discussions in the language
  (C) teaching in the language and using no English in class
  (D) not correcting errors at the start
  (E) using the language laboratory too early

170. [A] [B] [C] [D] [E]

171. Interpretation is a necessary element of learning. Which of these responses indicates pupil interpretation?

  (A) Mary asks to do supplementary reading.
  (B) John wants to make a report to the class.
  (C) Jack writes a creative composition.
  (D) Joan invites her father to speak to the class.
  (E) Alan asks if there are any rules that apply to the singular and plural forms of the verbs.

171. [A] [B] [C] [D] [E]

172. Jack's interest in becoming able to speak in front of the English class with confidence is an example of

  (A) motivation   (D) reinforcement
  (B) goal   (E) interpretation
  (C) insight

172. [A] [B] [C] [D] [E]

173. Most teachers should attempt to solve all *except one* of these:

  (A) increasing pupil interest in the subject
  (B) increasing pupil understanding
  (C) matching every pupil's performance with national norms
  (D) helping pupils set realistic goals
  (E) evaluating pupil achievement according to ability

173. [A] [B] [C] [D] [E]

174. One of the teacher's responsibilities is to recognize individual differences. *One* of these is the best example:

  (A) giving frequent tests for evaluation
  (B) grading on the curve

(C) using homogeneous grouping
(D) using committees for planning sessions
(E) allowing pupils to set their own goals

174. A B C D E

175. Which is the best kind of evaluation to encourage pupil participation?

(A) Daily quizzes
(B) Weekly tests
(C) Gold stars for achievement
(D) Teacher's praise
(E) Pupil's self-evaluation

175. A B C D E

176. Adolescence is a time of rapid growth. How many adolescents are definitely disturbed about their physical development?

(A) about 1 our of 6
(B) about 1 out of 8
(C) about 1 out of 3
(D) about 1 out of 10
(E) about 1 out of 5

176. A B C D E

177. Those persons who advocate the teaching of reading to babies believe that

(A) readiness depends upon the method used in teaching
(B) children can learn anything at anytime
(C) parents are the best teachers
(D) age six is too late to learn to read
(E) boys and girls can learn at the same rate

177. A B C D E

178. The rate at which a boy grows and develops muscular coordination affects his

(A) social learning
(B) height and weight
(C) competence in vocal music
(D) interest in art
(E) capacity to do arithmetic

178. A B C D E

179. A child's concern about his physical size depends most upon

(A) his age and grade level
(B) acceptance by his group
(C) acceptance by his teacher
(D) siblings in the family
(E) parental attitudes

179. A B C D E

180. Girls mature more rapidly than boys. A typical girl of eleven to thirteen years would be as mature as a boy who is

(A) one year younger
(B) two years younger
(C) one year older
(D) two years older
(E) three years older

180. A B C D E

PART 1: PROFESSIONAL EDUCATION EXAMINATION

181. The reading test scores for sixth graders would show that

   (A) most pupils exceeded the norm for their grade
   (B) most pupils were below grade norm
   (C) most pupils were near the norm with many at the high end of the scale
   (D) most pupils were near the norm with few at high and low ends of the scale
   (E) few pupils were near the grade norm

181. [A] [B] [C] [D] [E]

182. Early maturing children tend to

   (A) have more emotional problems
   (B) make poor school adjustment
   (C) play with older children
   (D) play with younger children
   (E) dislike physical activities

182. [A] [B] [C] [D] [E]

183. Middle-class children have more cultural pressure upon them than lower-class children because of

   (A) the emphasis upon early achievement
   (B) the emphasis upon group acceptance
   (C) the lack of love
   (D) more severe punishment (physically)
   (E) the large number of siblings

183. [A] [B] [C] [D] [E]

184. The peer group is most important in its influence upon

   (A) boys below the age of ten
   (B) girls below the age of twelve
   (C) adolescents
   (D) girls below the age of fifteen
   (E) boys at age fourteen

184. [A] [B] [C] [D] [E]

185. The "teachable moment" is of primary importance in the teaching of

   (A) typewriting   (D) the social studies
   (B) swimming   (E) modern languages
   (C) reading

185. [A] [B] [C] [D] [E]

186. When comparing European children with American children one usually finds that European children are

   (A) better scholars
   (B) slower in muscular development
   (C) taller
   (D) less influenced by peer groups
   (E) more concerned about peer groups

186. [A] [B] [C] [D] [E]

187. Undesirable attitudes toward authority may be learned in the home and transferred to the school through

(A) autocratic methods
(B) punitive parents
(C) indifferent parents
(D) sibling rivalry
(E) inconsistent and unpredictable parental acts

187. [A] [B] [C] [D] [E]

188. Children who are overprotected at home, at school seem to be

(A) overly aggressive
(B) selfish
(C) unable to work by themselves
(D) lacking in independence
(E) unable to set limitations upon themselves

188. [A] [B] [C] [D] [E]

189. Children who have serious difficulties in emotional adjustment most often come from homes in which the

(A) mother and father are consistently autocratic
(B) mother is submissive, father is domineering
(C) father is domineering, mother is affectionate
(D) father is a weak personality, mother is domineering
(E) mother is overprotective, father is indulgent

189. [A] [B] [C] [D] [E]

190. Parental rejection is

(A) demonstrated by the child's agressiveness
(B) demonstrated by the child's hostility
(C) shown by the child's shyness
(D) different in effect on individual children
(E) demonstrated by the child's lack of trust

190. [A] [B] [C] [D] [E]

191. An adolescent boy who makes a good adjustment to high school usually has a father who

(A) is competitive and adequate as a father
(B) is cooperative and easy-going
(C) is very indulgent to his son
(D) sets high goals for his son
(E) lets his wife run the family

191. [A] [B] [C] [D] [E]

192. A child who has been indulged and protected is likely to

PART 1: PROFESSIONAL EDUCATION EXAMINATION

    (A) be very self-reliant
    (B) be insecure
    (C) be low in self-discipline
    (D) be very agressive
    (E) be very friendly   192. [A][B][C][D][E]

193. The autocratic teacher impairs the child's development because

    (A) creativity is not permitted
    (B) the child must obey rules
    (C) opportunities for creative self-expression are reduced
    (D) the teacher makes all the important decisions
    (E) the child must do his work whether he wants to or not   193. [A][B][C][D][E]

194. If a teacher has a number of pupils who are under-achieving, she should

    (A) assume that they have emotional disturbances
    (B) expel them from the class
    (C) recommend their placement in a slow-learner's group
    (D) reduce the length of the assignment
    (E) change the teaching methods and content   194. [A][B][C][D][E]

195. If a pupil is highly motivated toward achievement, he is

    (A) over-achieving
    (B) very insecure
    (C) a perfectionist
    (D) trying to impress his parents
    (E) obtaining intrinsic rewards from his work   195. [A][B][C][D][E]

196. Any teacher who does a class study of a child should realize that all *except one* of these apply:

    (A) Behavior has multiple causes.
    (B) A single cause can produce different kinds of behavior.
    (C) Consistent behavior is normal behavior.
    (D) A child behaves as he perceives his world.
    (E) Behavior is an attempt to meet a need.   196. [A][B][C][D][E]

197. The best way to solve a child's discipline problem is to

(A) scold the child in front of the class
(B) keep the child very busy
(C) try to find the causes of the behavior
(D) remove the child from the classroom
(E) confer with the principal

197. When studying the interpersonal behavior of pupils in the fourth grade, a useful device is the

(A) sociogram
(B) Wetzel grid
(C) Wechsler test
(D) California Personality test
(E) Stanford-Binet test

199. Herbart's emphasis upon a curriculum which prepared pupils for present problems would find the greatest support from teachers of

(A) the languages
(B) English
(C) natural and social sciences
(D) speech
(E) home economics

200. The attitude of educators in traditional Latin grammar schools and classical universities toward the approach of Locke, Pestalozzi, and Herbart

(A) was one of rejection of the new subjects
(B) was one of acceptance of the new methodology
(C) was one of acceptance of the new subjects
(D) was one of experimentation with the new subjects
(E) was one of disinterest

PART 1: PROFESSIONAL EDUCATION EXAMINATION

Practice Test **2**

DIRECTIONS: Each of the questions or incomplete statements is followed by five suggested answers or completions. Select the *one* which is best.

1. The changing relationship of the teacher to the pupils is characterized by the increased use of group dynamics in the classroom. This is in contrast to traditional schools which relied mostly on

    (A) coaction
    (B) interaction
    (C) role playing
    (D) group processes
    (E) face-to-face relationships

2. One of the yearbooks of the Association for Supervision and Curriculum Development listed several basic concepts of cooperative learning. Which one of these would *not* be an example?

    (A) establishing rapport
    (B) group evaluation
    (C) a division of responsibility
    (D) making group decisions
    (E) coaction by teacher and pupils

3. The definition of a unit of work would *not* include one of the following:

    (A) the teacher is a taskmaster
    (B) a central theme
    (C) cooperative group planning
    (D) many types of experience
    (E) unified activities

4. When studying a child's social relations in the classroom, a rating by his peers will be helpful because

    (A) the teacher rates the child on her standards
    (B) children use different dimensions for rating others
    (C) the teacher may overlook some information
    (D) the teacher is prejudiced
    (E) teachers disagree among themselves when rating pupils

5. A student referred to the school psychologist by the teacher might be given an individual test such as the

    (A) Wechsler Intelligence Scale for Children
    (B) California Personality Test

(C) Stanford Achievement Test
(D) Sequential Tests of Educational Progress
(E) School and College Ability Test

5. [A] [B] [C] [D] [E]

6. Rousseau Believed that education should be

   (A) strict and rigid
   (B) paced to the unfolding design of the child
   (C) for mental discipline
   (D) for practical application
   (E) for the aesthetic senses

6. [A] [B] [C] [D] [E]

7. Children can learn to cope with failure. Those who receive training tend to

   (A) give up sooner
   (B) project
   (C) rationalize failure
   (D) give up quickly
   (E) try to solve problems without help

7. [A] [B] [C] [D] [E]

8. Psychologists who favor operant conditioning criticize current teaching techniques because of the

   (A) permissiveness
   (B) competition with others
   (C) immediate reinforcement
   (D) infrequent reinforcement
   (E) lack of insight

8. [A] [B] [C] [D] [E]

9. The activity program for meeting pupil needs in the classroom is characterized by

   (A) projects
   (B) teacher-pupil planning
   (C) flexibility in pupil assignments
   (D) self-evaluation
   (E) group evaluation

9. [A] [B] [C] [D] [E]

10. All teachers work with pupils who have both positive and negative educational sets toward their studies. A pupil moves more effectively toward educational goals if he

    (A) is receiving praise from the teacher
    (B) is punished for poor work
    (C) is thwarted every day in the classroom
    (D) is threatened with failure
    (E) is actively involved in group work

10. [A] [B] [C] [D] [E]

11. Current research on "group effect" on pupil attitudes shows that

    (A) pupils will not change their opinions to meet group standards
    (B) group ratings affect pupil attitudes
    (C) group ratings have little effect on individual pupils
    (D) teacher ratings have more effect than pupil ratings
    (E) group ratings have no effect on individual pupils

11. [A] [B] [C] [D] [E]

PART 1: PROFESSIONAL EDUCATION EXAMINATION

12. Social mobility increases the problems of school-age children. The more frequently a child moves, the

    (A) lower his age in a particular grade
    (B) lower his IQ
    (C) lower his arithmetic age
    (D) higher his age in a particular grade
    (E) more he dislikes school

    12. [A] [B] [C] [D] [E]

13. Successful students, when compared to unsuccessful students, tend to

    (A) have more realistic goals
    (B) have a higher IQ
    (C) have a lower mental age
    (D) have lower levels of aspiration
    (E) spend more hours in study

    13. [A] [B] [C] [D] [E]

14. School pressures to succeed are the heaviest on pupils from

    (A) the upper class   (D) all of these
    (B) the middle class   (E) none of these
    (C) the lower class

    14. [A] [B] [C] [D] [E]

15. Workbooks can be valuable resources for learning if the teacher uses them

    (A) for daily seatwork
    (B) to keep the class busy and quiet
    (C) to individualize instruction
    (D) for drill and practice
    (E) for slow learners only

    15. [A] [B] [C] [D] [E]

16. Learning listening functions may be more difficult for some children than learning to read because

    (A) they listen all of the time
    (B) they have had so much practice in listening
    (C) they tune out part of the auditory world
    (D) they have no control over the rate they must listen
    (E) they always listen purposefully

    16. [A] [B] [C] [D] [E]

17. The transition from manuscript to cursive writing is usually made in the

    (A) sixth grade   (D) third grade
    (B) fifth grade   (E) second grade
    (C) first grade

    17. [A] [B] [C] [D] [E]

18. The teacher would expect to find in the student's cumulative folder all *except one* of the following:

    (A) pupil's health record
    (B) pupil's home background check list

(C) standardized test scores
(D) copies of guidance counselor's conferences
(E) personality or anecdotal comments from teachers   18. [A] [B] [C] [D] [E]

19. The school program should be evaluated upon

(A) objective evidence
(B) teachers' comments and feelings about the school
(C) objectives formulated by the board of education
(D) criteria established by the supervisors
(E) the basis of parental satisfaction   19. [A] [B] [C] [D] [E]

20. The impact of automation will be felt in the schools by the

(A) loss of clerical workers
(B) demand for more skilled workers
(C) loss of some teachers
(D) mass production of textbooks
(E) increased drop-out rate   20. [A] [B] [C] [D] [E]

21. Terman's study of gifted children found that gifted children are

(A) smaller in height
(B) socially maladjusted
(C) lighter in weight
(D) less dependable
(E) above average in moral attitudes   21. [A] [B] [C] [D] [E]

22. When teaching co-educational social activities to pre-adolescent pupils one finds that the attitude of the boys toward the girls is typically one of

(A) contemptuous rejection   (D) exploitation
(B) tolerance   (E) affection
(C) hostility   22. [A] [B] [C] [D] [E]

23. During the 1960's experiments have been conducted with pupil-team teaching. Results show that

(A) pupils should prepare their own study guides
(B) a teacher must be part of the team
(C) this is an uneconomical way to use time
(D) pupils showed marked improvement in certain subjects
(E) pupils showed no improvement in any subject   23. [A] [B] [C] [D] [E]

24. Pupil-team teaching has possibilities not only for subject matter learnings but also for

(A) group dynamics
(B) parliamentary procedure
(C) group planning
(D) individual social development
(E) the teaching of attitudes and values   24. [A] [B] [C] [D] [E]

PART 1: PROFESSIONAL EDUCATION EXAMINATION

25. Much of the learning that takes place through problem and project methods is not evaluated by the teacher as it

    (A) does not involve individual pupils
    (B) involves the learning of good study habits
    (C) is immeasurable
    (D) is meaningless
    (E) is of little relevance

26. Twentieth century educational leaders have explored the use of teacher-centered and pupil-centered methods; now they are exploring the values of

    (A) group-centered methods
    (B) pupil interaction
    (C) educational media
    (D) the use of teachers' aides
    (E) parent tutors

27. All philosophy that underlies educational teaching and goals is based upon

    (A) man's search for knowledge
    (B) man's changing level of aspiration
    (C) man's intrinsic motivations
    (D) significant learnings
    (E) the search for knowledge of the good

28. Contemporary educational philosophy has rejected eighteenth and nineteenth century knowledge that was either *received* or *discovered* for the theory that knowledge is *constructed* because under the earlier philosophies

    (A) children were considered as little adults
    (B) heredity was more important than environment
    (C) schools were teacher-centered
    (D) the common man had a subordinate status
    (E) leadership was emphasized

29. Philosophers who preceded the twentieth century tended to place the leadership of societies in the hands of

    (A) the common men   (D) the elected elite
    (B) royalty   (E) the church
    (C) the elite few

30. All unit teaching involves both experience and subject matter. The difference is primarily one of

    (A) subject-matter   (D) information
    (B) emphasis   (E) interest
    (C) experience

COMMON EXAMINATION

31. The earliest use of testing instruments was based upon the philosophy that

    (A) nature was more important than nurture in individual differences
    (B) guidance could develop interests
    (C) good teaching would change aptitudes
    (D) level of aspiration could modify heredity
    (E) Failure would be reduced by aptitude testing

32. Scientific inquiry which emphasized the philosophy of determinism had its impact upon education through the use of mathematics for

    (A) mental discipline
    (B) making inferences and predictions
    (C) developing a mind set toward science
    (D) research techniques
    (E) the preparation of scientists

33. The teaching of biology underwent considerable changes when textbook writers began to include Darwin's

    (A) theory of natural selection
    (B) population and food ratio theory
    (C) theory of determinism
    (D) the immutability of the species
    (E) origin of fossils

34. The educational psychologists who attempt to improve learning by establishing a connection between a certain stimulus and a particular response were indebted for the first experimentation to

    (A) Bain   (D) Pavlov
    (B) Thorndike   (E) Cattell
    (C) Watson

35. The two psychologists who attempted to discover the unlearned forms of behavior were

    (A) Cattell and Watson   (D) Wundt and Galton
    (B) Watson and Thorndike   (E) Darwin and Bain
    (C) Pavlov and Watson

36. The knowledge of the good, according to Rousseau, came to the child

    (A) through education
    (B) through life in the family
    (C) by the example of his peers
    (D) through great literature
    (E) from the child's soul

37. A pupil's autobiography can help the teacher

    (A) understand the pupil's personality

PART 1: PROFESSIONAL EDUCATION EXAMINATION

    (B) understand the pupil's socio-economic background
    (C) gain insight into the pupil's motivation
    (D) discover the pupil's hobbies
    (E) obtain information about the pupil's interests and problems

37. [A] [B] [C] [D] [E]

38. John is an underachiever whose IQ was measured as 107, 100, and 110 on three different occasions. The teacher should assume that

    (A) he is rejected at home
    (B) he is slightly below normal in intelligence
    (C) he is slightly above normal in intelligence
    (D) he has problems which need diagnosis
    (E) he doesn't like school.

38. [A] [B] [C] [D] [E]

39. The catechumenal classes taught by Christian leaders were

    (A) in early Christian schools
    (B) established for the teaching of reading and writing
    (C) for the teaching of vernacular language only
    (D) for the perpetuation of the Christian doctrine among adults
    (E) for teaching Christian doctrine to adults and children

39. [A] [B] [C] [D] [E]

40. The early catechetical schools in Alexandria were taught by

    (A) many learned scholars   (D) Christian converts
    (B) Christian parents   (E) young missionaries
    (C) women teachers

40. [A] [B] [C] [D] [E]

41. The first use of the title chancellor in education was applied to the

    (A) catechetical school administrators
    (B) catechumenal class directors
    (C) supervisor of instruction in the cathedral schools
    (D) Alcuin of York
    (E) Charlemagne

41. [A] [B] [C] [D] [E]

42. Medieval scholars in the cathedral schools taught three branches of learning, namely

    (A) grammar, rhetoric, and dialectic
    (B) rhetoric, grammar, and music
    (C) grammar, music, and physical education
    (D) rhetoric, Latin, and music
    (E) music, Latin, and physical education

42. [A] [B] [C] [D] [E]

43. During the Middle Ages, formal education was

    (A) encouraged for all Christians
    (B) primarily for the clergy and the wellborn
    (C) accessible to all Christian boys

(D) denied to those who could not read Latin
(E) only for the priesthood

43. [A] [B] [C] [D] [E]

44. The activity curriculum is characterized by all *except one* of the following:

(A) a unitary group of activities
(B) flexible organization
(C) a fusion of subject-matter fields
(D) grouping of activities around centers of interest
(E) learning through activity

44. [A] [B] [C] [D] [E]

45. The philosopher who seeks a definition of reality is contemplating

(A) a metaphysical problem
(B) an epistemological problem
(C) the nature of the good
(D) a philosophical system
(E) a logical problem

45. [A] [B] [C] [D] [E]

46. In his understanding of the nature of man, Rousseau rejected

(A) the concept of natural goodness
(B) the unfolding design
(C) "wholeness" of the child
(D) the doctrine of original sin
(E) the natural man

46. [A] [B] [C] [D] [E]

47. Every local school should have an organization for curriculum improvement. An effective organization will

(A) control individual ideas
(B) utilize the experience of individual teachers
(C) be dominated by the principal
(D) be directed by the supervisors
(E) show little concern for staff morale

47. [A] [B] [C] [D] [E]

48. The real functional unit for all curriculum-planning is the

(A) community
(B) child
(C) individual classroom
(D) school district
(E) individual school

48. [A] [B] [C] [D] [E]

49. The main responsibility of the system-wide curriculum council is to

(A) maintain a unified but flexible program of instruction
(B) disregard the problems of individual schools
(C) furnish supervision for program implementation
(D) utilize preschool work conferences for in-service education
(E) permit complete freedom for individual school planning

49. [A] [B] [C] [D] [E]

PART 1: PROFESSIONAL EDUCATION EXAMINATION

50. The best time for curriculum work which involves all teachers in a system is

    (A) the hour after school
    (B) summer workshops
    (C) released time
    (D) the hour before school begins
    (E) regarding it as part of the teachers' load for which they are paid

51. The most effective teachers' meetings concern

    (A) the principal's agenda
    (B) individual teacher's problems
    (C) problems selected by a teachers' committee
    (D) behavioral problems
    (E) curriculum development

52. One response which is possessed by the neonate is

    (A) perspiration from heat
    (B) the ability to turn the head
    (C) the curiosity response with eye movement
    (D) canalization
    (E) the startle response

53. The psychological principle of differentiation relates to the fact that

    (A) each person is different
    (B) development proceeds from the general to the specific
    (C) development proceeds from the specific to the general
    (D) each child grows through different stages at different times
    (E) none of these

54. Plato's opinion of knowledge was that it was based upon the

    (A) sensory experiences
    (B) world of ideas
    (C) experimentation
    (D) previous learnings
    (E) recapitulation

55. The method of teaching which attempts to draw from the pupil the hidden truth is called the

    (A) Socratic method
    (B) Platonic approach
    (C) Herbartian technique
    (D) Dewey system
    (E) cognitive insight method

56. Plato encouraged the search for the knowledge of the good by the method of

    (A) deductive reasoning
    (B) contemplation
    (C) inductive reasoning
    (D) mental discipline
    (E) thwarting

57. The pressure of the group has led to conformity in our society. What examples of this do we see in the schools?

   (A) emphasis upon high achievement
   (B) rewards for scholastic attainment
   (C) emphasis upon group processes
   (D) return to the three R's
   (E) increased size of American high schools

58. During the last decade learning situations have changed. One of the most important changes has been the

   (A) use of class discussion at lower grade levels
   (B) uniformity of instruction at the junior high level
   (C) attention to problem-solving at all levels
   (D) evaluation of work by pupils
   (E) use of daily lesson plans by teachers

59. State educational standards now require a full-time school librarian when the enrollment is

   (A) over 500 pupils
   (B) between 200 to 500 pupils
   (C) over 600 pupils
   (D) over 1,000 pupils
   (E) over 750 pupils

60. The main purpose of the attendance officer is to

   (A) control the child
   (B) assist the school in controlling the child
   (C) find out *why* the child is not in school
   (D) assist the parents in controlling the child
   (E) look out for the child's welfare

61. The main function of the effective guidance program is to

   (A) furnish information to the teachers
   (B) coordinate home, school, and community
   (C) help pupils understand and use their abilities to achieve realistic goals
   (D) help pupils fit into existing school programs
   (E) counsel potential college students

62. The Reformation movement gave impetus to the universities for the purpose of

   (A) educating the laity
   (B) improving women's education
   (C) educating the masses
   (D) training the clergymen
   (E) giving a practical humanistic education

63. The method of acquiring knowledge which relied upon inductive reasoning was known as

PART 1: PROFESSIONAL EDUCATION EXAMINATION

(A) scholasticism
(B) realism
(C) rationalism
(D) idealism
(E) essentialism

63. [A] [B] [C] [D] [E]

64. The group leadership which produced the largest expression of individual differences in the Lippitt and White study was the

(A) autocratic
(B) democratic
(C) laissez-faire
(D) leader indifference
(E) pupil sub-leaders

64. [A] [B] [C] [D] [E]

65. Children tend to be conformists. The peer group tends to influence

(A) easy decisions more than difficult ones
(B) only difficult decisions
(C) difficult decisions more than easy ones
(D) few decisions of bright children
(E) few decisions of slow learners

65. [A] [B] [C] [D] [E]

66. When attempting to understand "acting out" behavior, the teacher must realize that the most important determinant of a child's behavior is his

(A) heredity
(B) temperament
(C) physique
(D) self-concept
(E) socio-economic background

66. [A] [B] [C] [D] [E]

67. The use of defense mechanisms is an attempt to

(A) protect the ego
(B) obtain id domination
(C) gain control of the superego
(D) overcome the will
(E) utilize the superego

67. [A] [B] [C] [D] [E]

68. The search of knowledge through specific problems which will be solved through the discovery process has been known in education as

(A) essentialism
(B) sense realism
(C) sense empiricism
(D) progressivism
(E) rationalism

68. [A] [B] [C] [D] [E]

69. The use of psychological testing is best left to

(A) the school psychologist and his staff
(B) the guidance counselors
(C) the school supervisors
(D) the classroom teacher
(E) clinical psychologists

69. [A] [B] [C] [D] [E]

70. Children's jokes and humor often show rebellion against adults by

(A) showing adult behavior as absurd

(B) imitating their mistakes
(C) misinterpreting adult comments
(D) all of these
(E) both A and C

70. A B C D E

71. Lippitt and White conducted a study in group behavior. The independent variable in their study was the

(A) age of pupils
(B) leader role
(C) effect of the leader on the group
(D) effect of the activity on the group
(E) effect of sustained effort on the group

71. A B C D E

72. Rousseau placed great faith in education which was found in the American philosophy of education which advocated

(A) education for the improvement of society
(B) education of the masses
(C) education of women
(D) higher education
(E) schools in the vernacular

72. A B C D E

73. The logical problem to the philosopher involves

(A) the validity of inferences drawn from certain premises
(B) a search for truth
(C) a search for reality
(D) a system of values
(E) categorical reasoning

73. A B C D E

74. Primitive supernaturalism was often misled by belief in

(A) the good
(B) divine guidance
(C) animism
(D) the evil of man
(E) man as a savage

74. A B C D E

75. The Greek teachers who spread the doctrine of naturalism were called

(A) Macedonians
(B) Spartans
(C) Sophists
(D) Philosophers
(E) followers of Plato

75. A B C D E

76. Plato's philosophy rejected naturalism and advocated

(A) essentialism
(B) supernaturalism
(C) materialism
(D) classical realism
(E) revelation

76. A B C D E

77. The scientific study of learning and pupil behavior led to certain changes in traditional subject-matter. One of these changes was the

PART 1: PROFESSIONAL EDUCATION EXAMINATION

   (A) introduction of modern languages
   (B) sequence of learning within a certain grade-level
   (C) setting of the same standards of performance for all
   (D) use of men teachers in the elementary schools
   (E) addition of geography to the social studies

77. [A] [B] [C] [D] [E]

78. After the days of Dewey, the learner was no longer considered to be

   (A) an active participant
   (B) trainable
   (C) a passive recipient of knowledge
   (D) motivated to learn
   (E) able to transfer his learning

78. [A] [B] [C] [D] [E]

79. Much emphasis was given in curriculum development, before World War II, to the

   (A) number of courses the teacher would teach
   (B) the class load
   (C) the number of minutes spent in class
   (D) real-life needs of the pupil
   (E) psychological testing for grad-placement

79. [A] [B] [C] [D] [E]

80. Current educational methods contradict Watson's belief that all normal individuals could learn similar new habits. This is demonstrated by the constant attempt to

   (A) meet individual differences
   (B) group by ability level
   (C) devise different grading systems
   (D) use summer programs
   (E) utilize guidance counselors

80. [A] [B] [C] [D] [E]

81. "Every stimulus must be given not to men or to children in general, but to a particular individual or group characterized by certain peculiarities." This statement has had much influence on education since World War II. It was made by

   (A) Watson   (D) Pressey
   (B) Wundt   (E) Thorndike
   (C) Freud

81. [A] [B] [C] [D] [E]

82. The testing instrument constructed by Binet and revised for American use by Terman is

   (A) a group test
   (B) an individual intelligence test
   (C) a preference test
   (D) an achievement test
   (E) a personality test

82. [A] [B] [C] [D] [E]

COMMON EXAMINATION

83. The knowledge of individual differences among children in their capacity to learn led to further development of tools to test the child's

    (A) special aptitudes
    (B) musical ability
    (C) motor skills
    (D) clerical ability
    (E) artistic interests

    83. [A] [B] [C] [D] [E]

84. The American educators who widely circulated the new methods of Herbart and Pestalozzi were

    (A) Dewey and Mann
    (B) Mann and Bernard
    (C) Bernard and Thorndike
    (D) Dewey and Binet
    (E) Binet and Bernard

    84. [A] [B] [C] [D] [E]

85. The teacher of units of work in correlated courses is usually most concerned about

    (A) fusion of information
    (B) economy of time
    (C) democratic planning
    (D) child-centered activities
    (E) subject-centered activities

    85. [A] [B] [C] [D] [E]

86. Sectarian education had been replaced by public control and support in America by the

    (A) last half of the seventeenth century
    (B) first half of the eighteenth century
    (C) last half of the eighteenth century
    (D) Civil War
    (E) end of the nineteenth century

    86. [A] [B] [C] [D] [E]

87. The stimulation of scientific discovery and its movement in Europe and America had a great impact upon education through the

    (A) establishment of state universities and research agencies
    (B) lengthened school day
    (C) education for women
    (D) primary grades of the elementary school
    (E) use of the academy for terminal education

    87. [A] [B] [C] [D] [E]

88. For years educators have been punishing undesirable behavior and rewarding desirable behavior largely due to the studies on stimulus and response conducted by

    (A) Wundt
    (B) Watson
    (C) Bain
    (D) Thorndike
    (E) Cattell

    88. [A] [B] [C] [D] [E]

89. Thorndike defined teaching as "the art of giving and withholding stimuli to produce or prevent certain responses." He urged the understanding and use of three laws of learning. One of these widely used laws was called the law of

PART 1: PROFESSIONAL EDUCATION EXAMINATION

(A) effect
(B) trial-and-error
(C) insight
(D) cognition
(E) reinforcement

89. Ⓐ Ⓑ Ⓒ Ⓓ Ⓔ

90. Children quarrel frequently. Which statement is true?

(A) Quarrels are of long duration.
(B) Quarrels occur only among boys.
(C) Quarrels become more verbal than physical with increasing age.
(D) Children carry grudges for several days.
(E) Quarrels over toys increase with age.

90. Ⓐ Ⓑ Ⓒ Ⓓ Ⓔ

91. All children must develop independent decision-making ability. Their ambivalent feelings toward their parents

(A) last a life-time
(B) end at puberty
(C) begin at adolescence
(D) last only during puberty
(E) reach their peak during the middle-childhood years

91. Ⓐ Ⓑ Ⓒ Ⓓ Ⓔ

92. Which pupil would have the most adjustment problems?

(A) The early maturing girl
(B) The early maturing boy
(C) The late maturing boy
(D) The late maturing girl
(E) Neither C or D

92. Ⓐ Ⓑ Ⓒ Ⓓ Ⓔ

93. The normal adolescent demonstrates his rebellion against authority by

(A) rejection of all adult values
(B) school truancy
(C) running away from home
(D) demanding more privileges than he can handle
(E) rejection of religious ideals

93. Ⓐ Ⓑ Ⓒ Ⓓ Ⓔ

94. Which is most likely to cause a speech defect in a child?

(A) Telling him that he stutters
(B) Being indifferent to his questions
(C) Teaching reading in infancy
(D) Ignoring readiness for school entrance
(E) Encouraging competitiveness

94. Ⓐ Ⓑ Ⓒ Ⓓ Ⓔ

95. The adolescent with a psychopathic personality would show all *except one* of these characteristics:

(A) lack of guilt about misbehavior
(B) concern for the rights of others

(C) failure to learn from experience
(D) poor judgment in decision-making
(E) disregard for school regulations   95.   A B C D E

96. The investigator who uses the cross-sectional approach in child study would

(A) study different children at different ages
(B) study one segment of personality at a time
(C) study only one age group at a time
(D) compare boys with girls of different ages
(E) compare children of the same age from different socio-economic groups   96.   A B C D E

97. The experimental method of child study

(A) works with children singly only
(B) ignores children's emotions
(C) ignores maturation levels
(D) is concerned only with intellectual development
(E) uses a control and experimental group   97.   A B C D E

98. Marks should

(A) be used as incentives
(B) not be used as ends in themselves
(C) reward good students
(D) punish poor students
(E) represent the normal curve   98.   A B C D E

99. Miss T attempts to make her tests reliable. She is trying to

(A) have her tests measure what has been taught
(B) make her test consistent
(C) make all questions equally difficult
(D) have some questions more difficult than others
(E) conform to a percentage distribution   99.   A B C D E

100. When a committee of teachers discuss the possibility of promotion or non-promotion for a pupil, the first question they usually ask concerns

(A) achievement age   (D) mental ability
(B) home conditions   (E) physiological maturity
(C) chronological age   100. A B C D E

101. The search for knowledge through research is based upon the philosophy of

(A) sense realism   (D) essentialism
(B) rationalism   (E) sense empiricism
(C) scientism   101. A B C D E

102. Locke believed that we obtain all of our ideas from

PART 1: PROFESSIONAL EDUCATION EXAMINATION

    (A) revelation
    (B) the senses
    (C) the mind
    (D) sensation and reflection
    (E) contemplation and revelation

103. The faculty psychologists thought there was a need to

    (A) discipline the mind
    (B) discipline the faculty of reason
    (C) discipline each faculty of the mind separately
    (D) discipline the mind as a whole
    (E) learn only by experience

104. One of the earliest pioneers in the scientific movement in education was

    (A) Dewey   (D) Herbart
    (B) Comenius   (E) Locke
    (C) Pestalozzi

105. When a teacher attempts to use group techniques in structuring learning situation she should keep in mind all *except one* of the following assumptions:

    (A) learning is affected by feelings of acceptance
    (B) play groups and study groups need to take into account children's feelings toward one another
    (C) sociometric methods would be of little assistance in understanding group structure
    (D) the group must have a goal to solidify it
    (E) discussions of leadership roles and member roles are essential

106. Much more teacher assistance in group work is necessary with younger children than with adolescents because young children

    (A) learn much more slowly
    (B) do not fit into groups very well
    (C) are more interested in self-expression than group participation
    (D) disagree more often
    (E) have little need for group goals

107. One group technique used by teachers is "brainstorming". This is a problem-solving technique which differs from class discussion mainly in that

    (A) proposed solutions are not criticized by the group
    (B) proposed solutions are analyzed by the group
    (C) the teacher does not participate in discussions
    (D) group leaders play a minor role
    (E) ideas have little value for group goals

108. Maximum pupil involvement in the learning situation is still hampered by the fact that

(A) pupils take too many tests
(B) teachers talk a lot and pupils talk little in class
(C) pupils talk too much in class
(D) pupils ask the teacher questions instead of listening
(E) too much time is spent in explanations   108. A B C D E

109. The use of films and audiovisual aids are most effective when used with

(A) bright children
(B) slow learners
(C) before and after discussion of information
(D) no prior discussion of information
(E) a follow-up test   109. A B C D E

110. To encourage pupil involvement in the learning situation some teachers use buzz groups. All *except one* of these statements is true about buzz groups.

(A) Buzz groups are useful as "warm-up" devices.
(B) A few students dominate the discussion.
(C) Small group discussions arouse interest in a new subject.
(D) Buzz groups spread pupil participation in discussion.
(E) Buzz groups can be initiated by stating a problem in the form of a question.   110. A B C D E

111. Teachers of today would disagree with Herbart in his belief that materials which have been taught to the pupil

(A) should be related to previous learnings
(B) could be retained indefinitely
(C) could be based upon principles
(D) could be applied in a practical manner
(E) should be introduced by a preparation of the pupil   111. A B C D E

112. The schools which were derived from the cathedral schools became well known in the United States as

(A) elementary schools
(B) Dame schools
(C) Latin grammar schools
(D) Sunday schools
(E) private academies   112. A B C D E

113. The Protestant Reformation spurred the efforts to teach reading

(A) to the elite
(B) in the vernacular
(C) in the Latin grammar schools
(D) in the elementary cathedral schools
(E) to adults   113. A B C D E

PART 1: PROFESSIONAL EDUCATION EXAMINATION

114. When counseling students, the "nondirective" counselor would

    (A) use his own ideas to guide the student
    (B) permit the student to lead the interview
    (C) tell the student what to do
    (D) suggest a parent conference
    (E) offer good advice

115. The use of the normal curve as a plan for distributing marks is

    (A) never justifiable
    (B) acceptable with large homogeneous groups
    (C) acceptable with small homogeneous groups
    (D) acceptable with large heterogeneous groups
    (E) an unacceptable marking system

116. The most dependable way to acquire knowledge was through the use of reason according to

    (A) the nominalists
    (B) Aristotelian logic
    (C) the classical realists
    (D) the scholasticists
    (E) revelation

117. Newtonian philosophy differed from that of Aristotle in Newton's emphasis upon

    (A) the search for universals
    (B) the concept of immanence
    (C) the uses of the senses to discover natural laws
    (D) the internal forces of nature
    (E) scientific inquiry

118. Education in Europe and America was significantly affected by the assertion of John Locke that

    (A) the mind contained all truth
    (B) mental discipline was essential to all learning
    (C) mathematics is the foundation for all science
    (D) the child is born conscious
    (E) the infant's mind is a *tabala rasa*

119. Lippitt and White found that the greatest amount of tension existed among group members under which kind of leadership?

    (A) autocratic
    (B) democratic
    (C) laissez-faire
    (D) leader indifference
    (E) pupil sub-leaders

COMMON EXAMINATION

120. The founding of vernacular reading schools by the Puritans in America was an outgrowth of the

    (A) Calvinistic doctrine
    (B) Protestant reformers
    (C) mental discipline concept
    (D) need for ministers
    (E) education for women

121. To American elementary school teachers trained in the Herbartian method of teaching the first important step was to

    (A) obtain and hold the pupil's attention
    (B) use oral-visual and tactile presentation of material
    (C) present a principle to the class
    (D) pretest
    (E) associate ideas

122. Aristotle's influence on the progress of science had its origin in the research center at

    (A) Alexandria
    (B) Rome
    (C) Antioch
    (D) Athens
    (E) Macedonia

123. Rationalism relied upon a certain method of reasoning for its acquisition of knowledge. It was known as

    (A) categorical
    (B) inductive reasoning
    (C) deductive reasoning
    (D) comparison
    (E) observation

124. The theoretical foundations of education in the Western world were based upon the early philosophy of

    (A) Luther
    (B) Pope Urban
    (C) Plato
    (D) Cicero
    (E) Socrates

125. Rousseau thought the first evil from which all other corruption arose was

    (A) the family
    (B) public education
    (C) the education of women
    (D) politics
    (E) ownership of land

126. Geometry was recommended for study by Plato

    (A) because it leads the mind from the objects of sense to truth
    (B) for contemplative purposes
    (C) for the study of the harmony of sounds
    (D) because of the power of dialectic
    (E) because it was a preparatory study

PART 1: PROFESSIONAL EDUCATION EXAMINATION

127. Studies of prejudice in children show that prejudice is firmly established by the age of

   (A) five
   (B) six
   (C) eight
   (D) ten
   (E) eleven

128. Children with high levels of anxiety tend to perform

   (A) poorly on both easy and difficult tasks
   (B) poorly only on difficult tasks
   (C) poorly on easy tasks, better on difficult tasks
   (D) poorly on difficult tasks, better on easy tasks
   (E) better on both easy and difficult tasks

129. The highest and final discipline which Plato recommended in his system of education was

   (A) geometry
   (B) music
   (C) physical education
   (D) dialectic
   (E) the sciences

130. Until the eighteenth century there was no shortage of teachers even without formal control of their education due to the

   (A) control of school enrollments
   (B) lack of demand for teachers
   (C) poor education of teachers
   (D) low standards of private education
   (E) number of women in education

131. The Pestalozzian and Herbartian methodologies brought major changes in the

   (A) attitude toward education
   (B) attitude toward teacher education
   (C) attitude toward textbooks
   (D) attitude toward administration
   (E) attitude toward the study of languages

132. Modern teachers of the language arts would agree with Rousseau that the young child

   (A) learns language by example
   (B) should be forced to drop his incorrect speech habits
   (C) learns language mostly from his peers
   (D) should not begin a second language until age twelve
   (E) conforms to adult standards before age six

133. The function of language to communicate ideas was first emphasized by

(A) Dewey
(B) Froebel
(C) Kilpatrick
(D) Bode
(E) Rousseau

133.

134. The concept of general education as seen by Plato would be offered to the learner through the study of

(A) the sciences
(B) mathmatics
(C) geometry
(D) music
(E) physical education

134.

135. During the dominance of scholasticism the university scholar had to become proficient in the use of

(A) romance languages
(B) Latin
(C) deductive logic
(D) inductive reasoning
(E) Greek

135.

136. The humanists attempted to improve the languages taught by the recovery of the manuscripts of

(A) Cicero
(B) Charlemagne
(C) Socrates
(D) church scholars
(E) none of these

136.

137. Plato viewed the study of arithmetic as

(A) the most important subject
(B) mental discipline
(C) life itself
(D) liberal education
(E) essential for all

137.

138. Plato's school would have used subject matter to

(A) prepare for a vocation
(B) study abstract ideas
(C) encourage education for all
(D) teach rote learning
(E) encourage individual differences

138.

139. The Hebrews gave the Western world the concept of the

(A) "otherworldly life"
(B) the knowledge of the good
(C) the human will
(D) value of human reason
(E) worth of philosophy

139.

140. Education which followed the Christian tradition

PART 1: PROFESSIONAL EDUCATION EXAMINATION

    (A) the human will   (D) contempation
    (B) rationalism   (E) essentialism
    (C) revealed knowledge

140. [A] [B] [C] [D] [E]

141. The work of the Swiss educator, Pestalozzi, was introduced in America after his successes

    (A) in Switzerland   (D) in France
    (B) with Prussian schools   (E) in Sweden
    (C) in England

141. [A] [B] [C] [D] [E]

142. The first philosopher to label the assimilation of percepts as *apperception* was

    (A) Binet   (D) Montessori
    (B) Thorndike   (E) Dewey
    (C) Herbart

142. [A] [B] [C] [D] [E]

143. The concern with the subconscious and the conscious in the learning process received much emphasis in American education through the work of

    (A) Dewey   (D) Sheldon
    (B) Freud   (E) Herbart
    (C) Thorndike

143. [A] [B] [C] [D] [E]

144. One of the first and most famous of the fifteenth century humanistic schools was supported by

    (A) the Prince of Mantua   (D) Pope Urban IV
    (B) Charlemagne   (E) the Cathedral of Paris
    (C) Alfred

144. [A] [B] [C] [D] [E]

145. During the seventeenth and eighteenth centuries a new subject received considerable interest in the preparatory, grammar schools and the universities. This was the outgrowth of the influence of Bacon and Descartes. The teaching of this subject is receiving renewed emphasis as a foundation for the sciences. It is the study of

    (A) Latin   (D) mathematics
    (B) algebra   (E) none of these
    (C) modern languages

145. [A] [B] [C] [D] [E]

146. The rationalist's philosophy of education is firmly grounded in the American schools and is expressed by those who

    (A) expect education to teach students to think
    (B) teach deductively
    (C) use the problem solving method
    (D) test by recall
    (E) use objective questions on examinations

146. [A] [B] [C] [D] [E]

COMMON EXAMINATION

147. Pestalozzi was convinced that the nurture of the intellectual potential of the child must be provided through

    (A) experiences with nature
    (B) sense impressions
    (C) group play
    (D) mental discipline
    (E) classical studies

148. Which part of speech does the young child use with the *least* correctness?

    (A) verbs
    (B) nouns
    (C) pronouns
    (D) adverbs
    (E) prepositions

149. Jealousy of a classmate's relation to the teacher may be manifested by

    (A) daydreaming
    (B) nail biting
    (C) withdrawing
    (D) high achievement
    (E) low test scores

150. The sense empiricists dominated education until well into the twentieth century with the philosophy that

    (A) subject matter must be imparted to all regardless of ability
    (B) the good life will follow the pupil's having the right knowledge
    (C) the pupil is mote important than the subject matter
    (D) scientific discoveries are of little significance to education
    (E) all subject matter must be correlated

151. It is possible for pupils from the lower socio-economic classes to obtain a good education mainly because of our system of

    (A) grouping
    (B) enrichment
    (C) acceleration
    (D) non-graded schools
    (E) public support for education

152. The University of Berlin furnished many men to United States institutions of learning to improve

    (A) scientific scholarship
    (B) teacher-training
    (C) grammar schools
    (D) elementary education
    (E) musical education

153. Teachers who use flexible lesson plans would not be using the system of presentation devised by

    (A) Dewey
    (B) Pestalozzi
    (C) Herbart
    (D) Skinner
    (E) Bruner

154. Teaching in the early twentieth century gave little thought to the

PART 1: PROFESSIONAL EDUCATION EXAMINATION

(A) psychological effects of the lesson on the pupils
(B) teacher's specialization
(C) future needs of the pupil
(D) practical aspects of subject matter
(E) educational reform

154. Ⓐ Ⓑ Ⓒ Ⓓ Ⓔ

155. The main criticism of the Herbartian method of teaching came from its

(A) emphasis upon modern languages
(B) emphasis upon grouping
(C) its lack of concern with children's interests
(D) its emphasis upon technique
(E) its use of pupil monitors

155. Ⓐ Ⓑ Ⓒ Ⓓ Ⓔ

156. The most famous higher technical school was established as university in 1810 at

(A) London
(B) Zurich
(C) Berlin
(D) Stockholm
(E) Copenhagen

156. Ⓐ Ⓑ Ⓒ Ⓓ Ⓔ

157. Modern educators refer to Rousseau's emphasis on the education by nature as the

(A) growth of insight
(B) maturation process
(C) social experience
(D) role of experience
(E) sense realism

157. Ⓐ Ⓑ Ⓒ Ⓓ Ⓔ

158. The inductive method of reasoning was described under the title of *Novum Organum*. This was written by

(A) Francis Bacon
(B) Aristotle
(C) Plato
(D) Leibnitz
(E) Spinoza

158. Ⓐ Ⓑ Ⓒ Ⓓ Ⓔ

159. The Age of Reason or the Enlightenment dominated the

(A) fifteenth century
(B) sixteenth centur
(C) seventeenth century
(D) eighteenth century
(E) nineteenth century

159. Ⓐ Ⓑ Ⓒ Ⓓ Ⓔ

160. Teacher-pupil planning can utilize pupils to determine all *except one* of the following:

(A) unit objectives
(B) necessary committees
(C) student activities
(D) leadership in group planning and implementation
(E) evaluation of pupil participation

160. Ⓐ Ⓑ Ⓒ Ⓓ Ⓔ

161. The young child can draw with a crayon before he can write with a regular-sized pencil. This illustrates the principle of

   (A) integration
   (B) coorination
   (C) handedness
   (D) differentiation
   (E) asynchronous growth

162. What does the child inherit?

   (A) insight
   (B) thinking ability
   (C) conditioning
   (D) functional subordination
   (E) his own combination of genes

163. The culminating activity of a unit usually is

   (A) a comprehensive evaluation of the work
   (B) a test to determine mastery of skills
   (C) a test to determine mastery of information
   (D) a summary of the pupil achievements
   (E) an assembly program

164. Curriculm builders before World War II were searching to find those habits and skills used by successful adults to arrange functional school programs. They were guided by the writings of such men as

   (A) Gates amd Watson
   (B) Terman and Binet
   (C) Judd and Charters
   (D) Spencer and Terman
   (E) Bain and Cattell

165. Those who are concerned with the improvement of mankind through the improvement of the environment are interested in

   (A) eugenics
   (B) conditioning
   (C) euthenics
   (D) canalization
   (E) growth gradients

166. One of the weaknesses of the child-rearing practice which emphasized the behavioristic approach was that it did not

   (A) use the organismic growth theory
   (B) differentiate according to sex differences
   (C) use the concept of permissiveness
   (D) believe in insight
   (E) consider maturation level

167. To determine habits, skills, and information most useful to successful adults, educational researchers use a technique called

PART 1: PROFESSIONAL EDUCATION EXAMINATION

    (A) correlation
    (B) measuring the central tendencies
    (C) making a frequency distribution
    (D) applying the mean
    (E) factor analysis

168. During the 1940's research came to play a more important part in curriculum-making through studies of the relationships between present-job requirements and school studies. This study of school-leavers used a special technique to obtain data. This is used today under the title of

    (A) personal interviews   (D) surveys
    (B) follow-up techniques   (E) cumulative records
    (C) questionnaires

169. The first curricula for the gifted emphasized some aspects of a program which are not too readily accepted in today's schools. One of these emphasized leadership and was characterized by

    (A) early graduation of the gifted
    (B) enrichment programs for the gifted
    (C) the dropping of grades for the gifted
    (D) study centers established for the gifted
    (E) an emphasis upon science for enrichment of the gifted

170. Teachers who believe that nature and nurture are both important and can change the learner

    (A) agree with the emphasis upon leadership for the gifted
    (B) disagree with the emphasis upon leadership only for the gifted
    (C) regard the IQ as constant
    (D) place little value upon motovation
    (E) regard the home as more important than the school

171. The child's speech indicates the ability to use the verb tenses first in this order:

    (A) past, then future
    (B) present, then past
    (C) present, future, then past
    (D) present, past, then future
    (E) either B or D

172. The Prussian national system of education demanded for the children of the common people

    (A) a knowledge of Latin
    (B) a classical education
    (C) the teaching of religion
    (D) studies in German language and literature
    (E) noncompulsory attendance

COMMON EXAMINATION

173. When teacher-training institutions were first established in America, teachers from other countries came to the United States to teach the new methods. Most of the teachers came from

   (A) England
   (B) Switzerland
   (C) France
   (D) Switzerland and Germany
   (E) England and Switzerland

   173. [A] [B] [C] [D] [E]

174. Methodology changes constantly; the first unified system of knowledge was proposed as early as the

   (A) seventeenth century
   (B) eighteenth century
   (C) nineteenth century
   (D) middle of the nineteenth century
   (E) turn of the twentieth century

   174. [A] [B] [C] [D] [E]

175. After World War I, curriculum makers who were seeking a more effective method of presentation for individual subjects began encouraging the use of

   (A) units
   (B) correlation
   (C) fusion
   (D) independent study
   (E) modular scheduling

   175. [A] [B] [C] [D] [E]

176. A teaching unit usually has

   (A) correlation between subjects
   (B) its base in the social studies
   (C) unrelated topics
   (D) correlated units
   (E) a central topic related to the unit as a whole

   176. [A] [B] [C] [D] [E]

177. The Age of Reason as the dominant intellectual theme of eighteenth century Europe was reflected in America by the

   (A) founding of state universities
   (B) founding of private academies
   (C) founding of utopian communities
   (D) political influence of the clergy
   (E) political platforms

   177. [A] [B] [C] [D] [E]

178. Rhetoric in the grammar schools founded by the scholastics would be known today as

   (A) grammar
   (B) literature
   (C) language arts
   (D) Latin
   (E) speech

   178. [A] [B] [C] [D] [E]

179. Educational methodology has for decades been concerned with the acquisition of knowledge through

PART 1: PROFESSIONAL EDUCATION EXAMINATION

(A) oral language
(B) deductive reasoning
(C) memory
(D) natural processes
(E) recall

179. [A] [B] [C] [D] [E]

180. The classical realists attached great importance to the search for

(A) universals
(B) truth
(C) the particular in contrast to the universal
(D) revealed truth
(E) rational method

180. [A] [B] [C] [D] [E]

181. The concept of the apperceptive mass was first introduced into American educational psychology by

(A) Binet
(B) Guthrie
(C) Herbart
(D) Lange
(E) Wundt

181. [A] [B] [C] [D] [E]

182. The American high school was preceded in development by the

(A) junior high school
(B) academy
(C) Latin Grammar School
(D) private school
(E) collegiate institute

182. [A] [B] [C] [D] [E]

183. The first responsibility for the training of teachers was delegated to

(A) local communities
(B) private colleges
(C) local school systems
(D) ecclesiastical authorities
(E) parents

183. [A] [B] [C] [D] [E]

184. Societies which have been ruled by an intellectual elite are of necessity also

(A) democratic
(B) laissez-faire
(C) autocratic
(D) socialistic
(E) communistic

184. [A] [B] [C] [D] [E]

185. All education begins with a set of goals. Those goals are implicit usually because we believe that the student should learn a particular set of skills or understandings. When the teacher evaluates the results of the teaching-learning experiences, the goals usually become

(A) mere results
(B) explicit goals
(C) the teacher's goals
(D) the pupil's goals
(E) the goals of society

185. [A] [B] [C] [D] [E]

COMMON EXAMINATION

186. If the teacher bases his evaluation program upon the scientific method the first basic step would probably be

   (A) determining the learners' goals
   (B) determining the teacher's goals
   (C) formulating the objectives of the curriculum
   (D) diagnosing individual differences
   (E) making a unit plan

187. Measurement, evaluation, and testing are not synonymous terms. Although *evaluation* is more inclusive than *measurement,* good measurement

   (A) is the basis of good evaluation
   (B) is required for good testing
   (C) involves the use of pupil progress reports
   (D) is based upon teacher's judgment
   (E) has little relationship to testing

188. Much of the success of a unit of work depends upon the orientation of the pupils to the work. Orientation involves all *except one* of these:

   (A) evaluation of the unit
   (B) seeing the significance of the work
   (C) relating the unit to past experiences
   (D) using community resources
   (E) a stimulating classroom environment

189. Parents who oppose grouping because it is undemocratic *object* on the grounds that

   (A) all children should study together
   (B) grouping creates class prejudice
   (C) children can learn from one another
   (D) grouping makes snobs of some children
   (E) each individual should decide his own course in life

190. Another name for the apperceptive mass is

   (A) area of consciousness (D) the mind
   (B) associated percepts   (E) the subconscious
   (C) memory

191. The beginning of the study of association psychology came about through the study of learning by

   (A) Binet   (D) Herbart
   (B) Thorndike   (E) Pestalozzi
   (C) Tolman

77

PART 1: PROFESSIONAL EDUCATION EXAMINATION

192. The order in which Comenius presented information was an attempt to develop understanding. He said that

    (A) sensory knowledge must follow the training of judgment
    (B) the printed word was less significant than the oral lecture
    (C) memory was the most important
    (D) knowledge is revealed
    (E) sensory knowledge must precede training for judgment

193. The training of mental faculties was essential according to Comenius so that

    (A) pupils would not make improper judgment
    (B) pupils would comprehend sooner
    (C) memory would be increased
    (D) learning would be accelerated
    (E) none of these

194. Pestalozzi in his educational ventures was primarily concerned with

    (A) children who were gifted
    (B) the education of boys
    (C) children of the working class
    (D) retarded children
    (E) innovations in the teaching of reading

195. Modern educators disagree with the scholastics and the rationalists in the use of

    (A) strict discipline with students
    (B) reason in the search for truth
    (C) dialectic as a major subject
    (D) authority
    (E) religious doctrine

196. In spite of the failure of Pestalozzi to finance his schools, his ideas were incorporated in the nineteenth century into the

    (A) state schools of Sweden
    (B) new national system of free schools in Prussia
    (C) private schools of England
    (D) private schools of America
    (E) new system of free schools in France

197. The Prussian school system became a model for other national systems because of the way in which

    (A) the free schools were administered
    (B) Rousseau's natural system of education was used
    (C) the free schools were established without destroying the classical schools
    (D) Pestalozzi's ideas were utilized
    (E) teacher education was state controlled

COMMON EXAMINATION

198. The elementary schools were so named because they were supposed to

   (A) teach young children
   (B) teach elementary subjects
   (C) teach at the beginners level
   (D) teach the elements of the new scientific subjects
   (E) extend beyond the kindergarten

   198. [A] [B] [C] [D] [E]

199. According to Aristotle, the child's knowledge begins on the

   (A) physical level
   (B) sensory level
   (C) rational level
   (D) contemplative level
   (E) insightful level

   199. [A] [B] [C] [D] [E]

200. The method of discovery was an important process in the acquistion of knowledge as viewed by

   (A) Dewey
   (B) Thorndike
   (C) Kilpatrick
   (D) Plato
   (E) Aristotle

   200. [A] [B] [C] [D] [E]

Practice Test 1 — Answers

#	Ans	#	Ans	#	Ans	#	Ans	#	Ans
1.	D	48.	C	95.	E	142.	C	189.	D
2.	E	49.	B	96.	C	143.	C	190.	D
3.	A	50.	A	97.	B	144.	E	191.	A
4.	C	51.	E	98.	B	145.	C	192.	C
5.	B	52.	C	99.	A	146.	D	193.	C
6.	E	53.	B	100.	D	147.	A	194.	E
7.	D	54.	D	101.	B	148.	C	195.	E
8.	C	55.	B	102.	A	149.	A	196.	C
9.	A	56.	B	103.	B	150.	C	197.	C
10.	D	57.	D	104.	D	151.	C	198.	A
11.	E	58.	A	105.	A	152.	C	199.	C
12.	C	59.	E	106.	B	153.	A	200.	A
13.	B	60.	E	107.	D	154.	B		
14.	E	61.	B	108.	C	155.	B		
15.	E	62.	A	109.	D	156.	E		
16.	E	63.	C	110.	D	157.	A		
17.	A	64.	C	111.	D	158.	D		
18.	D	65.	D	112.	A	159.	E		
19.	A	66.	B	113.	E	160.	B		
20.	B	67.	A	114.	B	161.	D		
21.	A	68.	D	115.	C	162.	B		
22.	C	69.	C	116.	D	163.	A		
23.	D	70.	D	117.	A	164.	C		
24.	C	71.	D	118.	A	165.	B		
25.	E	72.	A	119.	B	166.	D		
26.	B	73.	D	120.	B	167.	D		
27.	C	74.	E	121.	B	168.	B		
28.	D	75.	E	122.	D	169.	A		
29.	A	76.	A	123.	D	170.	D		
30.	C	77.	C	124.	B	171.	E		
31.	A	78.	C	125.	A	172.	B		
32.	C	79.	C	126.	C	173.	C		
33.	E	80.	B	127.	D	174.	E		
34.	E	81.	A	128.	E	175.	E		
35.	A	82.	A	129.	B	176.	C		
36.	C	83.	B	130.	B	177.	A		
37.	C	84.	B	131.	A	178.	A		
38.	C	85.	D	132.	E	179.	B		
39.	A	86.	C	133.	B	180.	D		
40.	A	87.	D	134.	D	181.	D		
41.	B	88.	B	135.	B	182.	C		
42.	B	89.	D	136.	B	183.	A		
43.	C	90.	E	137.	A	184.	C		
44.	B	91.	A	138.	B	185.	C		
45.	A	92.	A	139.	B	186.	D		
46.	E	93.	B	140.	C	187.	E		
47.	E	94.	A	141.	E	188.	D		

Practice Test 2 — Answers

1. A	48. E	95. B	142. C	189. E
2. E	49. A	96. A	143. E	190. B
3. A	50. E	97. E	144. A	191. D
4. B	51. C	98. B	145. D	192. E
5. A	52. E	99. B	146. A	193. A
6. B	53. B	100. C	147. B	194. C
7. E	54. B	101. E	148. C	195. B
8. D	55. A	102. D	149. B	196. B
9. C	56. B	103. C	150. B	197. C
10. E	57. C	104. B	151. E	198. D
11. B	58. C	105. C	152. A	199. B
12. D	59. B	106. C	153. C	200. E
13. A	60. C	107. A	154. A	
14. B	61. C	108. B	155. D	
15. C	62. D	109. C	156. C	
16. D	63. C	110. B	157. B	
17. D	64. B	111. B	158. A	
18. D	65. C	112. C	159. D	
19. A	66. D	113. B	160. D	
20. B	67. A	114. B	161. D	
21. E	68. C	115. D	162. E	
22. A	69. A	116. A	163. D	
23. D	70. D	117. C	164. C	
24. E	71. B	118. E	165. C	
25. B	72. A	119. A	166. E	
26. A	73. A	120. B	167. E	
27. E	74. C	121. A	168. B	
28. D	75. C	122. A	169. A	
29. C	76. D	123. B	170. B	
30. B	77. B	124. C	171. C	
31. A	78. C	125. E	172. D	
32. B	79. D	126. A	173. D	
33. A	80. A	127. E	174. E	
34. D	81. E	128. D	175. B	
35. B	82. B	129. D	176. E	
36. E	83. A	130. A	177. C	
37. E	84. B	131. B	178. B	
38. D	85. E	132. A	179. B	
39. E	86. E	133. E	180. A	
40. A	87. A	134. A	181. C	
41. C	88. D	135. C	182. B	
42. A	89. A	136. A	183. D	
43. B	90. C	137. B	184. C	
44. D	91. A	138. B	185. B	
45. A	92. C	139. A	186. C	
46. D	93. D	140. C	187. A	
47. B	94. A	141. B	188. A	

SELF-RATING PRACTICE TEXT CHART

DIRECTIONS: Record the number of your correct answers in the box under *Your Score*.

To convert your scores to percentages, use the following formula: $\dfrac{\text{YOUR SCORE}}{\text{TOTAL POSSIBLE}} \times 100 =$ Percent Right

PERCENTAGE RANGE	APPROXIMATE INTERPRETATION
84-100	Strong
74-83	Above Average
62-73	Average
50-61	Weak
0-49	Poor

Professional Education Examination of the Common Examination

	Total Possible	Your Score	Percent Right
Practice Test 1	200		
Practice Test 2	200		

General Education Examination of the Common Examination

	Total Possible	Your Score	Percent Right
Social Studies, Litertaure, and Fine Arts			
Practice Test 1	71		
Practice Test 2	70		
Practice Test 3	70		
Science and Mathematics			
Practice Test 1	24		
Practice Test 2	24		
Practice Test 3	24		
Written English Expression			
Practice Test 1 Part 1	30		
Part 2	20		
Practice Test 2 Part 1	30		
Part 2	20		

THE NATIONAL TEACHER EXAMINATION

Additional Aids to Review and Study

	Total Possible	Your Score	Percent Right
English Grammar and Usage			
Practice Test 1	15		
Practice Test 2	15		

Teaching Area Examinations

PERCENTAGE RANGE	APPROXIMATE INTERPRETATION
88-100	Strong
77-87	Above Average
65-76	Average
50-64	Weak
0-49	Poor

	Total Possible	Your Score	Percent Right
Art Education	20		
Biology and General Science	20		
Business Education	20		
Chemistry, Physics, and General Science	20		
Early Childhood Education	20		
Education in the Elementary School	20		
English Language and Literature	20		
Home Economics Education	20		
Industrial Arts	20		
Mathematics	20		
Music Education	20		
Physcial Education	20		
Social Studies Education	20		

Part 2
General Education Examination of the Common Examination

Social Studies, Literature, and Fine Arts
Science and Mathematics
Written English Expression

General Education Examination of the Common Examination

Social Studies, Literature, and Fine Arts

EXPLANATION: All questions are of the multiple-choice type with five possible answers from which you are to choose the one you believe to be the *best*. You are to blacken the lettered space for the one answer you select.

EXAMPLE:

John Greenleaf Whittier was an American

(A) novelist
(B) essayist
(E) short story writer
(D) poet
(E) playwright

SAMPLE ANSWER
[A] [B] [C] [D] ■

Practice Test 1

DIRECTIONS: Each of the questions or incomplete statements is followed by five suggested answers or completions. Select the one which is best.

1. The symphony form was developed during the

    (A) classical period
    (B) Romantic period
    (C) modern period
    (D) 18th Century
    (E) 17th Century

    1. [A] [B] [C] [D] [E]

2. Man's mode of living differs most according to the

    (A) geographic region
    (B) maintenance needs
    (C) psycho-social needs
    (D) climate
    (E) occupation

    2. [A] [B] [C] [D] [E]

3. The beginning of economic life stems from

    (A) human wants
    (B) national needs
    (C) political interests
    (D) the abundance of goods
    (E) unlimited productivity

    3. [A] [B] [C] [D] [E]

4. The main characteristic which distinguishes modern Western civilization from other civilizations is its

    (A) worldwide dissemination
    (B) narrow orientation

COMMON EXAMINATION

    (C) Protestant orientation
    (D) confinement to North and South America
    (E) confinement to the countries of Europe   4. [A] [B] [C] [D] [E]

5. When studying a painting one should observe carefully the real essence of the art which is

    (A) color   (D) perspective
    (B) form   (E) story
    (C) content   5. [A] [B] [C] [D] [E]

6. The satisfaction of human wants of necessity leads to conflicts in that

    (A) productivity is unlimited
    (B) the supply of goods is limited
    (C) natural resources are limited
    (D) research keeps ahead of human needs
    (E) each society has a cultural lag   6. [A] [B] [C] [D] [E]

7. The spread of Western civilization was greatly aided by

    (A) religious wars   (D) the rise of Hitler
    (B) commercial enterprise   (E) Christianity
    (C) the World Wars   7. [A] [B] [C] [D] [E]

8. The greatest achievement of the Europeans in the nineteenth century was the

    (A) rise of the Russian monarchy
    (B) French Revolution
    (C) colonization of distant lands
    (D) rise of the British empire
    (E) development of naval power   8. [A] [B] [C] [D] [E]

9. The European geographical expansion during the 19th century produced an unusual political organization called the

    (A) Socialist state   (D) nation-state
    (B) communist commune   (E) pure democracy
    (C) city-state   9. [A] [B] [C] [D] [E]

10. During the nineteenth century Great Britain had great influence on the other nations of Europe which helped to maintain

    (A) the growth of commerce   (D) trade agreements
    (B) colonial expansion   (E) the balance of power
    (C) political alliances   10. [A] [B] [C] [D] [E]

11. Consumer art tends to dull the observation and understanding of American great works of art because the consumer criticizes a painting on the basis of

PART 2: GENERAL EDUCATION EXAMINATION

(A) story
(B) form
(C) neither A nor B
(D) appeal to the eye
(D) unusual details

11. [A] [B] [C] [D] [E]

12. One of the main forces which operated during the twentieth century to upset the existing balance of power in Europe was the

(A) rapid development of technology
(B) growing number of new nations
(C) rise of powerful leaders
(D) decline of the monarchy
(E) growth of mercantilism

12. [A] [B] [C] [D] [E]

13. The main characteristic of rationalism was its

(A) rejection of authority and tradition
(B) rejection of religion
(C) rejection of absolutism
(D) rejection of religion
(E) acceptance of otherworldliness

13. [A] [B] [C] [D] [E]

14. The Italian poet, Petrarch, developed a type of poetry which contains fourteen lines. It came to be known as

(A) lyric poetry
(B) an ode
(C) a sonnet
(D) the elegy
(E) the song

14. [A] [B] [C] [D] [E]

15. Human wants seem to be capable of

(A) creating inherent drives
(B) easy fulfillment
(C) declining with age
(D) constant expansion
(E) expanding with age

15, [A] [B] [C] [D] [E]

16, The "Father of History" was the historian

(A) Clement
(B) Herodotus
(C) Hippocrates
(D) Plato
(E) Nevins

16. [A] [B] [C] [D] [E]

17. Most symphonies are written in the form of

(A) the concerto
(B) two movements
(C) the classical sonata
(D) three movements
(E) four movements

17. [A] [B] [C] [D] [E]

18. More important that the style of a literary work is its

(A) form
(B) content
(C) author
(D) appeal
(E) lyric quality

18. [A] [B] [C] [D] [E]

COMMON EXAMINATION

19. The most high-pitched instruments in the woodwind section of the orchestra are the the

    (A) oboes
    (B) bassoons
    (C) flutes
    (D) clarinets
    (E) saxophones

20. The migration of man was in early history determined primarily by the

    (A) location of water
    (B) location of land
    (C) location of mountains
    (D) location of natural resources
    (E) needs of man

21. Modern man is less dependent upon nature than primitive man because he can

    (A) preserve his food
    (B) modify and control his enviroment
    (C) migrate
    (D) produce synthetic
    (E) reduce disease

22. The most noted early English economist was

    (A) John Stuart Mill
    (B) John Milton
    (C) Francis Bacon
    (D) Adam Smith
    (E) Adam Smithsonian

23. Literary works become immortal when they possess the quality of

    (A) reality
    (B) emotionality
    (C) universality
    (D) inspiration
    (E) enrichment

24. The smallest subdivision of culture is called a

    (A) family
    (B) group
    (C) trait
    (D) clan
    (E) unit

25. Capitalism began to develop as absolutism declined mainly because of the rise of

    (A) essentialism
    (B) rationalism
    (C) big business
    (D) landed aristocracy
    (E) religious sanctions

26. In art, form is related to the

    (A) style or the design
    (B) color
    (C) content
    (D) story
    (E) perspective

PART 2: GENERAL EDUCATION EXAMINATION

27. By undermining the role of the nobility, the foundations of the modern state were laid by the

    (A) feudalistic lords
    (B) landed property owners
    (C) capitalistic enterprises
    (D) absolute monarchy
    (E) vested interests of commerce

28. Few societies have been able to

    (A) develop culture independent of other groups
    (B) develop their own systems of family life
    (C) write their own histories
    (D) have a unique cultural heritage
    (E) pattern experiences into a culture

29. Every society has both a material and non-material culture. The non-material culture consists of

    (A) language and tools
    (B) tools
    (C) communication
    (D) folkways and language
    (E) food, shelter, and clothing

30. The rise of the middle class was fostered by the

    (A) authority of the eighteenth-century Church
    (B) development of commerce and industry
    (C) increase in property ownership
    (D) forces of tradition
    (E) value of inherited wealth

31. The Phoenicians became the first great maritime people because of their

    (A) skill in shipbuilding
    (B) curiosity
    (C) resource of wood for shipbuilding
    (D) location
    (E) search for natural resources

32. Wealthy cities first naturally developed in

    (A) the plains regions
    (B) mountainous regions
    (C) fertile river valleys
    (D) along the seacoasts
    (E) in hilly regions

33. When Milton in England was writing *Paradise Lost,* an American author was writing on a similar subject, *The Day of Doom.* His name was

    (A) Longfellow
    (B) Whittier
    (C) Emerson
    (D) Wigglesworth
    (E) Byrd

34. After the Peace of Paris (1763), France had lost most of its holdings in North America. It only held

(A) Canada (D) two islands off Newfoundland
(B) Detroit (E) Montreal
(C) Quebec

34. [A] [B] [C] [D] [E]

35. The economist refers to all things that have utility as

(A) free goods (D) resources
(B) goods (E) products
(C) consumer goods

35. [A] [B] [C] [D] [E]

36. Group habits of action are called

(A) mores (D) taboos
(B) customs (E) folkways
(C) laws

36. [A] [B] [C] [D] [E]

37. The term that describes the feeling held by groups that their way of doing things and their culture is the best is

(A) a more (D) heliocentrism
(B) a taboo (E) patriotism
(C) ethnocentrism

37. [A] [B] [C] [D] [E]

38. Musical pitch is determine by

(A) force of vibration (D) type of vibration
(B) rate of vibration (E) contrast in volume
(C) length of vibration

38. [A] [B] [C] [D] [E]

39. Periodic reactions against rationalism have affected Western societies through movements which began at the end of the eighteenth century in the form of

(A) classicism (D) progressivism
(B) shcolasticism (E) Romanticism
(C) absolutism

39. [A] [B] [C] [D] [E]

40. The American colonies had a weekly newspaper published in Boston, as early as

(A) 1890 (D) 1704
(B) 1650 (E) 1802
(C) 1727

40. [A] [B] [C] [D] [E]

41. Some of the best writings about life in colonial America were written by

(A) Whittier (D) Smith
(B) Emerson (E) Webster
(C) Byrd

41. [A] [B] [C] [D] [E]

PART 2: GENERAL EDUCATION EXAMINATION

42. Very few goods are free. One of these is

    (A) air
    (B) water
    (C) oil
    (D) sunshine
    (E) electricity

43. Greek art was considered to be superior because of the emphasis upon

    (A) form
    (B) story
    (C) perspective
    (D) color
    (E) imitation of nature

44. If you attempt to understand a work of art in terms of communicating with the artist you must observe his use of

    (A) color and subject
    (B) color and perspective
    (C) form and content
    (D) story and color
    (E) style and color

45. The eighteenth century came to be called the Age of Enlightenment because of the

    (A) emphasis upon reason
    (B) decline of the aristocracy
    (C) decline of the monarchy
    (D) rise of the middle class
    (E) emphasis upon science

46. The first American poet to write about nature told how he felt about wild honeysuckle. The poet was

    (A) Longfellow
    (B) Teasdale
    (C) Freneau
    (D) Whittier
    (E) Poe

47. Culture is changed by the accumulation of culture traits. Every change thus adds to the complexity of the culture because

    (A) the new trait is unadaptable
    (B) new things are regarded with suspicion
    (C) new traits cause culture to spread
    (D) the new trait may not substitute for an old one
    (E) culture borrowing is unpopular

48. The most significant characteristic of an economic good is its

    (A) utility
    (B) requirement of labor
    (C) transferability
    (D) cost
    (E) scarcity

49. Communism is more than an economic system. Like socialism, facism, and syndicalism, it

92

(A) has its roots in labor problems
(B) is a complete social reorganization
(C) distributes authority among many leaders
(D) eliminates all elite persons
(E) limits the sovereignty of the state

49. [A] [B] [C] [D] [E]

50. The musical instrument which is most like the human voice is the

(A) viola
(B) flute
(C) cello
(D) violin
(E) harp

50. [A] [B] [C] [D] [E]

51. The modern short story is often traced back to the works of Boccaccio. His famous collection of tales was the

(A) Canterbury Tales
(B) Tales of the Falcon
(C) Tales at Midnight
(D) Tales of the Alhambra
(E) Decameron

51. [A] [B] [C] [D] [E]

52. Romanticism differs from rationalism in its emphasis upon

(A) democratic government
(B) the monarchy
(C) religion and custom
(D) man as a rational being
(E) middle class values

52. [A] [B] [C] [D] [E]

53. People today have considerable mobility. When people move on the same social level it is referred to as

(A) horizontal mobility
(B) vertical mobility
(C) group dynamics
(D) inaction
(E) social stability

53. [A] [B] [C] [D] [E]

54. In a fascist state, the will of the majority is

(A) replaced by the rule of a single man
(B) used to raise group standards
(C) utilized in the commune
(D) used through organized labor
(E) used to increase production

54. [A] [B] [C] [D] [E]

55. The viola usually is used in a quartet to

(A) double the melody an octave lower than the violin
(B) duplicate the melody of the cello
(C) play the main melody
(D) emphasize the beat
(E) give a foundation to the harmony

55. [A] [B] [C] [D] [E]

56. Although all governments differ, there are several similarities in the system of government. Governments are similar in all *except one* of these characteristics:

(A) authority
(B) teamwork
(C) regularized behavior
(D) control of crime
(E) control of the individual

56. [A] [B] [C] [D] [E]

PART 2: GENERAL EDUCATION EXAMINATION

57. The Stuarts of England and the Hohenzollerns of Germany ruled their respective countries by the theory that

    (A) the rights of the state are fixed
    (B) rulership is hereditary
    (C) divine right of kings is justified
    (D) the force theory is right for the people
    (D) the social contract theory is valid

    57. Ⓐ Ⓑ Ⓒ Ⓓ Ⓔ

58. Many people dislike modern art because they approach it

    (A) too cautiously   (D) with detachment
    (B) with uncertainty   (E) with a closed mind
    (C) with preconceived notions

    58. Ⓐ Ⓑ Ⓒ Ⓓ Ⓔ

59. The greatest concept developed during the "Age of Enlightenment" was

    (A) the Copernican theory   (D) Kepler's work on revolution
    (B) the foundation of mathematics (E) Laplace's concept of the world-machine
    (C) Newton's gravitational theory

    59. Ⓐ Ⓑ Ⓒ Ⓓ Ⓔ

60. The first major support for the experimental method was given by the Englishman

    (A) Thomas Malthus   (D) David Hume
    (B) John Locke   (E) Immanuel Kant
    (C) Lord Herbert

    60. Ⓐ Ⓑ Ⓒ Ⓓ Ⓔ

61. A modern musician who used the objectivity of classicism in his compositions was

    (A) Debussy   (D) Stravinsky
    (B) Ravel   (E) Berlioz
    (C) Schoenberg

    61. Ⓐ Ⓑ Ⓒ Ⓓ Ⓔ

62. One of the most active current American composers is

    (A) Strauss   (D) Johnson
    (B) Bernstein   (E) Franck
    (C) Stravinsky

    62. Ⓐ Ⓑ Ⓒ Ⓓ Ⓔ

63. Karl Marx rejected the capitalistic system on the grounds that

    (A) no system can be a pure democracy
    (B) the class system was evil
    (C) a small group profits from the efforts of labor
    (D) profits should only be taken by the government
    (E) industries should be controlled by the government

    63. Ⓐ Ⓑ Ⓒ Ⓓ Ⓔ

64. The conflicts among nations in recent times which have attempted to keep any one nation from dominating the scene have been affected by the theory of

(A) right makes might
(B) might makes right
(C) the balance of power
(D) the hunger motive
(E) the population drive

65. The classical period in music came to an end in 1827 with the death of

(A) Bach
(B) Gluck
(C) Lully
(D) Beethoven
(E) Monteverdi

66. The use of equity under the law is to

(A) protect the state
(B) limit the power of the federal government
(C) challenge the right of eminent domain
(D) enforce the rigidity of the law
(E) prevent individual injustice

67. The Council of Ministers of the U. S. S. R., according to the Soviet constitution, functions as the

(A) judiciary branch of power
(B) representative branch of government
(C) executive branch of state power
(D) Union government
(E) representatives of the Party

68. The tragic drama, the *Doll's House,* was written by Henrik Ibsen, a native of

(A) Holland
(B) France
(C) England
(D) Sweden
(E) Norway

69. There are four basic sources of international laws. More laws have been produced by

(A) the balance of power
(B) control of a country's navy
(C) the need for shipping lanes
(D) the need for export-import duties
(E) custom

70. Negotiating nations sometimes make less formal agreements regarding specific matters which take the form of

(A) protocols
(B) declarations
(C) armistices
(D) cartels
(E) conventions

71. Mediation of serious disputes is less advantageous than arbitration because under the rules of arbitration, the

(A) disputing parties agree to accept the arbitrator's decision

PART 2: GENERAL EDUCATION EXAMINATION

 (B) "gentlemen's agreement" cannot be used
 (C) negotiations are out "in the open"
 (D) settlement is by negotiation only
 (E) settlement is by involuntary action   71. [A][B][C][D][E]

Practice Test 2

DIRECTIONS: All questions are of the multiple-choice type with five possible answers from which you are to choose the *one* you believe to be the *best*. There are five sample answer spaces for each question. You are to blacken the lettered space for the *one* answer you select.

1. Certain characteristics of man can be explained by climate and geographical features of a particular region. This philosophy is known as

 (A) the Malthus theory   (D) geographical determinism
 (B) the law of diminishing returns   (E) humanism
 (C) the law of least resistance   1. [A][B][C][D][E]

2. To get the most from a painting one must be aware of form and story as well as

 (A) texture   (D) emotional impact
 (B) color   (E) purely visual aspects
 (C) details   2. [A][B][C][D][E]

3. John Locke conceived of knowledge as

 (A) based upon reason   (D) as the development of insight
 (B) obtained through revelation   (E) based upon experience
 (C) an inborn trait   3. [A][B][C][D][E]

4. Goethe, in his literary works, emphasized the theme that

 (A) man is innocent
 (B) man is inherently evil
 (C) man is eternally struggling for knowledge
 (D) creation is spontaneous
 (E) individualism is the most important trait   4. [A][B][C][D][E]

5. The poorest viewers of art are those persons who

 (A) take little time   (D) have done some painting
 (B) are intellectually alive   (E) avoid sensual experiences
 (C) are psychologically alive   5. [A][B][C][D][E]

6. The ballard form which originated in the days of feudalism is marked by certain characteristics. Among them is the ballad stanza with certain accented words and the

 (A) iambic pentameter   (D) abstract ideas
 (B) refrain   (E) emphasis upon lost love
 (C) complicated vocabulary   6. [A][B][C][D][E]

COMMON EXAMINATION

7. The character Jean Valjean was the hero in the novel

   (A) *Three Musketeers*
   (B) *Wilheim Meister*
   (C) *Les Miserables*
   (D) *The Count of Monte Cristo*
   (E) *David Copperfield*

8. The skill of a teacher can fulfill the definition of being scarce and useful and yet *not* be considered as

   (A) service
   (B) personal ability
   (C) an economic good
   (D) a material
   (E) a utility

9. The *Descent From the Cross* was painted by

   (A) Leonardo da Vinci
   (B) Michelangelo
   (C) Rembrandt
   (D) El Greco
   (E) Cezanne

10. Fichte, through his writings, greatly aided the transformation of German cultural nationalism into

    (A) colonialism
    (B) mercantilism
    (C) political nationalism
    (D) organic unity
    (E) socialism

11. The painter who wrote, "that painting is most praiseworthy which is most like the thing represented," was

    (A) Rembrandt
    (B) Picasso
    (C) Cezanne
    (D) Rubens
    (E) da Vinci

12. The use of dissonant chords in music creates the feeling of

    (A) relaxation
    (B) beauty
    (C) tension
    (D) confusion
    (E) fulfillment

13. Burke opposed the

    (A) destruction of institutions inherited from the past
    (B) dominance of middle class values
    (C) reliance upon tradition
    (D) reliance upon tradtional responsibilities of citezenship
    (E) any form of conformity

14. The "natural right" theory permitted the kings' exploitation of their subjects because when the people resisted they thought they were

PART 2: GENERAL EDUCATION EXAMINATION

    (A) subject to punishment
    (B) held under a common bond of fealty
    (C) obligated for servitude
    (D) under social contract obligations
    (E) rebelling against divine authority

15. *Anna Karenina* was a Russian novel depicting

    (A) the Revolution
    (B) the influency of Peter the Great
    (C) the time of Catherine the Great
    (D) pre-World War I aristocratic life
    (E) post-revolutionary Russia

16. In Burke's *Reflection on the French Revolution,* he contended that man

    (A) is endowed with certain inalienable rights
    (B) acquired rights in the community in which he is born
    (C) has rights that are abstract
    (D) develops the state deliberately
    (E) should regaard the state as a contract with the individual

17. Musical compositions are usually written in one of two kinds of time–*duple* or *triple*. In triple time with three beats to the bar, the accent in on the

    (A) first   (D) first and second
    (B) second   (E) first and third
    (C) third

18. Another name for four-four time is

    (A) legato   (D) free rhythm
    (B) common time   (E) halftime
    (C) double beat

19. In "The Devil and Daniel Webster," Jabez Stone sold his soul to the devil

    (A) as a lark   (D) to pay a debt
    (B) after a drunken spree   (E) to pay the mortgage on the farm
    (C) because of family illness and bad luck

20. The hypotheses that thesis produces antitheses which then is resolved into a syntheses was relevant to the philosophy of

    (A) Erasmus   (D) Hegel
    (B) Schiller   (E) Fichte
    (C) Burke

21. One of the best known paintings by da Vinci is the

COMMON EXAMINATION

(A) *Mona Lisa*
(B) *Discobolus*
(C) *Disrobing of Christ*
(D) *Madonna of the Rocks*
(E) *Sistine Madonna*

21. [A] [B] [C] [D] [E]

22. The present concept of the state

(A) has evolved over a period of time
(B) can be traced to the divine right theory
(C) came about through revolution
(D) is based on the socialistic theory
(E) shows little influence of the social contract theory

22. [A] [B] [C] [D] [E]

23. An oligarchy is government by

(A) a single monarch
(B) a group of leaders
(C) anarchy
(D) democratic action
(E) socialistic precepts

23. [A] [B] [C] [D] [E]

24. The tempo generally determines the duration of musical beats. *Allegro molto* means to play the piece

(A) solemnly
(B) slowly
(C) broadly
(D) very lively
(E) lively

24. [A] [B] [C] [D] [E]

25. Booth Tarkington's book, *Seventeen*, was greeted with indignation by adolescents because the characters

(A) had babyish speech
(B) were immature
(C) were immoral
(D) obeyed their parents
(E) fell in love

25. [A] [B] [C] [D] [E]

26. The musician who sees the word *accelerando* above a few bars will begin to play

(A) gradually slower
(B) leisurely
(C) very lively
(D) very quickly
(E) gradually faster

26. [A] [B] [C] [D] [E]

27. A good illustration of unitary state was the Third French Republic in that local officials.

(A) were directed by Napoleon
(B) were free of kingly control
(C) were heavily taxed
(D) exercised local control
(E) secured their authority from the central government.

27. [A] [B] [C] [D] [E]

28. England and the United States are democracies due to the

(A) two legislative houses
(B) authority of elected officials
(C) freedom of the citizens

PART 2: GENERAL EDUCATION EXAMINATION

(D) national elections
(E) authority of local governments

29. The American writer Edna St. Vincent Millay is best known for her

(A) novels
(B) detective plots
(C) sonnets
(D) lyric poetry
(E) essays

30. One main difference between modern totalitarian states and despotic monarchies is the

(A) interest of present states in education
(B) neglect of the masses in totalitarian states
(C) role of leadership
(D) delegation of authority
(E) restrictions on citizens

31. Economic goods differ from services in their

(A) materiality
(B) scarcity
(C) utility
(D) transferability
(E) productivity

32. Close analysis of the paintings of Rembrandt will reveal that every face he painted was

(A) a natural giant
(B) untrue to nature
(C) himself
(D) his brother
(E) photographic realism

33. It is unlikely that an entire musical composition would be marked *presstissimo* in tempo for this means to play it

(A) as solemnly as possible
(B) as quickly as possible
(C) as lively as possible
(D) faster than andante
(E) not as fast as allegro

34. One of the basic functions of government is to preserve the domestic peace. One nation which succumbed because it could not control internal discorder was

(A) Germany
(B) Russia in 1917
(C) Italy
(D) Franch
(E) Venezuela

35. A number of obligations of the state relate to its responsibility to promote the general welfare. An example is

(A) the education of the populace
(B) support of labor management relations

(C) laws regarding marriage
(D) regulatory laws prohibiting individual acts
(E) the federal income tax

35. [A] [B] [C] [D] [E]

36. The development of the town form of local government in the New England colonies was fostered by

(A) the Indian raids
(B) land unsuited for agricultural use
(C) the unfavorable climate
(D) the English populace
(E) the strict religious beliefs of the citizens

36. [A] [B] [C] [D] [E]

37. Economic goods that have a material quality can be classified as

(A) essential
(B) scarce
(C) useful
(D) services
(E) wealth

37. [A] [B] [C] [D] [E]

38. When describing the *timbre* of a musical instrument the musician is referring to

(A) the string family
(B) the woodwind family
(C) its range
(D) its color
(E) texture

38. [A] [B] [C] [D] [E]

39. In economics, land is a natural resouces

(A) essential as wealth
(B) created without labor
(C) nonessential for production
(D) of little use in consumption
(E) or free goods

39. [A] [B] [C] [D] [E]

40. The main difference between Oriental music and non-Oriental music is in its texture. In Oriental countries music generally has

(A) polyphonic texture
(B) slow scale passages
(C) monophonic texture
(D) harmonic fifth chords
(E) rapid tempo

40. [A] [B] [C] [D] [E]

41. European furniture has shown distinct characteristics during various historical periods. Ebony cabinets with intricate carvings were popular during the

(A) Renaissance
(B) Baroque period
(C) time of Louis XVI
(D) tiem of Louis XIII
(E) "Empire" period

41. [A] [B] [C] [D] [E]

42. Capital has its greatest economic value in that it

PART 2: GENERAL EDUCATION EXAMINATION

    (A) belongs to everybody   (D) is used to produce other goods
    (B) is government-controlled   (E) exploits labor
    (C) in non-materialistic

42. [A] [B] [C] [D] [E]

43. Pop art, in its attempt to portray the dehumanizing aspects of realism, becomes

    (A) idealism   (D) a protest against popular style
    (B) classical realism   (E) an art of realism
    (C) photographic realism

43. [A] [B] [C] [D] [E]

44. The German philosopher, Hegel, tried to reconcile

    (A) scholasticism with romanticism
    (B) romanticism with rationalism
    (C) conservatism with absolutism
    (D) scientism with romanticism
    (E) scholasticism with scientism

44. [A] [B] [C] [D] [E]

45. There are numerous classifications in the field of economics. Capital, which plays a brief part in the productive process, is classified as

    (A) free capital   (D) circulating capital
    (B) specialized capital   (E) wealth
    (C) fixed capital

45. [A] [B] [C] [D] [E]

46. The county form of government was best suited to the needs of the

    (A) New England colonies   (D) South
    (B) New York colony   (E) Middle Colonies
    (C) Connecticut settlement

46. [A] [B] [C] [D] [E]

47. The Virginia Bill of Rights embodied the principle that

    (A) all men have certain inherent rights
    (B) a democracy is not a republic
    (C) the people must be free
    (D) education is essential for general welfare
    (E) the legislative branch is the most powerful arm of government

47. [A] [B] [C] [D] [E]

48. The state of Maryland would not ratify the Articles of Confederation until

    (A) the role of Congress was defined
    (B) it established its own government
    (C) the western claims were clarified
    (D) each state had equal rights
    (E) Connecticut was accepted into the union

48. [A] [B] [C] [D] [E]

49. The best known American painter of regional scenes is

    (A) Andrew Wyeth   (D) Rockwell Kent
    (B) Norman Rockwell   (E) Edward Hopper
    (C) H. Bosch

49. [A] [B] [C] [D] [E]

COMMON EXAMINATION

50. According to the philosophy of Hegel, reason

    (A) was usually in error
    (B) was static and unchanging
    (C) was a fusion of contradictions
    (D) was a faculty existing in individuals
    (E) existed outside the *real*

51. Frank Lloyd Wright is best known for his contribution to

    (A) history
    (B) literature
    (C) politics
    (D) music
    (E) architecture

52. The significance of the Ordinances of 1785 and 1787 lies in the

    (A) plan for constitutional union
    (B) plan for territorial government
    (C) plan for colonial expansion
    (d) provision for the building of roads in western lands
    (E) provision for homesteading western lands

53. There are several kinds of income which a person may obtain. The type of income which is of *least* importance to an economist would be

    (A) money income
    (B) real income
    (C) capital gains
    (D) earned income
    (E) psychic income

54. Edmund Burke contributed greatly toward the shaping of

    (A) a conservative British political and social philosophy
    (B) British antagonism against the American colonies
    (C) the American Revolution
    (D) French pre-revolutionary philosophy
    (E) the social contract philosophy of government

55. The democratic form of government has always used private property as

    (A) an incentive to economic growth
    (B) a restriction upon the individual
    (C) a weapon against corporate expansion
    (D) a prohibition upon the use of free goods
    (E) a source of wealth

56. The composer of the well-known *Messiah* was

    (A) Wagner
    (B) Sullivan
    (C) Handel
    (D) Bach
    (E) Mozart

PART 2: GENERAL EDUCATION EXAMINATION

57. The development of the modern factory system has its origin in

    (A) the craft guilds
    (B) the English woolen industry
    (C) British iron and steel industries
    (D) Medieval breweries and tanneries
    (E) the expansion of coal mining

58. Mozart was a great composer who lived in the

    (A) fifteenth century
    (B) sixteenth century
    (C) seventeenth century
    (D) eighteenth century
    (E) nineteenth century

59. The economic characteristics of the modern era which began in the Middle Ages and accelerated progress into the 20th century came to be known as the

    (A) Protestant Reformation
    (B) Industrial Revolution
    (C) capitalistic state
    (D) socialistic form of economy
    (E) theory of mercantilism

60. The major difference between Egyptian, Greek, and Roman architecture is the Roman use of the

    (A) arch
    (B) ramp
    (C) lintel
    (D) embellishment
    (E) natural contour

61. The constitution limits the powers of the states in *one* of the following areas:

    (A) education
    (B) highways
    (C) welfare
    (D) ex post facto laws
    (E) use of "tokens" for sales taxes

62. Which one of the following compositions would not belong in a program of "absolute" or "pure" music?

    (A) Tschaikovsky's *Concerto in B-flat Minor, No. 1*
    (B) Moussorgsky's *Pictures at an Exhibition*
    (C) Mozart's *Symphony No. 40*
    (D) Mendelssohn's *Violin Concerto*
    (E) Beethoven's *Third Symphony*

63. The President of the U.S. may be removed through

    (A) recall
    (B) impeachment
    (C) investiture
    (D) filabuster
    (E) Congressional action

64. In the Soviet Union the legislative power is vested in the

(A) Council of Ministers
(B) Presidium
(C) Council of Nationalities
(D) Council of the Union
(E) Supreme Soviet

64. Ⓐ Ⓑ Ⓒ Ⓓ Ⓔ

65. The dramatist has one disadvantage over the novelist in that he

(A) must curtail a play's length
(B) has limited characterization
(C) must use a narrow plot
(D) cannot easily reveal the thoughts of his characters
(E) has limited settings for action

65. Ⓐ Ⓑ Ⓒ Ⓓ Ⓔ

66. Liszt developed the tone poem to a high degree of perfection. One of his most beautiful tone poems is

(A) *Les Preludes*
(B) *Fantasy*
(C) *Moonlight Sonata*
(D) *Eine Kleine Nachtmusik*
(E) *Eroica*

66. Ⓐ Ⓑ Ⓒ Ⓓ Ⓔ

67. Bach wrote the greatest works in

(A) cantata form
(B) contrapuntal form
(C) harmony and melody
(D) chamber sonata form
(E) oratorio form

67. Ⓐ Ⓑ Ⓒ Ⓓ Ⓔ

68. The Pan-American Union has its permanent headquarters in

(A) Washington D. C.
(B) New York City
(C) San Francisco
(D) Trinidad
(E) Ecuador

68. Ⓐ Ⓑ Ⓒ Ⓓ Ⓔ

69. Cultural lag exists in most societies due to the fact that

(A) transfer of training is small
(B) experiments are invalid
(C) human behavior is unpredictable
(D) the non-material lags behind material culture in growth rate
(E) in rapid change, folkways lose their importance

69. Ⓐ Ⓑ Ⓒ Ⓓ Ⓔ

70. The largest instrument in the string family is the

(A) cello
(B) violin
(C) viola
(D) double bass
(E) contrabassoon

70. Ⓐ Ⓑ Ⓒ Ⓓ Ⓔ

PART 2: GENERAL EDUCATION EXAMINATION

Practice Test 3

DIRECTIONS: All questions are of the multiple-choice type with five possible answers from which you are to choose the *one* you believe to be the best. There are five sample answer spaces for each question. You are to blacken the lettered space for the *one* answer you select.

1. The first major change which industrialization brought to manufacturing was the

    (A) introduction of child labor
    (B) British putting out or domestic system
    (C) British control of coal mining
    (D) mass production
    (E) building of huge factories

2. Polyphonic music requires more concentration by the listener than homophonic music because of its

    (A) tempo
    (B) independent melodies
    (C) timbre
    (D) harmonic chords
    (E) dissonance

3. The architecture of the Byzantine period is characterized by the use of

    (A) stained glass windows
    (B) chancels
    (C) columns
    (D) sculpture
    (E) the arch and vault

4. The greatest German composer of the opera form was

    (A) Bach
    (B) Brahms
    (C) Beethoven
    (D) Liszt
    (E) Wagner

5. The hold which Greek art has had upon students of art for centuries is primarily due to its

    (A) concern for reality
    (B) natural approach
    (C) ability to transcend reality
    (D) content
    (E) emotional impact

6. The most significant legislation of the congress of the Confederation was the

    (A) right of each state to one vote
    (B) bicameral legislature
    (C) provision for justice
    (D) the Northwest Ordinance
    (E) the Ordinance of 1785

7. The Constitution of the United States has been changed to meet the needs of a developing nation. The Constitution has been changed by all *except one* of the following ways:

(A) amendments
(B) statutes by legislative bodies
(C) court decisions
(D) presidential edict
(E) administrative interpretation

7. Ⓐ Ⓑ Ⓒ Ⓓ Ⓔ

8. The concerto is a form of music which often appears on musical programs. A concerto by definition is a musical composition which uses

   (A) a solo instrument
   (B) two stringed instruments
   (C) a piano and orchestra
   (D) a solo insturment with an orchestra
   (E) an orchestra and harp

8. Ⓐ Ⓑ Ⓒ Ⓓ Ⓔ

9. Karl Marx in his radical social and political philosophy drew the concept of historical evolution as a dialectical development from the nineteenth century writings of the conservative German

   (A) Fichte   (D) Hagerman
   (B) Hegel   (E) Herder
   (C) Stein

9. Ⓐ Ⓑ Ⓒ Ⓓ Ⓔ

10. The Congress of Vienna, 1814-1815, met for the purpose of

    (A) concluding the War of 1812
    (B) refining the Treaty of 1812
    (C) making naval agreements
    (D) settling shipping claims
    (E) settling boundaries after the Napoleonic Wars

10. Ⓐ Ⓑ Ⓒ Ⓓ Ⓔ

11. A musical composition for solo piano is usually called a

    (A) concerto   (D) overture
    (B) sonata   (E) prelude
    (C) symphony

11. Ⓐ Ⓑ Ⓒ Ⓓ Ⓔ

12. An amendment to the Constitution can be made by a

    (A) one-fourth vote of the Senate
    (B) two-thirds vote of both houses of Congress and ratified by three-fourths of the states
    (C) ratified by three-fourths of the states
    (D) presidential signature
    (E) Supreme Court regulation

12. Ⓐ Ⓑ Ⓒ Ⓓ Ⓔ

13. The realism in the paintings of Rembrandt is shown by his use of

    (A) romantic scenes   (D) everyday scenes
    (B) religious themes   (E) adventurous fantasies
    (C) flamboyant colors

13. Ⓐ Ⓑ Ⓒ Ⓓ Ⓔ

PART 2: GENERAL EDUCATION EXAMINATION

14. The movements of a symphony are differentiated by

    (A) use of different instruments
    (B) use of solo instrument in the third movement
    (C) mood and tempo
    (D) intensity
    (E) tempo

15. Admirers of the scientific method consider the greatest historical writer of modern times to be the German historian

    (A) Herder
    (B) Hagerman
    (C) Fichte
    (D) Ranke
    (E) Hegel

16. Early Christian art differed from secular works through its emphasis upon

    (A) idealized qualities
    (B) form
    (C) emotionalism
    (D) copying the real world
    (E) spiritual mysticism

17. A "Gentlemen's agreement" in business has often

    (A) hampered the use of capital goods
    (B) controlled the sale of consumer goods
    (C) interfered with competitive prices
    (D) controlled the amount of production
    (E) hampered the collection of income taxes

18. The U. S. Constitution failed to provide for

    (A) the Presidential veto power
    (B) a federal annual budget
    (C) state's rights
    (D) the election of a president
    (E) the election of a vice-president

19. Epic hero tales have been written in periods of cultural growth but not in primitive times. One of the best known of epics is the *Iliad* and *Odyssey* which was written by

    (A) Sappho
    (B) Plato
    (C) Cid
    (D) Roland
    (E) Homer

20. A summary of the religious faith of the Middle Ages is found in the *Divine Comedy* written by

    (A) Seigfried
    (B) Chaucer
    (C) Malory
    (D) Swift
    (E) Dante

COMMON EXAMINATION

21. The art of pre-historic artists is characterized by

    (A) carving
    (B) drawing
    (C) metalwork
    (D) etching
    (E) carving and drawing

22. Program music differs from absolute music in its attempt to

    (A) portray an idea
    (B) be music for its own sake
    (C) be relaxing to the listener
    (D) by symbolic
    (E) be idealistic

23. Production, according to the economist, is the

    (A) manufacutre of consumer goods
    (B) creation of utility
    (C) creation of wealth
    (D) creation of capital
    (E) creation of form utility

24. The greatest weakness of the Articles of Confederation arose from the

    (A) lack of an executive department of government
    (B) small number of states in the union
    (C) lack of amending procedures
    (D) lack of funds to operate the government
    (E) jealously among the states

25. The art of the Renaissance period reflected

    (A) the spirit of mysticism
    (B) the revealed nature of truth
    (C) classical idealism
    (D) idealism
    (E) surrealism

26. If advertising is effective it will increase the desiredness for goods and thus create

    (A) time utility
    (B) place utility
    (C) possession utility
    (D) new consumer goods
    (E) new maintenance needs

27. The U. S. government, as structured under the Consittution, was

    (A) an oligarchy
    (B) a pure democracy
    (C) a socialistic state
    (D) a representative democracy
    (E) a patronage system

PART 2: GENERAL EDUCATION EXAMINATION

28. Great impetus was given to the Industrial Revolution in the nineteenth century by the

    (A) building of roads
    (B) division of labor
    (C) use of machinery
    (D) decline of craft guilds
    (E) development of the railroads

29. Which one of the following compositions would be classified as program music?

    (A) Beethoven's *Piano Concerto No. 4 in G Major*
    (B) Brahm's *Symphony No. 1 in C Minor*
    (C) Prokofieff's *Peter and the Wolf*
    (D) Ravel's *Concerto in G Major for Piano and Orchestra*
    (E) Handel's *Messiah*

30. The chief executive of the United States must be a

    (A) member of the majority party in Congress
    (B) resident of the same state as the vice-president
    (C) citizen of the United States
    (D) male, twenty-five years old or older
    (E) veteran, as he commands the armed forces

31. One of the most essential factors in production consists of

    (A) natural resources
    (B) labor
    (C) construction area
    (D) wealth
    (E) stocks and bonds

32. While Virgil's *Aeneid* was a fictitious epic, Homer's *Iliad* and *Odyssey* were based upon

    (A) folk legends
    (B) Roman history
    (C) a prehistoric ode
    (D) worship of the gods
    (E) the fall of Carthage

33. The American nation is a federal state due to the power of the central government and the states. The Amendment which safeguards the authority of the states is the

    (A) Fifth Amendment
    (B) Tenth Amendment
    (C) Twelfth Amendment
    (D) Twentieth Amendment
    (E) Twenty-first Amendment

34. Absolute music has its particular appeal because while it doesn't tell a story it

    (A) is monophonic
    (B) utilizes harmony
    (C) uses abstract symbols
    (D) expresses human emotions
    (E) employs melody and harmony

COMMON EXAMINATION

35. A comedy is a play in which

    (A) the hero dies
    (B) the hero triumphs
    (C) the climax is uncertain
    (D) several characters take the lead
    (E) some characters have happy endings

36. The business executive who has a salary of $50,000 a year is *not* an enterpriser unless he

    (A) is the corporation president
    (B) contributes his services
    (C) also takes risks through ownership
    (D) directs the production of goods
    (E) is an innovator

37. American Indians have had certain restrictions and rights. In 1924, they were

    (A) classified as wards of the government
    (B) given full citizenship
    (C) considered as aliens
    (D) classified as stateless persons
    (E) classified as dependents

38. According to Jefferson, the role of government

    (A) was limited only by the Constitution
    (B) was limited by popular needs
    (C) was to have rule by the intellectual elite
    (D) was limited to maintenance of order and peace
    (E) implied strong federal control

39. A naturalized citizen cannot

    (A) hold public office
    (B) serve in the armed forces
    (C) become President of the United States
    (D) lose his state citizenship
    (E) vote in the presidential primaries

40. Expressionist painters like Van Gogh depict the world as the

    (A) artist sees it
    (B) artist feels it
    (C) world should be
    (D) visual perspective
    (E) world of nature

41. The treaty-making power of the Chief Executive is limited by

    (A) Senate approval
    (B) Congressional approval
    (C) Supreme Court approval
    (D) Constitutional amendment
    (E) power of the ambassadors

PART 2: GENERAL EDUCATION EXAMINATION

42. Prior to the nomination of the presidential candidate, each political party must

    (A) select a candidate
    (B) run its candidate in several state primaries
    (C) adopt a platform
    (D) let the public see and hear the candidates
    (E) sense popular appeal

43. The voters select the President by

    (A) voting the straight ticket
    (B) splitting ballot
    (C) selecting the President in the primary
    (D) casting their ballots for electors
    (E) a direct vote

44. A composition for orchestra in one movement is called

    (A) a concerto grosso
    (B) a symphony
    (C) a sonata allegro
    (D) an overture
    (E) a suite

45. It is possible to receive the largest number of popular votes and still not win the presidential election. This can happen when

    (A) the opposition candidate obtains the most electoral votes
    (B) the vice-presidential candidate receives more votes
    (C) the popular vote in small states is small
    (D) the voters do not select all the electors
    (E) voters improperly register

46. A United States senator must be at least

    (A) twenty-four years old
    (B) thirty-two years old
    (C) twenty-eight years old
    (D) thirty-five years old
    (E) thirty years old

47. One of the outstanding composers of the Renaissance (1400-1600) was

    (A) Bach
    (B) Haydn
    (C) Purcell
    (D) Palestrina
    (E) Mozart

48. To the cubist painter, the most important factor is

    (A) color
    (B) texture
    (C) structure
    (D) shape
    (E) line

49. The President can remove from office

    (A) anyone employed by the government
    (B) only members of his cabinet
    (C) only high-ranking officers of the armed forces
    (D) appointed officials, except civil service employees
    (E) only ambassadors and consuls   49. Ⓐ Ⓑ Ⓒ Ⓓ Ⓔ

50. The madrigal is a choral work which flourished in the

    (A) sixteenth century   (D) fifteenth century
    (B) twelfth century   (E) eighteenth century
    (C) thirteenth century   50. Ⓐ Ⓑ Ⓒ Ⓓ Ⓔ

51. The influence of African art is evident in the work of the Cubist artist

    (A) Cezanne   (D) Leger
    (B) Braque   (E) Delaunay
    (C) Picasso   51. Ⓐ Ⓑ Ⓒ Ⓓ Ⓔ

52. A United States' Representative must be

    (A) a resident of the district from which he is elected
    (B) a man with political experience
    (C) a citizen of the United States
    (D) twenty-five years of age
    (E) thirty years of age   52. Ⓐ Ⓑ Ⓒ Ⓓ Ⓔ

53. A dramatic composition, based upon a religious text, for orchestra, chorus, and soloists is

    (A) a concerto   (D) a madrigal
    (B) a symphonic poem   (E) an oratorio
    (C) a motet   53. Ⓐ Ⓑ Ⓒ Ⓓ Ⓔ

54. Impressionism had its origin in the work of

    (A) nineteenth century French painters   (D) Daumier
    (B) Goya   (E) Chardin
    (C) Corot   54. Ⓐ Ⓑ Ⓒ Ⓓ Ⓔ

55. The Constitution provides that all bills of revenue must

    (A) be initiated by the President
    (B) come from the House
    (C) originate in the Senate
    (D) originate with the appropriations
    (E) be presented first in the committee of the national budget 55. Ⓐ Ⓑ Ⓒ Ⓓ Ⓔ

PART 2: GENERAL EDUCATION EXAMINATION

56. Members of Congress have certain immunities. However, a Congressman can be arrested for

    (A) a felony
    (B) a misdemeanor
    (C) verbal attack against another member
    (D) verbal attack on the President
    (E) absence from office

57. Many pressure groups function in Washington. Each group maintains its own influential

    (A) publicity representatives   (D) campaign directors
    (B) senatorial leaders   (E) representatives in the House
    (C) lobbyists

58. The Impressionist movement emphasized the

    (A) emotional   (D) ordinary
    (B) unemotional   (E) idealistic
    (C) subjectivity

59. The federal judiciary consists of three main courts - the district court, the Supreme Court, and the

    (A) probate court   (D) municipal court
    (B) court of appeals   (E) juvenile court
    (C) circuit court

60. One of the most often demonstrated forms of cooperation between federal and state governments is in

    (A) road building   (D) military affairs
    (B) income taxes   (E) liquor tax collection
    (C) parochial education

61. The powers of the federal government are delegated by the Constitution; the rights of the states are

    (A) imposed by state consitutions
    (B) reserved by the Constitution
    (C) guaranteed by the state constitutions
    (D) delegated by the Constitution
    (E) delegated by state legislatures

62. An example of interstate cooperation which serves the public is the

    (A) Boulder Dam project
    (B) federal highways
    (C) teacher retirement acts

(D) import duties on goods
(E) acceptance of education credits

63. The famous *Overture of 1812* was composed by

(A) Tschaikovsky
(B) Moussorgsky
(C) Schubert
(D) Stravinsky
(E) Haydn

64. Modern music which uses the twelve tones of the chromatic scales is characterized by

(A) atonality
(B) dominant chords
(C) the dominant fifth
(D) the tonic chord
(E) the C-major key

65. One significant reason for the establishment of a judicial system as the third branch of government is that

(A) the federal government is affected by the political affiliation of the leaders
(B) the federal government has only powers delegated to it by the Constitution
(C) the states can challenge the role of the federal government
(D) citizens can sue the government
(E) the federal government is involved in foreign relations

66. The short story has its origin in the prose tales written by Boccaccio in

(A) Italy
(B) England
(C) Finland
(D) France
(E) Scotland

67. The most important difference between the Classical and Romantic musical compositions is the Romantic emphasis upon

(A) structure
(B) harmony
(C) expressing emotions
(D) size and grandeur
(E) restraint of emotions

68. Since 1823, the Monroe Doctrine has supported the development of South American countries through its intention that

(A) European countries may not engage in free trade
(B) European countries may no longer colonize South America
(C) European labor may not be used to flood South American markets
(D) South American products may enjoy free import status
(E) raw materials from North American may be shipped to South America

PART 2: GENERAL EDUCATION EXAMINATION

69. The largest instrument in the string family is the

    (A) cello
    (B) violin
    (C) double bass
    (D) viola
    (E) contrabassoon

70. Harmony in music is similar in painting to the use of

    (A) perspective
    (B) color
    (C) form
    (D) texture
    (E) sensual impact

SCIENCE AND MATHEMATICS

Practice Test 1

1. According to Aristotelian logic we can argue deductively that if

   All adolescents are rebellious,
   Johnny is a pre-adolescent

   (A) Johnny is rebellious.
   (B) Johnny might be rebellious.
   (C) Some adolescents are not rebellious.
   (D) Johnny is not rebellious.
   (E) The statement is unreliable.

2. A needle will float upon the surface of the water due to

   (A) gravity
   (B) density
   (C) weight
   (D) elasticity
   (E) surface tension

3. In statistics, the average score can be determined by

   (A) the mean
   (B) the standard deviation
   (C) the median
   (D) (A), (C), and (E)
   (E) the mode

4. Logic is primarily concerned with

   (A) valid inference
   (B) individual judgment
   (C) inductive systems
   (D) analogy
   (E) theoretical concepts

COMMON EXAMINATION

5. A 15-pound lead ball and a 5-pound iron ball are dropped simultaneously from a height of 25 feet.

    (A) The iron ball reaches the ground first.
    (B) The lead ball reaches the ground first.
    (C) Both balls reach the ground at the same time.
    (D) Air pressure determine which ball reaches the ground first.
    (E) Air currents determine which ball reaches the ground first.

6. In algebraic symbols, $x^2 - y^2$ equals

    (A) xy^2
    (B) $(x+y)(x-y)$
    (C) $x - y^2$
    (D) $x^2 - y$
    (E) $(x^2 + y)(x - y)$

7. In a storage battery the flow of electrons

    (A) comes from the negative terminal
    (B) comes from the positive terminal
    (C) comes from either terminal
    (D) depends upon voltage
    (E) no definite terminal

8. Two co-planar lines are parallel if

    (A) their slopes are negative reciprocals of each other
    (B) they intersect
    (C) their slopes differ
    (D) they have the same slope
    (E) they coincide

9. The corpuscular theory that light was made up of tine particles was formulated by

    (A) Franklin
    (B) Newton
    (C) Bacon
    (D) Roemer
    (E) Galileo

10. An atom or a group of atoms carrying an excess electric charge is called

    (A) a proton
    (B) an ion
    (C) a neutron
    (D) a meson
    (E) a molecule

11. The slope of a horizontal line is zero, but the slope of a vertical line is

    (A) dependent upon the x coordinate
    (B) dependent upon the y coordinate

117

PART 2: GENERAL EDUCATION EXAMINATION

(C) in constant variation
(D) undefined
(E) impossible to measure

11. [A] [B] [C] [D] [E]

12. A needle is stroked from its head to its point, using the north pole as its magnet. The polarity of the point of the needles is

(A) north
(B) northeast
(C) south
(D) southwest
(E) south, southwest

12. [A] [B] [C] [D] [E]

13. A scientific theory is

(A) a law
(B) an hypothesis
(C) indirect evidence
(D) a logical guess
(E) direct evidence

13. [A] [B] [C] [D] [E]

14. One of the most often used forms of logical argument is the

(A) category
(B) inference
(C) syllogism
(D) hypothesis
(E) synthesis

14. [A] [B] [C] [D] [E]

15. Air pressure at sea level is approximately

(A) 16 lbs./sq. in.
(B) 14.7 lbs./sq. in.
(C) 1 lb./sq. in.
(D) 15.8 lbs./sq. in.
(E) 20.1 lbs./sq. in.

15. [A] [B] [C] [D] [E]

16. The theory that the earth is a part of a solar system with the sun at its center was first expressed by

(A) Galileo
(B) Copernicus
(C) Bacon
(D) Helio
(E) Aristotle

16. [A] [B] [C] [D] [E]

17. A prime number may be defined as a natural number that has two factors, itself and

(A) 2
(B) 1
(C) 3
(D) 5
(E) 10

17. [A] [B] [C] [D] [E]

18. Air provides oxygen which is necessary for life and, also performs one other very essential function. It

(A) keeps water vapor from rising

(B) diffuses the heat rays of the sun
(C) contains the oceans by air pressure
(D) diffuses dust particular
(E) keeps smog from rising

18. [A][B][C][D][E]

19. In relation to the solar system, the earth

(A) is the largest planet
(B) is the smallest planet
(C) is nearest the sun
(D) is in the center of the planets in order
(E) has no special distinction

19. [A][B][C][D][E]

20. According to the metric system, 10 millimeters is equal to

(A) 1 gram
(B) 1 liter
(C) 1 meter
(D) 1 kilometer
(E) 1 centimeter

20. [A][B][C][D][E]

21. If the sun were to "black out" for any period of time

(A) the earth would be cooler
(B) all life would eventually cease
(C) primitive life would survive
(D) the ocean would lose its tides
(E) water would cover the earth

21. [A][B][C][D][E]

22. Which one of the following has no relationship to the other four concepts?

(A) evaporation
(B) gravity
(C) Mach number
(D) sound barrier
(E) supersonic

22. [A][B][C][D][E]

23. Intersecting lines are lines which

(A) have no points in common
(B) have the same length
(C) are parallel
(D) have at least one point in common
(E) have two points in common

23. [A][B][C][D][E]

24. The scale which uses a spring balance demonstrates the application of

(A) Boyle's Law
(B) Galileo's Principle
(C) Hooke's Law
(D) Pascal's Law
(E) Archimedes' Law

24. [A][B][C][D][E]

PART 2: GENERAL EDUCATION EXAMINATION

Practice Test 2

1. Mathematics has a dual nature. It can be studied

    (A) as a theoretical subject
    (B) as mental discipline
    (C) in its applications to other knowledge
    (D) as both (A) and (B)
    (E) as both (A) and (C)

2. When electrons can move freely from atom to atom, the substance is

    (A) charged   (D) a repellent
    (B) neutral   (E) a conductor
    (C) an insulator

3. Applied mathematics is

    (A) an empirical study   (D) purely philosophical in nature
    (B) a theoretical study   (E) the study of theoretical structure
    (C) based upon formal logic

4. When polarization occurs in a cell

    (A) the EMF decreases   (D) the current increases
    (B) the EMF increases   (E) the current decreases
    (C) the EMF is unchanged

5. If x, y, and z are natural numbers, then $x(y + z)$ equals

    (A) xyz (D) $xy + 2x$
    (B) $xy + z$ (E) $x(yz)$
    (C) $xy + xz$

6. The pull of gravity on the moon, as compared with the pull of gravity on the earth is

    (A) only 1/10th that of the earth
    (B) only 1/6th that of earth
    (C) only 1/4th that of earth
    (D) only 1/20th that of earth
    (E) only 1/3rd that of earth

7. If a gas is at a constant temperature, the relation between the *density* and the *pressure* is

COMMON EXAMINATION

(A) without relation
(B) an inverse relationship
(E) a direct relationship
(D) immeasurable
(E) unpredictable

7. A B C D E

8. It is possible to factor the expression $3a + 3b + 3c$. The answer is

(A) $3(a+b+c)$
(B) $9(a+b+c)$
(C) $9a + 9b + 9c$
(D) $27abc$
(E) $9abc$

8. A B C D E

9. If a planet has water, carbon dioxide, and chlorophyll, photosynthesis can take place if

(A) air is available
(B) light is available
(C) energy is available
(D) sunlight is present
(E) heat is available

9. A B C D E

10. There are three main divisions of materials on the earth: (1) the atmosphere, (2) the hydrosphere, and (3) the

(A) oceans
(B) mountains
(C) lithosphere
(D) hemisphere
(E) water vapor

10. A B C D E

11. The concept of a one-to-one correspondence can be used is determining the size of a set of objects. If we count the names of all persons in the history class, our answer will be correct if

(A) all persons are present
(B) the names are listed only once
(C) the names are listed by sex
(D) those persons absent will not be counted
(E) persons with similar names are counted once

11. A B C D E

12. The oxidation of food in the cells is

(A) osmosis
(B) respiration
(C) digestion
(D) the food chain
(E) diffusion

12. A B C D E

13. At one time, the earth was regarded as the center of the universe. This theory was called the

(A) Heliocentric theory
(B) Solar plexus theory
(C) Geocentric theory
(D) Galilean theory
(E) Copernican theory

13. A B C D E

PART 2: GENERAL EDUCATION EXAMINATION

14. When factoring the following expression, $(x^2 + 13x + 42)$, the answer is

    (A) $(3x + 55)$
    (B) $(x + 6)(x + 7)$
    (C) $(2x - 13)$
    (D) $(x^2 - 13 + 42)$
    (E) $(3x - 13 - 42)$

15. Pure water is a compound of

    (A) one atom of hydrogen to two atoms of oxygen
    (B) two atoms of hydrogen to two atoms of oxygen
    (C) two atoms of hydrogen to one atom of oxygen
    (D) one atom of nitrogen to two atoms of hydrogen
    (E) one atom of nitrogen to one atom of oxygen

16. Which *one* of the following does not represent a chemical change?

    (A) adding water to sodium peroxide
    (B) mixing iron and sulfur
    (C) decomposing water by electricity
    (D) producing hydrogen from iron and hydrochloric acid
    (E) forming mercuric oxide from mercury and oxygen

17. When testing for divisibility, an integer is divisible by three of and only if

    (A) the last digit is three
    (B) the sum of its digits is a number divisible by three
    (C) the last digit is one
    (D) the sum of its digits is nine
    (E) the last two digits form a number divisible by three

18. The earth makes one complete rotation on its axis every

    (A) month
    (B) 365¼ days
    (C) twenty-four hours
    (D) twelve hours
    (E) week

19. Ashton was the first scientist to use the term *isotope*. All of these statements *except one* are true about isotopes:

    (A) These are forms of the same element that differ only in atomic weight.
    (B) Isotopes are present in an element in unequal amounts.
    (C) The atomic weight of an element is the average of the atomic weight of its isotopes.
    (D) The atomic weight of an element is a whole number because of its isotopes.
    (E) The atomic weight of an element is not a whole number because of its isotopes.

COMMON EXAMINATION

20. Which of the following is incorrectly represented as a decimal?

   (A) 7/100 = .07
   (B) 2 1/2 % = .25
   (C) 35/100 = .35
   (D) 150 % = 1.50
   (E) 1/3 = .33 1/3

   20.

21. Molecules of a compound can be divided into particles not having the properties of the original substance. These particles are called

   (A) ions
   (B) neutrons
   (C) atoms
   (D) electrons
   (E) protons

   21.

22. Without the anther, no flower would reproduce because it would be without

   (A) pollen
   (B) sepals
   (C) pedicels
   (D) receptacles
   (E) ovaries

   22.

23. Which *one* of the following statements is false?

   (A) -2 is the square root of 4
   (B) every positive number has exactly one positive square root
   (C) -2 equals $\sqrt{4}$
   (D) $\sqrt{4}$ equals 2
   (E) 2 is the square root of 4

   23.

24. Nuclear fission involves all *except one* of these:

   (A) splitting of heavy atoms such as U^{235} and Pu^{239}
   (B) nuclear chain reaction
   (C) fission fragments are vaporized and ionic
   (D) synchrotrons and linear accelerators
   (E) explosions are caused by retention of too many neutrons within fissionable material

   24.

Practice Test 3

DIRECTIONS: Select the best answer from the five possible choices.

1. The longest division of time in the geologic timetable is the

   (A) period
   (B) century
   (C) era
   (D) epoch
   (E) millenium

   1.

PART 2: GENERAL EDUCATION EXAMINATION

2. If x, y, and z are natural numbers, and if $x + z$ equals $y + z$, then x equals

   (A) xyz
   (B) yz
   (C) z
   (D) y
   (E) none of these

3. The bending of a ray of light as it passes from one medium to another is called

   (A) convection
   (B) refraction
   (C) lumination
   (D) reflection
   (E) illumination

4. The speed of light is

   (A) 175,000 mi./ sec.
   (B) 2,000 mi./sec.
   (C) 175 mi./sec.
   (D) 186,000 mi./sec.
   (E) 5,280 mi./sec.

5. In mathematical logic, if we assume that $\Phi \rightarrow \Psi$ is true, and we are then informed that Φ is true, we can conclude that

   (A) Ψ is false
   (B) the statement is in error
   (C) this is impossible
   (D) Ψ is true also
   (E) the answer is invalid

6. The electric meter measures

   (A) watts
   (B) volts
   (C) amperes
   (D) kilowatts
   (E) kilowatt-hours

7. If we had mercury and water at sea level where the atmospheric pressure is 14.7 pounds per square inch, the column of mercury would be raised about 30 inches. Since mercury is 13.6 times as dense as water, how high can a column of water be raised?

   (A) 200 inches
   (B) ten feet
   (C) 20 feet
   (D) 325 feet
   (E) 34 feet

8. Classes can be given a geometrical interpretation by the use of circles in

   (A) class diagrams
   (B) Venn diagrams
   (C) two circles
   (D) demonstrating uncommon elements
   (E) showing relative size

9. If the temperature in a classroom is 72 degrees F., the dew point will be

   (A) 75°F
   (B) 72°F
   (C) below 72°F
   (D) 60°F
   (E) 80°F

COMMON EXAMINATION

10. The inclination of the earth on its axis results in

    (A) night and day
    (B) the tides
    (C) changes in phases of the moon
    (D) seasonal variations in climate
    (E) changes in temperature

    10. [A] [B] [C] [D] [E]

11. If we factor the algebraic expression 3a + 3b which answer is correct?

    (A) 3ab
    (B) 6ab
    (C) 9ab
    (D) 3 (a + b)
    (E) 3 (ab)

    11. [A] [B] [C] [D] [E]

12. The winter solstice begins on December 21 when the sun's direct rays reach

    (A) the equator
    (B) the North Pole
    (C) the Tropic of Cancer
    (D) the Tropic of Capricorn
    (E) the South Pole

    12. [A] [B] [C] [D] [E]

13. What is the product of 3 times 5 hr. 36 min. 30 sec?

    (A) 15 hr. 108 min. 30 sec.
    (B) 16 hr. 42 min.
    (C) 15 hr. 36 min. 30 sec.
    (D) 16 hr. 41 min. 30 sec.
    (E) none of these

    13. [A] [B] [C] [D] [E]

14. Mountains have contributed to the problems of man. Their influence is demonstrated by the

    (A) progress in mountainous regions
    (B) backwardness of Appalachian areas
    (C) wealth created by the natural resources
    (D) frequent migrations from mountainous regions
    (E) barriers to transportation

    14. [A] [B] [C] [D] [E]

15. The answer to the problem: subtract 6 gal. 3 qt. 2 pt. from 9 gal. 1 pt. is:

    (A) 2 gal. 1 qt. 1 pt.
    (B) 1 gal. 2 qt. 1 pt.
    (C) 2 gal. 2 pt.
    (D) 1 gal. 1 qt. 1 pt.
    (E) 3 gal.

    15. [A] [B] [C] [D] [E]

16. Substances which can affect chemical reactions but are not changed by these reactions are

    (A) catalysts
    (B) covalent bonds
    (C) corrdinate bonds
    (D) resonance bonds
    (E) radicals

    16. [A] [B] [C] [D] [E]

17. Fifteen is 20% of what number?

125

PART 2: GENERAL EDUCATION EXAMINATION

(A) 100
(B) 75
(C) 70
(D) 65
(E) 66 2/3

18. The active elements which are either *metals* or *non-metals* can be distinguished by all except one of these:

(A) metals are malleable
(B) nonmetals are ductile
(C) nonmetals are gaseous or soft solids
(D) atoms of nonmetals usually have 5 to 7 electrons in their outer shells
(E) metals are good conductors of electricity

19. Bacteria were among the first forms of life on the earth. Today they are the most abundant form of life. They are characterized by all *except one* of these:

(A) They live invisibly everywhere
(B) Most bacteria are harmless
(C) Certain bacteria have flagella
(D) They have two simple cells
(E) Their cell has no organized nucleus

20. All of these numbers, *except* one, are approximate numbers. Which one is an exact number?

(A) Harry weighs 190 pounds.
(B) There are 5,280 feet in a mile.
(C) There were 35 students in the classroom.
(D) Katie is 5 feet 6 inches tall.
(E) We drove 16 miles to the game.

21. Every flower has four sets of parts. One of these does *not* apply:

(A) stamens
(B) pistil
(C) sepal
(D) petal
(E) anther

22. Animal life in its primitive form is represented today by tiny one-celled animals called

(A) protozoa
(B) fossils
(C) collenterates
(D) arthropods
(E) invertebrates

23. Rational numbers are

(A) percentages of whole numbers
(B) sets of whole numbers
(C) negative whole numbers
(D) ratios of whole numbers
(E) real numbers

COMMON EXAMINATION

24. The scale of electronegativity does *not* include the concept of

    (A) flourine as having the highest tendency to attract shared electrons
    (B) ionization potentials of atoms
    (C) energy released when an electron is added to an atom
    (D) the tendency of a dipole to turn in an electric field
    (E) the chemical bonds of inert elements

WRITTEN ENGLISH EXPRESSION

Practice Test 1

PART 1

DIRECTIONS: Four parts of the sentences below are underlined and lettered. Decide whether any of the underlined parts contains a word use, grammatical construction, or incorrect or omitted punctuation which should not be used in carefully written English. Designate this error by selecting the letter printed beneath the incorrect underlined portion and blacken the corresponding space on the answer sheet. Blacken space E if there are no errors in the sentence. *No sentence contains more than one error.*

EXAMPLE

She spoke <u>loudly</u> and <u>fearlessly</u> to <u>we</u> <u>students</u>. <u>No error</u>
       A   B   C   D   E

1. I <u>saw</u> a horse <u>hitched</u> to a <u>carnival</u> wagon, <u>with two white feet and a spot on</u>
   A   B   C   D
<u>his forehead</u>. <u>No error</u>
                  E

2. I <u>think</u> that <u>anybody</u> should be <u>allowed</u> to attend the game if <u>they</u> wish to.
   A   B   C   D
No error
E

3. I know that <u>either Mary or Jane were</u> here, because <u>she</u> left a <u>note</u> for us.
               A   B   C   D
No error
E

4. <u>Neither</u> my father <u>or</u> my brother would <u>take</u> me to the basketball game
   A   B   C
without my mother <u>or</u> sister. <u>No error</u>
                D   E

5. The new committee <u>agreed</u> that <u>everyone</u> <u>should</u> stand on <u>their</u> own feet.
                            A   B   C   D
No error
E

PART 2: GENERAL EDUCATION EXAMINATION

6. Mrs. Brown is one of those women who never has time to visit her
                        A   B   C
   children's classrooms. No error   6. [A] [B] [C] [D] [E]
        D   E

7. Everybody who was tired went to their room early in the evening. No error   7. [A] [B] [C] [D] [E]
               A   B   C   D   E

8. The two girls, Mary and Josephine, attended Stone and Robinson's
                         A   B   C
   Business College. No error   8. [A] [B] [C] [D] [E]
       D   E

9. It was difficult for Tom and Joe to decorate the tree because most of
            A   B   C
   the tree's trimmings were tinsel. No error   9. [A] [B] [C] [D] [E]
           D   E

10. I said that the principal, feeling as strongly as he does, could not talk to
           A   B   C   D
    the students without scolding them. No error   10. [A] [B] [C] [D] [E]
                                 E

11. Marjory, who was very talented, received the highest honors, but Jane
                     A   B
    was awarded the blue ribbon for effort. No error   11. [A] [B] [C] [D] [E]
        C   D   E

12. The storm struck early, but after we had closed the door,
                                  A
    the house was warmer and the wind did not sound so loudly. No error   12. [A] [B] [C] [D] [E]
           B   C   D   E

13. When the weather permits the small boys of the community
                         A   B
    having formed teams, play games of football in Snyder Park which has a
          C   D
    football field. No error   13. [A] [B] [C] [D] [E]
                 E

14. The frost on the window pane conceals the garage from me in the
           A   B   C
    wintertime. No error   14. [A] [B] [C] [D] [E]
       D   E

15. For several reasons, the twins, John and Joe, had arrived early on
                         A   B
    July 4, 1969 to see the fireworks. No error   15. [A] [B] [C] [D] [E]
       C   D   E

16. "Come in," he said politely, "and tell me what you know about it." No error   16. [A] [B] [C] [D] [E]
        A   B   C   D   E

COMMON EXAMINATION

17. Many people were present, of course, the usual large number of
                                  A   B

    visitors, actors, and stars; but they were so busy that they did not notice
                C   D

    the lateness of the hour. No error   17. [A] [B] [C] [D] [E]
                            E

18. "Jerry, he said, "it is difficult to come to love a dog and then to lose him.
        A   B   C   D

    No error   18. [A] [B] [C] [D] [E]
    E

19. I will go to college; (assuming I get the money); in which case I will
                A   B   C   D

    write you a letter. No error   19. [A] [B] [C] [D] [E]
                  E

20. John's schedule included the following courses: History, English, and
                                    A   B   C

    French. No error   20. [A] [B] [C] [D] [E]
    D   E

21. The principal, as well as the supervisors, were present at the banquet
           A   B C

    on Thursday. No error   21. [A] [B] [C] [D] [E]
       D   E

22. He is expected to accept the invitation for around ten o'clock on Friday.
           A   B   C   D

    No error   22. [A] [B] [C] [D] [E]
    E

23. Nothing can be more surprising than the sound made by the grasshopper-lark,
                                                         A

    which seems to be close by though a considerable distance; and when close
      B   C   D

    at hand, is scarcely any louder than when the bird is a great way off. No error 23. [A] [B] [C] [D] [E]
                                                                     E

24. The common deity of the English people was Woden, the war god, the
                           A   B   C

    guardian of lands and boundaries; whom every tribe thought to be the
                                       D

    first ancestor of its kings. No error   24. [A] [B] [C] [D] [E]
                            E

25. John was very nervous as he sat waiting for the time to begin his speech;
                                                        A

    he was bashful and timid, and he felt unprepared to speak before so large
           B   C   D

    an audience. No error   25. [A] [B] [C] [D] [E]
                E

PART 2: GENERAL EDUCATION EXAMINATION

26. She was going to try to get all the women to vote for Betty—and she had
                    A   B

    begun to think that Betty was spiteful and dishonest, at least, that is the
                                                       C   D

    way Betty behaved toward her. No error
                                   E

    26. [A] [B] [C] [D] [E]

27. During the fox hunt he rode a big horse, which didn't mind him and as a
               A

    result got into everybody's way, and very nearly caused an accident when
                    B   C

    it refused to jump over a low fence; Earl rode up and caught the horse by
                                      C

    the bridle before it could kick George as he was lying on the ground below.
                                           D

    No error
    E

    27. [A] [B] [C] [D] [E]

28. Father advised my brother neither to be a borrower nor to be a lender.
           A   B   C   D

    No error
    E

    28. [A] [B] [C] [D] [E]

29. I like walking over the fields and to swim in the pond. No error
          A   B   C   D   E

    29. [A] [B] [C] [D] [E]

30. John who hadn't even been there was one of those arrested, although
         A   B   C

    Mary told the police that he had not participated in the crime. No error
                        D   E

    30. [A] [B] [C] [D] [E]

PART 2

DIRECTIONS: In each of the following sentences some part of the sentence or the entire sentence is underlined. Five ways of writing the underlined portion are given beneath each sentence. The first way (A) repeats the original and the other four ways are all different. Select the *best* answer from the five suggestions — if you choose (A) you accept the sentence as written.

EXAMPLE

Sinclair Lewis' novel Babbitt which satirized American materialism, won Lewis the Nobel Prize for Literature.
  (A) Sinclair Lewis' novel Babbitt
  (B) Sinclair Lewises novel Babbitt
  (C) Sinclair Lewises' novel Babbitt
  (D) Sinclair Lewis' novel Babbitt,
  (E) Sinclair Lewises' novel Babbitt,

[A] [B] [C] ■ [E]

1. We looked at the rabbit in the hutch that Ted was feeding.

   (A) in the hutch that Ted was feeding
   (B) that Ted was feeding

COMMON EXAMINATION

    (C) rabbit that Ted was feeding in the hutch
    (D) in the hutch Ted was feeding
    (E) rabbit in the hutch.

1. [A] [B] [C] [D] [E]

2. American myth to the contrary, right-wing extremism is, <u>to paraphrase Rap Brown, "as American as Cherry Pie."</u>

    (A) to paraphrase Rap Brown, "as American as Cherry Pie."
    (B) to paraphrase Rap Brown, "as American as cherry pie."
    (C) to paraphrase Rap Brown, "As American as cherry pie."
    (D) to paraphrase Rap Brown; "as American as cherry pie".
    (E) to paraphrase, Rap Brown, "as American as cherry pie."

2. [A] [B] [C] [D] [E]

3. The students are learning how to get along with others, <u>to depend on oneself, and managing their own money.</u>

    (A) to depend on oneself, and managing their own money.
    (B) to depend on themselves and manage their own money
    (C) to depend on oneself, and manage their own money
    (D) to depend on themselves, and to manage their own money
    (E) depending on themselves, and managing their own money

3. [A] [B] [C] [D] [E]

4. <u>"What could be more probable," said Dr. Brown,"</u>than that addicts and junkies were attempting to use the "hard sell" on disturbed adolescents."

    (A) "What could be more probable," said Dr. Brown,
    (B) What should be more probable, said Dr. Brown,
    (C) What could be more possible, said Dr. Brown,
    (D) "What could be more possible said Dr. Brown,"
    (E) "Dr. Brown said, what could be more probable?"

4. [A] [B] [C] [D] [E]

5. Never boo a bad performance — <u>just call out "Bad luck!"</u> or "Better luck next time!"

    (A) Never boo a bad performance — just call out "Bad luck!"
    (B) Never boo a bad performance, just call out "Bad luck!"
    (C) Never boo a bad performance (just call out "Bad luck!")
    (D) You should never boo a bad performance; just call out "Bad luck!"
    (E) You should never boo a bad performance; "just call out bad luck!"

5. [A] [B] [C] [D] [E]

6. <u>I, being only a small girl at the time,</u> didn't understand why my parents were divoced.

    (A) I, being only a small girl at the time,
    (B) I, being only a small girl, at the time
    (C) I being only a small girl, at the time
    (D) I, being only a small girl, at the time
    (E) I being only a small girl at the time

6. [A] [B] [C] [D] [E]

PART 2: GENERAL EDUCATION EXAMINATION

7. Johnny, <u>needing a haircut and denying it, went to the barbershop, with his mother.</u>

   (A) needing a haircut and denying it, went to the barbershop, with his mother.
   (B) needing a haircut, and denying it, went to the barbershop with his mother.
   (C) needing a haircut and denying it went to the barbershop with his mother.
   (D) needing a haircut and denying it went to the barbershop, with his mother.
   (E) needing a haircut and denying it, went to the barbershop with his mother.   7. [A] [B] [C] [D] [E]

8. You should see that the tank is full, <u>the sparkplugs cleaned, the points adjusted</u>; and then your car will be ready to go.

   (A) the sparkplugs cleaned, the pointed adjusted;
   (B) the sparkplugs cleaned; the points adjusted;
   (C) the sparkplugs cleaned and the points adjusted;
   (D) that the sparkplugs are cleaned and the points adjusted;
   (E) that the sparkplugs are cleaned, and the points adjusted;   8. [A] [B] [C] [D] [E]

9. <u>George planned to go—whether he was invited or not; his wife had more sense.</u>

   (A) George planned to go—whether he was invited or not;
   (B) George planned to go, whether he was invited or not,
   (C) George planned to go. Whether he was invited or not,
   (D) Whether he was invited or not, George planned to go,
   (E) Whether he was invited or not—George planned to go.   9. [A] [B] [C] [D] [E]

10. <u>What we need is a list of students broken down alphabetically.</u>

    (A) What we need is a list of students broken down alphabetically.
    (B) What we need is a list of broken down students alphabetically.
    (C) What we need is a broken down list of students.
    (D) What we need is an alphabetical list of students.
    (E) What we need is an alphabetical students' list.   10. [A] [B] [C] [D] [E]

11. <u>Squandering everything on new clothes, the money was never repaid.</u>

    (A) Squandering everything on new clothes, the money was never repaid.
    (B) Squandering everything on new clothes—the money was never repaid.
    (C) Squandered on new clothes, the money was never repaid.
    (D) Squandering everything on new clothes; the money was never repaid.
    (E) Squandered on new clothes (the money was never repaid).   11. [A] [B] [C] [D] [E]

12. <u>Finally arriving home, discovering how weary he was,</u> he collapsed in a chair in the living room.

    (A) Finally arriving home, discovering how weary he was,
    (B) Finally arriving home; discovering how weary he was—
    (C) Finally arriving home—discovering how weary he was—
    (D) Finally arriving home; discovering how weary he was,
    (E) Arriving home, he finally discovered how weary he was,   12. [A] [B] [C] [D] [E]

COMMON EXAMINATION

13. Harry finally wrote the story; a long disjointed piece without beginning or end, without any sustaining idea—without, in fact, much of an idea at all.

    (A) Harry finally wrote the story; a long disjointed piece without beginning or end, without any sustaining idea—
    (B) Harry finally wrote the story, a long disjointed piece without beginning or end, without any sustaining idea—
    (C) Harry finally wrote the story—a long disjointed piece without beginning or end—without any sustaining idea;
    (D) Harry finally wrote the story, a long disjointed piece without beginning or end, without any sustaining idea—;
    (E) Finally Harry wrote the story, a long disjointed piece without beginning or end; without any sustaining idea—

    13. [A] [B] [C] [D] [E]

14. Her interests included: many books, the arranging of flowers—the care of the house and yard, and the old folks in the village.

    (A) Her interests included: many books, the arranging of flowers—
    (B) Her interests included many books, the arranging of flowers—
    (C) Included among her interests were: the arranging of flowers—
    (D) Included among her interests were—many books, the arranging of flowers,
    (E) Her interests included many books, the arranging of flowers,

    14. [A] [B] [C] [D] [E]

15. Me and Sally got throwed off of the horse in Herman's pasture.

    (A) Me and Sally got throwed off of the horse in Herman's pasture.
    (B) Me and Sally got thrown off of the horse in Herman's pasture.
    (C) Sally and me got thrown off of the horse in Herman's pasture.
    (D) While riding a horse in Herman's pasture, Sally and I were thrown.
    (E) While riding a horse in Herman's pasture, Sally and me were thrown.

    15. [A] [B] [C] [D] [E]

16. While flying low, the windmills were seen.

    (A) While flying low, the windmills were seen.
    (B) While flying low—the windmills were seen.
    (C) We saw the windmills flying low.
    (D) While flying low, we saw the windmills.
    (E) While flying low (we saw the windmills).

    16. [A] [B] [C] [D] [E]

17. The fact that the professor had travelled in Russia, this added interest to his course.

    (A) The fact that the professor had travelled in Russia, this added interest to his course.
    (B) The fact that the professor had traveled in Russia added interest to his course.
    (C) That the professor had been in Russia added interest to his course.
    (D) Traveling in Russia, the professor added interest to his course.
    (E) While traveling in Russia, the professor added interest to his course.

    17. [A] [B] [C] [D] [E]

PART 2: GENERAL EDUCATION EXAMINATION

18. Some biologists have admitted that in some of their laboratory experiments how they did not understand what they were doing with the plants.

    (A) Some biologists have admitted that in some of their laboratory experiments how they did not understand what they were doing with the plants.
    (B) Some biologists have admitted in some of their laboratory experiments how they did not understand what they were doing with the plants.
    (C) Some biologists have admitted that in some of their laboratory experiments they did not understand what they were doing with the plants.
    (D) In some laboratory experiments biologists admitted that they did not know what they were doing with the plants.
    (E) In some laboratory experiments biologists admitted how that they did not know what they were doing with the plants.

    18. [A] [B] [C] [D] [E]

19. Jogging is a form of exercise that if you did it on a regular basis you will have improved health and circulation.

    (A) Jogging is a form of exercise that if you did it on a regular basis you will have improved health and circulation.
    (B) Jogging is a form of exercise that if done on a regular basis you will have improved health and circulation.
    (C) If you do jogging as a form of exercise on a regular basis you will improve your health and circulation.
    (D) If you jog as a form of exercise on a regular basis, you will improve your health and circulation.
    (E) Jogging is a form of exercise if done on a regular basis will improve your health and circulation.

    19. [A] [B] [C] [D] [E]

20. Because his secretary forgot to remind him of the appointment was why Mr. Browning did not speak at the noon luncheon of the club.

    (A) Because his secretary forgot to remind him of the appointment was why Mr. Browning did not speak at the noon luncheon of the club.
    (B) Mr. Browning did not speak at the noon luncheon of the club because his secretary forgot to remind him of the appointment.
    (C) Because of his secretary's forgetting to remind him of the appointment, Mr. Browning did not speak at the noon luncheon of the club.
    (D) Why Mr. Browning did not speak at the noon luncheon of the club was because his secretary forgot to remind him.
    (E) His secretary's forgetting about the appointment was why Mr. Browning did not speak at the noon luncheon of the club.

    20. [A] [B] [C] [D] [E]

COMMON EXAMINATION

Practice Test 2

PART 1

DIRECTIONS: Four parts of the sentences below are underlined and lettered. Decide whether any of the underlined parts contains a word use, grammatical construction, or incorrect or omitted punctuation which should not be used in carefully written English. Designate this error by selecting the letter printed beneath the incorrect underlined portion and blacken the corresponding space on the answer sheet. Blacken space E if there are no errors in the sentence. *No sentence contains more than one error.*

EXAMPLE

The teacher <u>introduced</u> a <u>new</u> <u>innovation.</u> <u>No error</u>
    A   B C D   E

[A ■ C D E]

1. I <u>think</u> <u>that</u> <u>if</u> I make the Honor Roll <u>that</u> I will shout for joy. <u>No error</u>
  A B C   D   E

1. [A B C D E]

2. The <u>thought patterns</u> of creative <u>persons</u> <u>also</u> differ <u>in that</u> they take
    A   B C   D

 delight in taking risks, while non-creative persons strive to obtain the right

 answers. <u>No error</u>
     E

2. [A B C D E]

3. An <u>ideal</u> <u>childrens</u> story <u>should have</u> a plot <u>and</u> narrative continuity. <u>No error</u>
  A   B   C   D   E

3. [A B C D E]

4. <u>In the history</u> of the <u>United States,</u> there has not been a single
   A   B   C

 <u>generation of peace.</u> <u>No error</u>
    D   E

4. [A B C D E]

5. Five committee members <u>were</u> at the last meeting <u>but not agreeing</u> <u>to plan</u>
          A   B   C   D

 the program. <u>No error</u>
       E

5. [A B C D E]

6. <u>To listen</u> to <u>romantic music</u> and <u>painting</u> seascapes <u>are two pastimes</u> Marie
  A   B   C   D

 enjoys. <u>No error</u>
    E

6. [A B C D E]

7. <u>During the week</u> Selma was a <u>wife,</u> <u>mother,</u> and <u>grandmother</u> at times.
   A   B   C   D

 <u>No error</u>
  E

7. [A B C D E]

135

PART 2: GENERAL EDUCATION EXAMINATION

8. When hungry, Sally gave her pet cat, Mittens, some food. No error
        A   B   C   D   E
                                                                               8. A B C D E

9. Tom will get to the game before you will get to the game. No error
       A   B   C   D   E
                                                                               9. A B C D E

10. I can swim across the pool if you can swim across the pool. No error
         A   B   C   D   E
                                                                              10. A B C D E

11. When Mrs. Brown was visiting relatives, Mrs. Brown always worried about
        A   B   C   D
    gaining weight. No error
                    E   11. A B C D E

12. The instructor neither had sound knowledge of Latin American history
                       A   B
    and he did not understand the system of government. No error
            C   D   E   12. A B C D E

13. Being the son of a senator, the girls showed great romantic interest. No error
        A   B   C   D   E   13. A B C D E

14. She decided to get plenty of exercise and eating plenty of nutritious food
          A   B   C   D
    for good health. No error
                         E   14. A B C D E

15. He climbed up to the top of Mount Everest. No error
       A   B   C   D   E   15. A B C D E

16. She heard a lot of talk about ways to bring about an increase in class
        A   B   C   D
    attendance. No error
                 E   16. A B C D E

17. Because of the weather, I was unable to attend. No error
           A   B   C   D   E   17. A B C D E

18. She told her mother, "I will call inside of a week." No error
         A   B   C   D   E   18. A B C D E

19. Mary said, "I have nothing to say in regards to his suggestion." No error
        A   B   C   D   E   19. A B C D E

20. After much thought, the teacher replied, "I was very pleased with his reply."
          A   B   C   D
    No error
     E   20. A B C D E

21. The clouds gathered swiftly; it looks as though it may rain. No error
              A   B   C   D   E   21. A B C D E

COMMON EXAMINATION

22. When a man has a plan of life to hope and work toward, he will be happy.
         A   B   C   D
    No error
       E

    22. [A] [B] [C] [D] [E]

23. You should not miss an opportunity for to further your musical education.
            A   B   C   D
    No error
       E

    23. [A] [B] [C] [D] [E]

24. Federal aid to parochial schools is opposed to in the Consitution,
                      A   B   C
    but some is used anyway. No error
           D   E

    24. [A] [B] [C] [D] [E]

25. Understanding parents and teachers are needed to help every child
                                 A   B
    how to select the best career. No error
        C   D   E

    25. [A] [B] [C] [D] [E]

26. The principal did not know upon what he used as a basis for his criticism.
                A   B   C   D
    No error
       E

    26. [A] [B] [C] [D] [E]

27. Neither his interest nor aptitude for medical school brought him happiness.
        A   B C   D
    No error
       E

    27. [A] [B] [C] [D] [E]

28. What affect did the new law have upon you and your family? No error
         A   B   C   D   E

    28. [A] [B] [C] [D] [E]

29. His suggestion to eliminate one place on the committee was all together
        A   B   C
    unpopular with the mayor. No error
        D   E

    29. [A] [B] [C] [D] [E]

30. "It is difficult to choose between the books by Dickens," Juliet said,
        A   B   C
    with feeling. No error
        D   E

    30. [A] [B] [C] [D] [E]

PART 2

DIRECTIONS: In each of the following sentences some part of the sentence or the entire sentence is underlined. Five ways of writing the underlined portion are given beneath each sentence. The first way (A) repeats the original and the other four ways are all different. Select the *best* answer from the five suggestions—if you choose (A) you accept the sentence as written.

1. Besides the librarian, only the first assistance librarian has access to the audio-visual files.

PART 2: GENERAL EDUCATION EXAMINATION

(A) Besides the librarian, only the first assistant librarian has access to the audio-visual files.
(B) Beside the librarian, only the first assistant librarian have access to the audio-visual files.
(C) Besides the librarian, only the first assistant librarian have excess to the audio-visual files.
(D) Beside the librarian only the first assistant librarian, have access to the audio-visual files.
(E) Beside the librarian, only the first assistant librarian have excess to the audio-visual files.

1. A B C D E

2. Mr. Scott is younger than any teacher in the high school.

(A) Mr. Scott is younger than any teacher in the high school.
(B) Mr. Scott is the youngest teacher in the school.
(C) The high school's youngest teacher is Mr. Scott.
(D) Mr. Scott is the high school's youngest teacher.
(E) Mr. Scott is younger than any other teacher in the high school.

2. A B C D E

3. Attending a small college is different from attending a large state university.

(A) Attending a small college is different from attending a large state university.
(B) Attending a small college is different than attending a large state university.
(C) Attending a small college is different than a large state university.
(D) Attending a large state university is different than a small college.
(E) Attending a small college is so different from attending a large state university.

3. A B C D E

4. George is as ambitious or perhaps more ambitious than Tom.

(A) George is as ambitious or perhaps more ambitious than Tom.
(B) George is as ambitious as or perhaps more ambitious than Tom.
(C) George and Tom are as ambitious as each other.
(D) George is so ambitious or perhaps more ambitious than Tom.
(E) George is ambitious; so is Tom.

4. A B C D E

5. The most popular oratorio by Handel is The Messiah.

(A) The most popular oratorio by Handel is The Messiah.
(B) The most popular oratorio by Handel is THE MESSIAH.
(C) The most popular oratorio by Handel is "The Messiah."
(D) The most popular oratorio by Handel is The Messiah.
(E) The most popular oratorio by Handel is the messiah.

5. A B C D E

6. 535 people voted against the school bond issue.

(A) 535 people voted against the school bond issue.
(B) Five hundred and thirty-five people voted against the school bond issue.
(C) About 535 people voted against the school bond issue.
(D) Around 535 people voted against the school bond issue.
(E) 535 people voted against the school's bond issue.

6. A B C D E

COMMON EXAMINATION

7. The countdown for the space launch began <u>at six o'clock A.M.</u>

    (A) The countdown for the space launch began at six o'clock A.M.
    (B) The count down for the space launch began at six o'clock a.m.
    (C) The countdown for the space launch began at 6 o'clock A.M.
    (D) The countdown for the space launch began at 6:00 A.M.
    (E) The countdown for the space launch began at six A.M.

    7. Ⓐ Ⓑ Ⓒ Ⓓ Ⓔ

8. <u>Art History is so interesting that</u> I recommended it to my best friends.

    (A) Art History is so interesting that I recommended it to my best friends.
    (B) Art history is so very interesting that I recommended it to my best friends.
    (C) Art history is so interesting that I recommended the taking of it to my be best friends.
    (D) Art History is so very interesting I recommended it to my best friends.
    (E) The History of Art is so very interesting I recommended it to my best friends.

    8. Ⓐ Ⓑ Ⓒ Ⓓ Ⓔ

9. <u>Some contemporary novels are a study of good and evil and so on with some modern poetry.</u>

    (A) Some contemporary novels are a study of good and evil and so on with some modern poetry.
    (B) Contemporary novels are a study of good and evil and so on with some modern poetry.
    (C) Some contemporary novels contain a study of good and evil; this is also true of some modern poetry.
    (D) Contemporary novels and modern poetry contain a study of good and evil.
    (E) Good and evil is contained in contemporary novels and poetry.

    9. Ⓐ Ⓑ Ⓒ Ⓓ Ⓔ

10. <u>After a hour in the detention room, all the students felt miserably.</u>

    (A) After a hour in the detention room, all the students felt miserably.
    (B) After an hour in the detention room, all the students felt miserably.
    (C) After an hour in the detention room, all the students felt miserable.
    (D) After being an hour in the detention room, all the students felt miserably.
    (E) All the students felt miserably after being an hour in the detention room.

    10. Ⓐ Ⓑ Ⓒ Ⓓ Ⓔ

11. <u>John Jones hasn't hardly any peers</u> in the field of mathematical analysis.

    (A) John Jones hasn't hardly any peers in the field of mathematical analysis.
    (B) John Jones hasn't any peers in the field of mathematical analysis.
    (C) In the field of mathematical analysis John Jones has hardly any peers.
    (D) John Jones has hardly any peers in the field mathematical analysis.
    (E) John Jones hasn't got any peers in the field of mathematical analysis.

    11. Ⓐ Ⓑ Ⓒ Ⓓ Ⓔ

12. At the end of the hike, <u>even the cold food tasted well to the tired Boy Scouts.</u>

    (A) At the end of the hike, even the cold food tasted well to the tired Boy Scouts.

PART 2: GENERAL EDUCATION EXAMINATION

    (B) At the end of the hike, the cold food tasted well to the tired Boy Scouts.
    (C) At the end of the hike, even the cold food tasted good to the tired Boy Scouts.
    (D) At the end of the hike, the cold food tasted good to the tired Boy Schouts.
    (E) At the end of the hike, the cold food tasted quite well to the tired Boy Scouts.

12. [A] [B] [C] [D] [E]

13. "He was a mighty intelligent dog and his training was real appropriate," Sandy commented at the field trials.

    (A) "He was a mighty intelligent dog and his training was real appropriate," Sandy commented at the field trials.
    (B) "He was a mighty intelligent dog and his training was appropriate," Sandy commented at the field trials.
    (C) "He was an intelligent dog and his training was most appropriate," Sandy commented at the field trials.
    (D) "He was an especially intelligent dog and his training was very appropriate," Sandy commented at the field trials.
    (E) "He was an intelligent dog and his training was very appropriate," Sandy commented at the field trials.

13. [A] [B] [C] [D] [E]

14. "I haven't scarcely any time left at all," Mary replied anxiously.

    (A) "I haven't scarcely any time left at all," Mary replied anxiously.
    (B) "I have scarcely any time left at all," Mary replied anxiously.
    (C) "I have scarcely no time left at all," Mary replied anxiously.
    (D) "I have little time left at all," Mary replied anxiously.
    (E) "I haven't any time left at all," Mary replied anxiously.

14. [A] [B] [C] [D] [E]

15. The Dean of the University of Michigan Law School gave law instruction at the summer seminar to several hundred people.

    (A) The Dean of the University of Michigan Law School gave law instruction at the summer seminar to several hundred people.
    (B) The University of Michigan Law School Dean gave law instruction at the summer seminar to several hundred people.
    (C) The University of Michigan Law School Dean gave instruction in law at the summer seminar to several hundred people.
    (D) The Dean of the University of Michigan Law School gave instruction in law at the summer seminar to several hundred people.
    (E) The Dean of the University of Michigan Law School gave instruction in law to several hundred people at the summer seminar.

15. [A] [B] [C] [D] [E]

16. The mayor felt securely enough to accuse the Treasurer openly of bribery.

    (A) The mayor felt securely enough to accuse the Treasurer openly of bribery.
    (B) The mayor felt securely enough to accuse the treasurer openly of bribery.
    (C) The mayor felt securely enough to openly accuse the treasurer of bribery.
    (D) The mayor felt secure enough to accuse openly the treasurer of bribery.
    (E) The mayor felt secure enough openly to accuse the treasurer of bribery.

16. [A] [B] [C] [D] [E]

COMMON EXAMINATION

17. Professor Johnson was wary of discussing racism in class—<u>because several students had previously misquoted him.</u>

   (A) Professor Johnson was wary of discussing racism in class—because several students had previously misquoted him.
   (B) Professor Johnson was wary of discussing racism in class because several students previously had misquoted him.
   (C) Professor Johnson was wary of discussing racism in class, because several students previously had misquoted him.
   (D) Professor Johnson was wary of discussing racism in class because (several students previously had misquoted him).
   (E) Because several students previously had misquoted him Professor Johnson was wary of discussing racism in class.

   17. [A] [B] [C] [D] [E]

18. <u>The trust fund established for my mother and I is administered by an attorney who we both trust.</u>

   (A) The trust fund established for my mother and I is administered by an attorney who we both trust.
   (B) The trust fund established for my mother and me is administered by an attorney who we both trust.
   (C) The trust fund established for my mother and me is administered by an attorney who we both trust.
   (D) The trust fund established for my mother and me is administered by an attorney whom we both trust.
   (E) The trust fund established for my mother and I is administered by an attorney whom we both trust.

   18. [A] [B] [C] [D] [E]

19. My minister told me that he could not permit the youth club to meet in the church; still, <u>I believe that he had good reasons for denying the request.</u>

   (A) My minister told me that he could not permit the youth club to meet in the church; still, I believe that he had good reasons for denying the request.
   (B) My minister told me that he could not allow the youth club to meet in the church; still, I believe that he had good reasons for denial of the request.
   (C) My minister said to me that he could not allow the youth club to meet in the church, still, I believe that he had good reasons for denial of the request.
   (D) My minister told me that he could not permit the youth club to meet in the church—still; I believe that he had good reasons for denying the request.
   (E) My minister told me that he could not permit the youth club to meet in the church: still; I believe that he had good reasons for denying the request.

   19. [A] [B] [C] [D] [E]

20. <u>Parents are always asked questions by their children and they can't give correct answers.</u>

   (A) Parents are always asked questions by their children and they can't give correct answers.

141

PART 2: GENERAL EDUCATION EXAMINATION

(B) Parents always are asked questions by their children and they can't give correct answers.
(C) Parents always are asked questions by their children and the parents can't give correct answers.
(D) Parents are always asked questions by their children which the parents can't give correct answers.
(E) Parents always are asked questions, some of which they cannot answer, by their children.

20. Ⓐ Ⓑ Ⓒ Ⓓ Ⓔ

Practice Test 1 — Answers

SOCIAL STUDIES, LITERATURE, AND FINE ARTS

1. D		19. C		37. C		55. A
2. A		20. D		38. B		56. E
3. A		21. B		39. E		57. C
4. A		22. D		40. D		58. E
5. B		23. C		41. C		59. C
6. B		24. C		42. D		60. B
7. B		25. B		43. A		61. D
8. C		26. A		44. C		62. B
9. D		27. D		45. A		63. C
10. E		28. A		46. C		64. C
11. A		29. D		47. D		65. D
12. A		30. B		48. C		66. E
13. A		31. D		49. B		67. C
14. C		32. C		50. D		68. E
15. D		33. D		51. E		69. E
16. B		34. D		52. C		70. E
17. E		35. B		53. A		71. A
18. B		36. E		54. A		

Practice Test 2 — Answers

SOCIAL STUDIES, LITERATURE, AND FINE ARTS

1. D		19. C		37. E		55. A
2. D		20. D		38. D		56. C
3. E		21. A		39. B		57. B
4. C		22. A		40. C		58. D
5. E		23. B		41. B		59. B
6. B		24. D		42. D		60. A
7. C		25. A		43. D		61. D
8. C		26. E		44. B		62. B
9. C		27. E		45. D		63. B
10. C		28. B		46. D		64. E
11. E		29. D		47. A		65. D
12. C		30. A		48. C		66. A
13. A		31. A		49. A		67. B
14. E		32. C		50. C		68. A
15. D		33. B		51. E		69. D
16. B		34. B		52. B		70. D
17. A		35. A		53. E		
18. B		36. B		54. A		

Practice Test 3 — Answers

SOCIAL STUDIES, LITERATURE, AND FINE ARTS

1.	B	19.	E	37.	B	55.	B
2.	B	20.	E	38.	D	56.	A
3.	E	21.	E	39.	C	57.	C
4.	E	22.	A	40.	B	58.	B
5.	C	23.	B	41.	A	59.	B
6.	D	24.	A	42.	C	60.	A
7.	D	25.	C	43.	D	61.	B
8.	D	26.	C	44.	D	62.	A
9.	B	27.	D	45.	A	63.	A
10.	E	28.	E	46.	E	64.	A
11.	B	29.	C	47.	D	65.	B
12.	B	30.	C	48.	C	66.	A
13.	D	31.	B	49.	D	67.	C
14.	C	32.	A	50.	A	68.	B
15.	D	33.	B	51.	C	69.	C
16.	E	34.	D	52.	D	70.	A
17.	C	35.	B	53.	E		
18.	B	36.	C	54.	A		

Practice Test 1 — Answers

SCIENCE AND MATHEMATICS

1.	D	7.	B	13.	D	19.	E
2.	E	8.	D	14.	C	20.	E
3.	D	9.	B	15.	B	21.	B
4.	A	10.	B	16.	B	22.	A
5.	C	11.	D	17.	B	23.	D
6.	B	12.	C	18.	B	24.	C

Practice Test 2 — Answers

SCIENCE AND MATHEMATICS

1.	E	7.	B	13.	C	19.	D
2.	E	8.	A	14.	B	20.	B
3.	C	9.	D	15.	C	21.	C
4.	A	10.	C	16.	B	22.	A
5.	C	11.	B	17.	B	23.	C
6.	B	12.	B	18.	C	24.	C

Practice Test 3 — Answers

SCIENCE AND MATHEMATICS

1. C
2. D
3. B
4. D
5. D
6. E
7. E
8. E
9. C
10. D
11. D
12. D
13. D
14. B
15. A
16. A
17. B
18. B
19. D
20. C
21. E
22. A
23. D
24. E

Practice Test 1 — Answers

WRITTEN ENGLISH EXPRESSION

PART 1

1. D
2. D
3. B
4. B
5. D
6. E
7. C
8. C
9. D
10. E
11. E
12. D
13. B
14. C
15. D
16. E
17. E
18. A
19. A
20. B
21. C
22. C
23. E
24. D
25. E
26. E
27. C
28. E
29. D
30. A

PART 2

1. C
2. B
3. D
4. A
5. A
6. A
7. E
8. A
9. A
10. D
11. C
12. A
13. B
14. E
15. D
16. D
17. B
18. C
19. D
20. B

145

Practice Test 2 — Answers

WRITTEN ENGLISH EXPRESSION

PART 1

1. D
2. D
3. B
4. E
5. C
6. C
7. E
8. A
9. D
10. D
11. C
12. C
13. C
14. D
15. C
16. D
17. E
18. C
19. C
20. E
21. E
22. D
23. B
24. C
25. C
26. B
27. B
28. A
29. C
30. C

PART 2

1. A
2. E
3. A
4. B
5. D
6. B
7. D
8. A
9. C
10. C
11. B
12. D
13. D
14. B
15. E
16. E
17. B
18. D
19. A
20. E

Part 3
Additional Aids to Review and Study

Psychological Foundations of Education

Topics for Review

FUNCTION OF EDUCATIONAL PSYCHOLOGY

Contribution of Psychology to Education
Scientific Approaches to Educational Problems
Contribution of Research to Learning Theories
Process of Development
Nature of Educational Growth
Limitations of Educational Psychology
Application of Psychology Principles
Psychology of Effective Teaching

GROWTH AND DEVELOPMENT

Relationship of Heredity and Environment
Growth, Development, and Maturation
Developmental Patterns
Fundamental Needs of Children
Child Study Points of View
Major Developmental Tasks
Need Deprivation
Child Study Techniques, Longitudinal and Cross-Sectional

THEORIES OF CHILD DEVELOPMENT

Adlerian Point of View
Behaviorist Point of View
Developmental Maturational Point of View
Jean Piaget's Point of View
Organismic Point of View
Psychoanalytic Point of View
Use of Theories to Interpret Behavior and Misbehavior
Sociometric Point of View
Social Learning Interpersonal Point of View
Use of Theories to Understand Human Development

MOTOR DEVELOPMENT

Trends in Physical Growth
Development of Locomotion
Motor Performance and Interests and Attitudes
Relation Between Physical and Mental Ability
Environmental Influences on Physical Development
Motor Development and Educational Activities
Motor Development and Personality

SOCIAL DEVELOPMENT

Social Responses of the Young Child
Companionship and Friendship
Group Activities in the Preschool Years
Process of Self Discovery
Social Perception
Social Development During Early Childhood
Social Development During Later Childhood
Social Responses of the Adolescent
Socioeconomic Background and Social Development
Adult Influences and Social Learnings
Attitudes Toward Self
Development of a Self Image
Influence of the Peers on Adolescent Behavior
Leadership
Boy-Girl Relationships
Social Skills and Behavior
Prejudice
Influence of Education Upon Social Development

EMOTIONAL DEVELOPMENT

Definition of Emotions
Infantile Emotional Reactions
Control of Specific Emotions
Need for Affection
Parent-Child Relationships
Maturation and Learning in Emotional Development
Emotional Problems of Childhood

PSYCHOLOGICAL FOUNDATIONS OF EDUCATION

Temperamental Predispositions
Coping Behavior

DEVELOPMENT OF COGNITIVE FUNCTIONS: INTELLECTUAL DEVELOPMENT

Physical Bases of Mental Development
Mental Ability and Heredity Influences
Concepts of Intelligence
Twin Studies
Cultural Deprivation
Memory
Awareness
Intellectual Elements in Children's Thinking
Development of Concepts
Levels of Thinking
Learning and Thinking
Individual Differences in Mental Growth
Biological Nature and Experience

THE MEASUREMENT OF INTELLIGENCE

Nature of Intelligence
Intelligent Behavior and Environmental Factors
Growth of Intelligence
Theories of Intelligence
Predicting Mental Growth
The Constancy of the I.Q.
Measuring Intelligence

EVALUATION OF THE LEARNER

Interpreting Test Results to Parents and Pupils
Testing for Readiness
Maturation and Learning
Giftedness
Creativity
Mental Retardation
Aptitude Testing
Personality Tests and Their Use
Standardized Tests
Evaluation of Pupil's School Achievement
Teacher-Made Test Techniques
Statistics Through Correlation
Reliability of Tests
Test Validity

THEORIES OF LEARNING

Mental discipline-faculty psychology
Key persons: St. Augustine, John Calvin, Jonathan Edwards; contemporary: Hebraic-Christian fundamentalists
Mental discipline-classical tradition
Key persons: Plato, Aristotle; contemporary: R.E. Brennan and Mortimer J. Adler
Natural unfoldment-romantic naturalism
Key persons: J. Rousseau and F. Froebel; contemporary: extreme progressivists
Apperception-structuralism
Key persons: J. Herbart, W. Wundt, and E. Titchener; contemporary: many educators and administrators
S-R Bond-connectionism
Key persons: E.L. Thorndike; contemporary: J.M. Stephens and A.I. Gates
Conditioning-behaviorism
Key persons: J.B. Watson; contemporary: B.F. Skinner and E.R. Guthrie
Reinforcement-reinforcement
Key persons: C.L. Hull; contemporary: K.W. Spence
Goal insight-Gestalt psychology
Key persons: M. Wertheimer and K. Koffka; contemporary: W. Kohler and E. E. Bayles
Cognitive-field-field psychology or relativism
Key persons: Kurt Lewin, E. C. Tooman and J. S. Bruner; comtemporary: R. G. Barker, A. W. Combs, and H. F. Wright
The implications of these theories for educational practices and curriculum.

THE LEARNING PROCESS

Definition of Learning
Definition of Thinking
How is Problem-Solving Demonstrated?
Deductive and Inductive Reasoning
Insight and Intuition
Operant Conditioning
Behavior and Determinism
Respondent or Reflexive Conditioning
Extinction
Teaching Machines
Programmed Learning
Transfer of Learning

PSYCHOLOGY OF LEARNING AREAS

Learning and Teaching Specific Skills
Effective Study Habits
Attitudes, Interests, and Motivation
Modifying Attitudes

PART 3: ADDITIONAL AIDS TO REVIEW AND STUDY

Teaching Mathematical Concepts
Scientific Method of Reasoning
Improving Retention

PERSONALITY AND CHARACTER DEVELOPMENT

Definition of Personality
Theories of Personality
Biographical and Clinical Approach-Gessell
Topological Approach-Lewin
Constitutional Approach-Sheldon
Psychoanalytic Approach-Freud
Social-psychoanalytic Approach-Murray
Gestalt-Adlerian Approach-Adler
Phenomenological Approach-Rogers, Maslow, Combs, Kelley
Organismic Approach-Olson
Defense Mechanisms of Children
Home, School, and Community and Personality Development
Personality Assessment Tools and Criteria
Rating Scales
Personality Inventories
Projective Methods
Direct Observation

EXCEPTIONAL CHILDREN

The Gifted
Slow Learners
Mentally Retarded
Creative-Divergent Thinkers
Physically Handicapped
Culturally Handicapped
Emotionally Disturbed
Children With Problems-Behavior (Acting Out)
Individual Differences in Learning
Pacing
Promotion
Ungraded Schools
Acceleration
Flexible Grouping
School Adjustment of Exceptional Children

MENTAL HYGIENE IN THE SCHOOLS

Personal Adjustment Techniques
Function of Mental Hygiene in the Classroom
Guidance for Learner Adjustment

Societal Foundations of Education

Topics for Review

THE SCHOOL AND SOCIETY
Education in the American Setting
Early American Schools
Debt to European Education
Industrial Revolution and American Schools
American Ideals and Their Effect on Education
Dynamics of Change in American Society

CONTROL OF AMERICAN SCHOOLS
Philosophy of Local Control
Control at the State Level
Federal Aid to Education
Changing Roles of Local, State, and Federal Control

FINANCING AMERICAN EDUCATION
Local Support of Public Schools
State Support of Public Schools
Federal Support of Public Education
Cost and Quality of Education
New Methods of Financial Support for Education

IDEOLOGY AND EDUCATION
Democracy and Education
Totalitarianism and Education

National Control of Education
Conservative, Liberal, Radical, and Reactionary in Relation to Education

CHALLENGES TO AMERICAN EDUCATION
Education in a Changing Society
Adaptations to Change
School Organization
Curriculum
Instructional Methods
Community School and Community Education
Changing Role of Technical Education
Changing Role of Educational Organizations
The National Education Association
State Associations
The American Federation of Teachers

LEGAL FOUNDATIONS OF EDUCATION
Role of the State Legislature
State Departments of Education
Boards of Regents
State School Officers
Role of Private Schools in the Total System
Courts and Education
Local School Boards and Authority

Teaching Principles and Practices

Topics for Review

THE TEACHER IN THE CLASSROOM

Non-directed Learning
Directed Learning
Dominated Learning
Learning Objectives
Laboratory Approaches and Learning
Classical conditioning
Instrumental Learning
Selective learning
Rote learning
Discrimination learning
Problem-solving
Maturation and Readiness
Transfer of Training
Current Research on Learning

REINFORCEMENT AND LEARNING

Emitted Behavior
Respondent Behavior
Primary and Secondary Reinforces
Negative Reinforcement
Reward and Punishment
Delay in Reinforcement
Anticipatory Goal Responses
Extinction of Behavior
Motivation and Reinforcement

MOTIVATION

Need Systems
Conceptual Systems - Murray
Hierarchy of Needs
Anxiety as Motivation
Interest and Motives
Level of Aspiration and Goal-seeking Behavior

TRANSFER OF TRAINING

Level of Learning and Amount of Transfer
Utility and Transfer
Difficulty of Task and Transfer
Interference with Learning
Principles and Learning Sets
Transfer Mechanisms
Overlearning and Transfer
Retention Curves
Theories of Forgetting

TEACHER AND PUPIL ATTITUDES

Imitative Behavior
Habitual Responses
Prejudice
Measurement Devices for Attitudes
Group Pressures and Peer Relations
Resistance to Attitudinal Changes
Learning Problems and Resistance to Change

MEASUREMENT OF INTELLIGENCE AND APTITUDES

Current Research on Measurement and Evaluation
Intelligence: Relation to Academic Achievement
Constancy of the I.Q.
School Achievement, Predictor of Future Success

EDUCATION AND TECHNOLOGY

Audio-visual aids to learning
Use of Teaching Machines for Subject Areas
Programmed Learning and Creativity
Research on Educational Television

SELECTED REFERENCES

INDIVIDUAL DIFFERENCES

Exceptional Children
Range of Individual Differences
Problems of Grouping
The Gifted Child
The Slow Learner

PUPILS ADJUSTMENT

Defense Mechanisms
Nonadjustive Reactions
Social Adjustment
Peer Relations
School Adjustment
Discipline and Motivation

THE SCHOOL CURRICULUM

Objectives of Language Arts Programs
Objectives of Teaching the Sciences
Problems of Modern Language Instruction
Teaching the New Mathematics
New Trends in Social Studies
Junior High School Curriculum
Articulating the School Curriculum

CO-CURRICULAR ACTIVITIES

Place in the School Program
Objectives
Special Problems

Professional Education

SELECTED REFERENCES

Bany, Mary A., and Johnson, Lois V. *Classroom Group Behavior, Group Dynamics in Education.* New York: Macmillan, 1964.

Lembo, John M. *The Psychology of Effective Classroom Instruction.* Columbus, Ohio: Charles E. Merrill, 1969. (Paperback).

Ornstein, Allan C. and Haugen, Earl S. *How to Teach Disadvantaged Youth.* New York: David McKay, 1968. (Paperback).

McCollough, Celeste, and Van Atta, Loche. *Statistical Concepts, A Program for Self-Instruction.* New York: McGraw-Hill, 1963.

Smith, G. Milton. *A Simplified Guide to Statistics for Psychology and Education,* Third Edition. New York: Holt, Rinehart & Winston, 1962.

Stephens, Thomas M. *Directive Teaching of Children with Learning and Behavioral Handicaps.* Columbus, Ohio: Charles E. Merrill, 1970. (Paperback).

Storen, Helen F. *The Disadvantaged Early Adolescent: More Effective Teaching.* New York: McGraw-Hill, 1968.

PART 3: ADDITIONAL AIDS TO REVIEW AND STUDY

Psychological Foundations of Education

SELECTED REFERENCES

Allport, G. W. *Becoming. Basic Considerations for a Psychology of Personality.* New Haven, Conn.: Yale University Press, 1955.

Allport, G. W. *The Nature of Prejudice.* Reading, Mass.: Addison-Wesley, 1954.

Allport, G. W. *Personality and Social Encounter.* Boston: Beacon Press, 1960.

Allport, G. W. *Personality: A Psychological Interpretation.* New York: Holt, Rinehart and Winston; 1937.

Anastasi, Anne. *Differential Psychology,* 3d Ed. New York: Macmillan, 1958.

Ausubel, D. P. *Theory and Problems of Child Development.* New York: Grune & Stratton, 1958.

Baker, H. J. *Introduction to Exceptional Children.* 3d Ed. New York: Macmillan, 1959.

Baller, W. R. and Charles, D. C. *The Psychology of Human Growth and Development.* New York: Holt, Rinehart and Winston, 1961.

Bernard, H. W. *Mental Health for Classroom Teachers.* 2d Ed. New York: McGraw-Hill, 1961.

Bettelheim, B. *Love is not Enough: The Treatment of Emotionally Disturbed Children.* Glencoe, Ill.: Free Press, 1950.

Bigge, M. L. *Learning Theories for Teachers.* New York: Harper and Row, 1964.

Bloom, B. S. *Stability and Change in Human Characteristics.* New York: Wiley, 1964.

Britton, E. C., and Winans, J. M. *Growing From Infancy to Adulthood.* New York: Appleton-Century-Crofts, 1958.

Carmichael, L. (ed.) *Manual of Child Psychology.* New York: Wiley, 1954.

Cole, Luella. *The Psychology of Adolescence.* New York: Rhinehart, 1948.

Cronbach, L. J. *Essentials of Psychological Testing.* 2d. Ed. New York: Harper, 1960.

Crow, L. D., and Crow, Alice. *Educational Psychology.* New Revised Edition. New York: American Book, 1963

Cruikshank, W. M., and Johnson, G. O. *Education of Exceptional Children and Youth.* Englewood Cliffs, N. J.: Prentice-Hall, 1958.

Deese, J. *The Psychology of Learning.* New York: McGraw-Hill, 1952.

Diamond, S. *Personality and Temperament.* New York: Harper & Row, 1957.

Dinkmeyer, D. C. *Child Development - The Emerging Self.* Englewood Cliffs, N. J.: Prentice-Hall, 1965.

SELECTED REFERENCES

Duvall, Evelyn M. *Family Development.* 2d Ed. Philadelphia: Lippincott, 1962.

Erikson, E. H. *Childhood and Society.* New York: Norton, 1950.

Eysenck, H. J. *Dimensions of Personality.* London: Routledge, 1947.

Flanagan, Geraldine L. *The First Nine Months of Life.* New York: Simon and Schuster, 1962.

Flavell, J. H. *Developmental Psychology of Jean Piaget.* Princeton, N. J.: Van Nostrand, 1963.

Frandsen, A. N. *Educational Psychology.* New York: McGraw-Hill, 1961.

Gagne, R. M. *Conditions of Learning.* New York: Holt, Rinehart, and Winston, 1965.

Garrison, K. C. *Psychology of Exceptional Children.* 3d Ed. New York: Ronald Press, 1959.

Guthrie, E. R. *The Psychology of Learning,* Rev. Ed. New York: Harper, 1952.

Hall, C. C., and Lindzey, G. *Theories of Personality.* New York: Wiley, 1957.

Hildreth, Gertrude H. *Learning the Three R's.* Minneapolis, Minnesota: Educational Publishers, 1947.

Hilgard, E. R. *Theories of Learning.* 2d Ed. New York: Appleton-Century-Crofts, 1956.

Hunt, J. McV. *Intelligence and Experiance.* New York: Ronald, 1961.

Hurlock, Elizabeth B. *Child Development.* New York: McGraw-Hill, 1964.

Hutt, M. L., and Gibby, R. G., *The Mentally Retared Child.* Boston: Allyn and Bacon, 1958.

Ingram, C. P. *Educating the Slow-Learning Child.* ed Ed. New York: Ronald Press, 1960.

Jenkins, Gladys G., Shacter, Helen, and Bauer, W. W. *These are Your Children.* Chicago: Scott, Foresman, 1953.

Jersild, A. T. *Child Psychology.* 5th Ed. Englewood Cliffs, N. J.: Prentice-Hall, 1960.

Jersild, A. T., and Tasch, R. J. *Children's Interests and What They Suggest for Education.* New York: Bureau of Publications, Teachers College, Columbia University, 1949.

Jones, H. E. *Development in Adolescence.* New York: Appleton-Century-Crofts, 1935.

Kirk, S. A., and Johnson, G. O. *Educating the Retarded Children.* Boston: Houghton Mifflin, 1951.

Klausmeier, H. J., and Goodwin, W. *Learning and Human Abilities - Educational Psychology.* New York: Harper & Row, 1961.

Kneller, G. F. *The Art and Science of Creativity.* New York: Holt, Rinehart and Winston, 1965.

Kounin, J. S., and Wright, H. F. (eds.) *Child Behavior and Development.* New York: McGraw-Hill, 1943.

PART 3: ADDITIONAL AIDS TO REVIEW AND STUDY

Lane, H., and Beauchano, Mary. *Human Relations in Teaching.* Englewood Cliffs, N. J. : Prentice-Hall, 1955.

Lindgren, H. C. *Educational Psychology in the Classroom.* 3d ed. New York, Wiley, 1967.

Lindzey, C. (ed.) *Assessment of Human Motives.* New York: Rinehart, 1958.

Maslow, A. H. *Motivation and Personality.* New York: Harper & Row, 1954.

May, R. *Man's Search for Himself.* New York: Norton, 1953.

McClelland, D., Atkinson, J. W., Clark, R. A., and Lowell, E. L. *The Achievement Motive.* New York: Appleton-Century-Crofts, 1953.

McGraw, Myrtle B. *Growth, a Study of Johnny and Jimmy.* New York: Appleton-Century-Crofts, 1935.

Mowrer, O. H. *Learning Theory and Behavior.* New York: Wiley, 1960a.

Mowrer, O. H. *Learning Theory and the Symbolic Processes.* New York: Wiley, 1960b.

Murphy, G. *Human Potentialities.* New York: Basic Books, 1958.

Olson, W. C. *Child Development.* 2d Ed. Boston: Heath, 1959.

Pressey, S. L., Robinson, F. P., and Horrocks, J. E. *Psychology in Education.* New York: Harcourt, Brace, 1951.

Redl, F., and Wattenburg, W. W. *Mental Hygiene in Teaching.* New York: Harcourt, Brace, 1951.

Redl, F., and Wineman, D. *Children Who Hate.* Glencoe, Ill.: Free Press, 1951.

Russell, D. H. *Children's Thinking.* Boston: Ginn, 1956.

Spence, K. W. *Behavior Theory and Conditioning.* New Haven, Conn: Yale University Press, 1956.

Stott, L. H., *Child Development, An Individual Longitudinal Approach.* New York: Holt, Rinehart, 1967.

Strang, Ruth. *An Introduction to Child Study.* 3d Ed. New York: Macmillan, 1951.

Strang, Ruth. *Helping Children Solve Problems.* Chicago: Science Research, 1953.

Symonds, P. M. *The Dynamics of Human Adjustment.* New York: Appleton-Century-Crofts, 1946.

Terman, L. M., and Oden, Melita H. *Genetic Studies of Genius, Vol. 5, The Gifted Group at Midlife: Thirty-Five Years' Followup of the Superior Child.* Stanford, Calif. : Stanford University Press, 1959.

Terman, L. M., and Merrill, Maud A. *Measuring Intelligence.* Boston: Houghton Mifflin, 1937.

Thorndike, E. L. *Human Learning.* New York: Century, 1931.

SELECTED REFERENCES

Thorpe, L. P. *The Psychology of Mental Health.* 2d Ed. New York: Ronald Press, 1960.

Tolman, E. C. *Collected Papers in Psychology.* Berkeley, California: University of California Press, 1951.

Witty, P. *The Gifted Child.* Boston: Heath, 1051.

Woodworth, R. S. *Dynamics of Behavior.* New York: Holt, 1958.

Wright, B. A. *Physical Disability - A Psychological Approach.* New York: Harper, 1960.

Societal Foundations of Education

SELECTED REFERENCES

Allen, H. P. *The Federal Government and Education.* New York: McGraw-Hill, 1950.

Arndt, C. O., and Everett, Samuel, (eds.) *Education for a World Society.* New York: Harper, 1951.

Bartky, J. A. *Social Issues in Public Education.* Boston: Houghton-Mifflin, 1963.

Barzun, Jacques. *Teacher in America.* Boston: Little, Brown, 1944.

Bell, B. I. *Crisis in Education.* New York: McGraw-Hill, 1949.

Bestor, A. E. *The Educational Waste Lands.* Urbana: University of Illinois Press, 1953.

Belth, Marc. *Education as a Discipline.* Boston: Allyn and Bacon, 1965.

Brameld, Theodore. *Education as Power.* New York: Holt, Rinehart, and Winston, 1965.

Brameld, Theodore. *Patterns of Educational Philosophy.* Yonkers-on-the-Hudson, N. Y.: World, 1950.

Broudy, H. S. *Building a Philosophy of Education.* New York: Prentice-Hall, 1960.

Broudy, H. S., and Freel, E. L. *Psychology for General Education.* New York: Longmans, Green, 1956.

Brumbaugh, R. S. and Lawrence, N. M. *Philosophers on Education.* Boston: Houghton Mifflin, 1963.

Bulletins of the Council on Basic Education, 725 15th St., N. W., Washington, D. C.

Burke, A. J. *Financing Public School in the United States.* New York: Harper, 1951.

Butts, R. F. *A Cultural History of Western Education,* 2nd ed. New York: McGraw-Hill, 1955.

Butts, R. F., and Cremin, L. A. *A History of Education in American Culture.* New York: Holt, 1953.

Butts, R. F. *The American Tradition in Religion and Education.* Boston: The Beacon Press, 1950.

Caswell, H. L. (ed.) *The American High School.* New York: Harper, 1946.

PART 3: ADDITIONAL AIDS TO REVIEW AND STUDY

Childs, J. L. *Education and Morals.* New York: Appleton-Century-Crofts, 1950.

Conant, J. B. *Education in a Divided World.* Cambridge, Mass.: Harvard University Press, 1948.

Conant, J. B. *The American Hifh School Today.* New York: McGraw-Hill, 1959.

Counts, G. S. *Dare the School Build a New Social Order?* New York: John Day, 1952.

Counts, G. S. *The Challenge of Soviet Education.* New York: McGraw-Hill, 1957.

Cremin, L; A. *The American Common School.* New York: Bureau of Publications, Teachers College, Columbia University, 1951.

Cressman, G. R. and Benda, H. W. *Public Education in America.* New York: Appleton-Century-Crofts, 1961.

Cubberly, E. P. *Public Education in the United States.* Boston: Houghton Mifflin, 1947.

Cubberly, E. P. *The History of Education.* Boston: Houghton Mifflin, 1948.

Curti, Merle. *The Growth of American Thought.* New York: Harper, 1943.

Curtie, Merle. *The Social Ideas of American Educators.* New York: Scribner, 1954.

Dewey, John. *Democracy and Education.* New York: Macmillan, 1938.

Dewey, John. *Human Nature and Conduct.* New York: Holt, 1922.

Drake, W. E. *The American School in Transition.* New York: Prentice-Hall, 1955.

Duggan, Stephen. *A Student's Textbook in the History of Education.* New York: Appleton-Century-Crofts, 1948.

Eby, Frederick. *The Development of Modern Education.* New York: Prentice-Hall, 1952.

Educational Policies Commision. *Education for all American Children.* Washington, D. C.: National Education Association, 1944.

Educational Policies Commission. *Education for all American Youth.* Washington, D. C.: National Education Association, 1944.

Educational Policies Commission. *The Structure and Administration of Education in American Democracy.* Washington, D. C.: National Education Association, 1938.

Edwards, Newton, and Richey, H. G. *The School in the American Social Order.* 2nd. ed. Boston: Houghton-Mifflin, 1963.

Ehlers, H. J. and Lee, G. D. *Crucial Issues in Education.* 3rd ed. New York: Holt, Rinehart, and Winston, 1964.

SELECTED REFERENCES

Elsbree, W. S. *The American Teacher.* New York: American Book, 1939.

Fine, Benjamin. *Our Children are Cheated.* New York: Holt, 1947.

Frank, Lawrence. *Nature and Human Nature.* New Brunswick, N. J.: Rutgers University Press, 1951.

Frankena, W. K. *Philosophy of Education.* New York: Macmillan, 1965.

Full, Harold (ed.) *Controversy in American Education.* New York: Macmillan, 1967.

Good, H. G. *History of American Education.* New York: Macmillan, 1962.

Good, H. G. *A History of Western Education.* New York: Macmillan, 1949.

Greider, Calvin and Romine, Stephen. *American Education - An Introduction to the Teaching Profession.* New York: Ronald Press, 1965.

Gross, R. E. (ed.) *Heritage of American Education.* Boston: Allyn and Bacon, 1962.

Haan, Aubrey, and Haan, Norma. *Readings in Professional Education - An Interdisciplinary Approach.* Boston: Allyn and Bacon, 1963.

Halsey, A. H., Floud, Sean, and Anderson, C. A.. *Education, Economy, and Society. A Reader in Sociology of Education.* New York: Macmillan, 1965.

Hansen, K. H. *Public Education in American Society.* Englewood Cliffs, N. J.: Prentice-Hall, 1956.

Harris, S. E. *How Shall We Pay for Education?* New York: Harper, 1948.

Havighurst, R. J. and Newgarten, B. L. *Society and Education.* 3rd ed. Boston: Allyn and Bacon, 1967.

Henderson, S. V. P. *Introduction to Philosophy of Education.* Chicago: University of Chicago Press, 1947.

Hillway, Tyrus. *Education in American Society.* Boston: Houghton Mifflin, 1961.

Hook, Sidney. *Education for Modern Man.* New York: The Dial Press, 1946.

Hopstadter, Richard, and Smith, William (eds.) *American Higher Education.* Chicago: University of Chicago Press, 1961.

Hutchins, R. M. *The Higher Learning in America.* New Haven: Yale University Press, 1936.

Johns, R. L., and Morphet, E. L., (eds.) *Problems and Issues in Public School Finance.* New York: Bureau of Publication, Teachers College, Columbia University, 1952.

Johnston, Bernard (ed.) *Issues in Education: An Anthology of Controversy.* Boston: Houghton Mifflin, 1964.

Kearney, N. C. *Elementary School Objectives.* New York: Russell Sage Foundation, 1953.

Kelley, E. C., and Rasey, M. I. *Education and the Nature of Man.* New York: Harper, 1952.

Kilpatrick, W. H. *Philosphy of Education.* New York: Macmillan, 1963.

PART 3: ADDITIONAL AIDS TO REVIEW AND STUDY

Kimball, S. T., and McClellan, J. E. *Education and the New America.* New York: Random House.

Knight, E. W. *Education in the United States,* 3rd. rev. ed. Boston: Ginn, 1951.

Koerner, J. D. (ed.) *The Case for Basic Education.* Boston: Little, Brown, 1959.

Kvaraceus, W. C., and Gibson, J. S., and Curtain, T. J. *Poverty, Education, and Race Relations.* Boston: Allyn and Bacon, 1967.

Lee, G. C. *An Introduction to Education in Modern America.* New York: Holt, 1953.

Lee, M. J., and Lee, D. M. *The Child and His Curriculum.* New York: Appleton-Century-Crofts, 1950.

Leonard, J. P. *Developing the Secondary School Curriculum.* New York: Rinehart, 1946.

Lieberman, Myron. *The Future of Public Educatoin.* University of Chicago Press, 1960.

Mayer, Frederick. *A History of Educational Thought.* Columbus, Ohio: Charles Merrill Books, 1960.

McConnell, T. R. (ed.) *General Education.* Chicago: University of Chicago Press, 1952.

McLendon, J. C. (ed.) *Social Foundations of Education.* New York: Macmillan, 1966.

Menge, J. W. and Faunce, R. C. *Working Together For Better Schools.* New York: American Book, 1953.

Moore, C. B. and Cole, W. E. *Sociology in Educational Practice.* Boston: Houghton Mifflin, 1952.

Morris, Van Cleve. *Philosophy and the American School.* Boston: Houghton Mifflin, 1961.

Mort, P. R., and Reusser, W. C. *Public School Finance.* New York: McGraw-Hill, 1951.

Myers, A. F., and Williams, C. O. *Education in a Democracy.* 4th ed. New York: Prentice-Hall, 1954.

Myers, E. D. *Education in the Perspective of History.* New York: Harper, 1960.

Mulhern, James. *A History of Education.* New York: Ronald Press, 1959.

Nakosteen, Mehdi. *The History and Philosophy of Education.* New York: Ronald Press, 1965.

National Education Association. Commission on the Reorganization of Secondary Education. *The Cardinal Principles of Secondary Education.* U. S. Bureau of Education Bulletin, Washington, D. C., 1918.

National Society for the Study of Education. *Fifty-Fourth Yearbook, Part I. Modern Philosophies and Education.* Chicago: University of Chicago Press, 1955.

National Society for the Study of Education. *Forty-First Yearbook, Part I. Philosophies of Education.* Bloomington, Ill. : Public School Publishing Company, 1942.

Phenix, P. H. *Philosophy of Education.* New York: Holt, Rinehart, and Winston, 1958.

Price, Kinsley. *Education and Philosophical Thought.* 2nd ed. Boston: Allyn and Bacon, 1967.

SELECTED REFERENCES

Ragan, W. B. *Modern Elementary Curriculum*. New York: Dryden, 1953.

Rasey, M. I. *It Takes Time*. New York: Harper, 1953.

Reinhardt, Emma. *American Education: An Introduction*. New York: Harper, 1954.

Rickover, H. G. *Education and Freedom*. New York: Dutton, 1959.

Roe, Anne. *The Making of a Scientist*. New York: Dodd, Mead, 1953.

Rudman, H. C. *The School and State in the USSR*. New York: Macmillan, 1967.

Rugg, H. and Brooks, B. M. *The Teacher in School and Society*. New York: World Book, 1950.

Rusk, R. R. *The Philosophical Bases of Education*. Boston: Houghton Mifflin, 1956.

Russell, J. E. *Change and Challenge in American Education*. Boston: Houghton Mifflin, 1964.

Sayers, E. V., and Madden, Ward. *Education and Democratic Faith*. New York: Appleton-Century-Crofts, 1959.

Schneider, H. W. *A History of American Philosphy*. New York: Columbia University Press, 1946.

Scott, C. W., and Hill, C. M. *Public Education Under Criticism*. New York: Prentice-Hall, 1954.

Shane, H. C. (ed.) *The American Elementary School*. New York: Harper, 1953.

Smith, Huston. *The Purposes of Higher Education*. New York: Harper, 1955.

Smith, Mortimer. *And Madly Teach*. Chicago: Regnery, 1949.

Smith, Mortimer. *The Diminished Mind*. Chicago: Regnery, 1952.

Smith, O. B., Stanley, W. O., and Shores, H. J. *Fundamentals of Curriculum Development*. New York: World Book, 1950.

Spears, Harold. *The Teacher and Curriculum Planning*. Englewood Cliffs, N. J.: Prentice-Hall, 1951.

Stratemeyer, F. B., Forkner, H. L., and McKim, M. G. *Developing a Curriculum for Modern Living*. New York: Bureau of Publications, Teachers College, Columbia University, 1947.

The Harvard Committee, Report of. *General Education in a Free Society*. Cambridge, Mass.: Harvard University Press, 1945.

Thut, I. N. *The Story of Education:* Philosophical and Historical Foundations. New York: McGraw-Hill, 1957.

Tyler, R. W. (ed.) *Social Forces Influencing American Education*. Chicago: University of Chicago Press, 1961.

Ulich, Robert. *History of Educational Thought*. New York: American Book, 1950.

Washburned, Carleton. *What is Progressive Education?* New York: John Day, 1952.

PART 3: ADDITIONAL AIDS TO REVIEW AND STUDY

Weber, C. O. *Basic Philosophies of Education.* New York: Holt, Rinehart, and Winston, 1960.

Wegener, F. C. *An Organic Philosophy of Education.* Dubuque, Iowa: W. C. Brown, 1957.

Wild, John. *Introduction to Realistic Philosophy.* New York: Harper, 1948.

Williams, Robin. *American Society.* 2nd ed. New York: Knopf, 1950.

Willing, M. H., and others. *Schools and our Democratic Society.* New York: Harper, 1951.

Woodring, Paul. *A Fourth of a Nation.* New York: McGraw-Hill, 1957.

Woody, Thomas. *Life and Education in Early Society.* New York: Macmillan, 1949.

Wynne, J. P. *Theories of Education.* New York: Harper, 1963.

Yauch, Wilbur. *How Good is Your School?* New York: Harper, 1951.

Teaching Principles And Practices

SELECTED REFERENCES

Amidon, Edmund and Hunter, Elizabeth. *Improving Teaching: The Analysis of Classroom Verbal Interaction.* New York: Holt, Rinehart, and Winston, 1966.

Anderson, R. C., and Ausubel, D. P. *Readings in the Psychology of Cognition.* New York: Holt, Rinehart, and Winston, 1965.

Anderson, V. E. *Principles and Procedures of Curriculum Improvement.* New York: Ronald Press, 1965.

Anderson, V. E., and Gruhn, W. T. *Principles and Practices of Secondary Education.* New York: Ronald Press, 1962.

Barnard, J. D. *Rethinking Science Education.* Chicago: University of Chicago Press, 1960.

Beck, Robert, Cook, Walter, and Kearney, Nolan. *Curriculum in the Modern Elementary School.* 2nd ed. Englewood Cliffs, N. J.: Prentice-Hall, 1960.

Biddle, B. J. and Ellena, W. J. *Contemporary Research on Teacher Effectiveness.* New York: Holt, Rinehart, and Winston, 1964.

Boroughs, Homer Jr., Foster, C. D. and Salyer, R. C., Jr. *Introduction to Secondary School Teaching.* New York: Ronald Press, 1964.

Brembeck, C. S. *The Discovery of Teaching.* Englewood Cliffs, N. J.: Prentice-Hall, 1962.

Brink, W. G. (ed.) *Adapting the Secondary School Program to the Needs of Youth.* Chicago: University of Chicago Press, 1953.

SELECTED REFERENCES

Brown, E. J., and Phelps, A. T. *Managing the Classroom - The Teacher's Part in School Administration.* New York: Ronald Press, 1961.

Brueckner, L. J. and Bond, G. L. *The Diagnosis and Treatment of Learning Difficulties.* New York: Appleton-Century-Crofts.

Butler, F. A. *The Improvement of Teaching in Secondary Schools.* Chicago: University of Chicago Press, 1954.

Burton, W. H. *The Guidance of Learning Activities.* New York: Appleton-Century-Crofts, 1962.

Canavan, P. J. *The Way to Reading Improvement.* Boston: Allyn and Bacon, 1966.

Chamberlain, L. M., and Kindred, L. W. *The Teacher and School Organization.* 4th ed. Englewood Cliffs, N. J.: Prentice-Hall, 1966.

Collier, C. C., and Walsh, W. H. *Teaching in the Modern Elementary School.* New York: Macmillan, 1967.

Corsini, R. J. and Howard, D. D. *Critical Incidents in Teaching.* Englewood Cliffs, N. J.: Prentice-Hall, 1964.

Cruikshank, W. M., and Johnson, G. O. *Education of Exceptional Children and Youth.* 2nd ed. Englewood Cliffs, N. J.: Prentice-Hall, 1967.

DeHaan, R. F., and Havighurst, R. J. *Educating Gifted Children.* Chicago: University of Chicago Press, 1958.

De Kieffer, Robert, and Cochran, L. W. *Manual of Audio-Visual Techniques.* 2nd ed. Englewood Cliffs, N. J.: Prentice-Hall, 1962.

Doll, R. C. *Curriculum Improvement: Decision-Making and Process.* Boston: Allyn and Bacon, 1964.

Douglass, H. R. *The High School Curriculum.* New York: Ronald Press, 1964.

Downey, L. W. *The Secondary Phase of Education.* New York: Ginn, 1965.

Dressel, P. L. (ed.) *The Integration of Educational Experiences.* Chicago: University of Chicago Press, 1958.

Ebel, R. L. *Measuring Educational Achievement.* Englewood Cliffs, N. J.: Prentice-Hall, 1965.

Eisner, E. W., and Ecker, D. W. *Readings in Art Education: A Primary Source Book.* New York: Ginn, 1966.

Fraser, D. M., and West, Edith. *Sosial Studies in Secondary Schools: Curriculum and Methods.* New York: Ronald Press, 1961.

Green, E. J. *The Learning Process and Programmed Instruction.* New York: Holt, Rinehart, and Winston, 1962.

Hook, J. N. *The Teaching of High School English.* New York: Ronald Press, 1965.

PART 3: ADDITIONAL AIDS TO REVIEW AND STUDY

Hass, Glen and Wiles, Kimball. *Readings in Curriculum.* Boston: Allyn and Bacon, 1965.

Havighurst, R. J. *Education in Metropolitan Areas.* Boston: Allyn and Bacon, 1966.

Hill, W. F. *Learning: A Survey of Psychological Interpretations.* San Francisco: Chandler, 1963.

Hoover, K. H. *Learning and Teaching in the Secondary School.* Boston: Allyn and Bacon, 1964.

Jackson, P. W. *Classroom Life.* New York: Holt, Rinehart, and Winston, 1967.

Karmel, L. J. *Testing in Our Schools.* New York: Macmillan, 1966.

Kerber, A. F., and Bommarito, B. T. *Schools and the Urban Crisis.* New York: Holt, Rinehart, and Winston, 1965.

Kirk, S. A. (ed.) *The Education of Exceptional Children.* Chicago: University of Chicago Press, 1950.

Lane, Howard, and Beauchamp, Mary. *Human Relations in Teaching: The Dynamics of Helping Children Grow.* Englewood Cliffs, N. J.: Prentice-Hall, 1955.

La Salle, Dorothy, and Geer, Gladys. *Health Instruction in Today's Schools.* Englewood Cliffs, N. J.: Prentice-Hall, 1955.

Lazarfeld, Paul, and Sieber, S. D. *Organizing Educational Research.* Englewood Cliffs, N. J.: Prentice-Hall, 1964.

Massialas, B. G., and Kazamias, A. M. *Crucial Issues in the Teaching of Social Studies: A Book of Readings.* Englewood Cliffs, N. J.: Prentice-Hall, 1964.

McGrath, G. D., Jelinek, J. J., and Wochner, R. E. *Educational Research Methods.* New York: Ronald Press, 1963.

Michaelis, J. U. *The Social Sciences: Foundations of the Social Studies.* Boston: Allyn and Bacon, 1965.

Miel, Alice. *Changing the Curriculum.* New York: Appleton-Century-Crofts.

Miller, A. G., and Whitcomb, Virginia. *Physical Education in the Elementary School Curriculum.* 2nd ed. Englewood Cliffs, N. J.: Prentice-Hall, 1963.

Mills, H. H., and Douglass, H. R. *Teaching in High School.* New York: Ronald Press, 1957.

Moffatt, M. P. *Social Studies Instruction.* 3rd ed. Englewood Cliffs, N. J.: Prentice-Hall, 1963.

Morrison, H. C. *The Practice of Teaching in the Secondary School.* rev. ed. Chicago: University of Chicago Press, 1931.

Morsey, R. J. *Improving English Instruction.* Boston: Allyn and Bacon, 1965.

Neagley, R. L., and Evans, N. D. *Handbook for Effective Supervision of Instruction.* Englewood Cliffs, N. J.: Prentice-Hall, 1964.

Ohmer, M. M., Wucoin, C. V., and Cortez, M. J. *Elementary Contemporary Mathematics.* New York: Ginn, 1964.

Petersen, D. G., and Hayden, V. D. *Teaching and Learning in the Elementary School.* New York: Appleton-Century-Crofts.

Petty, W. T. *Improving Your Spelling Program.* San Francisco: Chandler, 1959.

Preston, R. C. *Social Studies in the Elementary School.* Chicago: University of Chicago Press, 1957.

Raths, J. D., Pancella, J. R., and Van Ness, J. S. *Studying Teaching.* Englewood Cliffs, N. J. : Prentice-Hall. 1967.

Rivlin, H. N. *Teaching Adolescents in Secondary Schools.* 2nd ed. New York: Appleton-Century-Crofts, 1961.

Russell, D. H. *Children Learn to Read.* 2nd ed. New York: Ginn, 1961.

Smith, J. A. *Setting Conditions for Creative Teaching in the Elementary School.* Boston: Allyn and Bacon, 1966.

Smith, K. U., and Smith, M. F. *Cybernetic Principles of Learning and Educational Design.* New York: Holt, Rinehart, and Winston, 1966.

Stanley, J. C. *Measurement in Today's Schools.* 4th ed. Englewood Cliffs, N. J. : Prentice-Hall, 1964.

Stephens, J. M. *The Process of Schooling.* New York: Holt, Rinehart, and Winston, 1967.

Stoops, Emery, and Rafferty, Maxwell Jr. *Practices and Trends in School Administration.* New York: Ginn, 1961.

Taylor, B. L., McMahill, D. R., and Taylor, L. O. *The American Secondary School.* New York: Appleton-Century-Crofts.

Thomas, L. G., Kinnery, L. B., and Coladarci, A. P., Fielstra, H. A., and Thomas, F. W. *Perspective on Teaching: An Introduction to Public Education.* Englewood Cliffs, N. J. : Prentice-Hall, 1961.

Thurber, W. A., and Collette, A. T. *Teaching Science in Today's Secondary Schools.* 2nd ed. Boston: Allyn and Bacon, 1964.

Verduin, John. *Cooperative Curriculum Improvement.* Englewood Cliffs, N. J. : Prentice-Hall, 1967.

Walton, John. *Toward Better Teaching in the Secondary Schools.* Boston: Allyn and Bacon, 1966.

Famous Writers

Addison, Joseph (1672-1719) England; with Richard Steele edited *The Spectator*

Aesop (sixth century B. C.) Greece; Fables

PART 3: ADDITIONAL AIDS TO REVIEW AND STUDY

Alcott, Louisa May (1832-1888) America; *Little Women* and *Little Men*

Aldrich, Thomas Bailey (1836-1907) America; poet, journalist

Aristophanes (444-380 B. C.) Greece; Comedies

Arnold, Matthew (1822-1888) England; poet, critic

Aurelius, Marcus (121-180) Italy; emperor, stoic philosopher

Bacon, Francis (1561-1626) England; essayist

Balzac, Honore de (1799-1850) France; novelist

Barrie, Sir James M. (1860-1937) Scotland; novelist and playwright

Bjornson, Bjornstjerne (1832-1910) Norway; novelist, poet, playwright

Boccaccio, Giovanni (1313-1375) France and Italy; poet, writer

Bronte, Charlotte (1816-1855) England; novelist

Browning, Elizabeth Barrett (1806-1861) England; poet

Browning, Robert (1812-1889) England; poet

Burke, Edmund (1729-1797) England; orator

Burns, Robert (1759-1796) Scotland; poet

Byron, Lord (George Gordon, 1788-1824) England; poet

Campion, Thomas (1567-1620) England; poet, composer

Carducci, Giosue (1836-1907) Italy; poet

Carman, Bliss (1861-1929) Canada; poet, editor

Carroll, Lewis (Charles L. Dodgson, 1832-1898); *Alice in Wonderland*

Catullus, Caius Valerius (84-54 B. C.) Italy; greatest Latin poet

Cervantes, Miguel De Saavedra (1547-1616) Spain; *Don Quixote*

Chekhov, Anton (1860-1904) Russia; plays, short stories

Chesterfield, Lord (Philip Dormer Stanhope, 1694-1773) England; Letters to his son

Cicero, Marcus Tullius (106-43 B. C.) Italy; orations

FAMOUS WRITERS

Confucius (Kung Fu-tsze, 551-484 B. C.) China; philosopher

Conrad, Joseph (Theodor Jozef Konrad Korzenioxski, 1857-1924); Russia: novels and stories

Cowper, William (1731-1800) England; poet

D'Annunzio, Gabriele (1863-1938) Italy; novelist, poet, dramatist, and journalist

Dante Alighieri (1265-1321) Italy; *Divina Commedia*

Day, Clarence (1874-1935) America; Author– –family life

Dickens, Charles (1812-1870) England; novelist

Dickinson, Emily (1830-1886) America; poet

Drachmann, Holgar (1846-1908) Denmark; Poet and author

Dumas, Alexandre (1802-1870) France; Novelist

Dunsany, Lord (1878-1937) Ireland; Author-fantasies

Emerson, Ralph Waldo (1803-1882) America; Essayist, poet

Erskine, John (1879-1951) America; Author

Erskine, Thomas (1750-1823) England; Author, lawyer

Euripides (480-406 B. C.) Greece; Dramatist

Field, Eugene (1830-1886) America; Journalist, poet

Fontaine, Jean de la (1621-1695) France; Fabulist

Foster, Stephen (1826-1864) America; Songwriter

Frost, Robert (1875-1967) America; Poet

Galsworthy, John (1867-1933) England; Novelist, dramatist

Gaskell, Elizabeth (1810-1865) England; Novelist

Gellert, Christian (1715-1769) Germany; Poet, moralist

Goethe, Johann Wolfgang (1746-1832) Germany; dramatist, poet, critic

Gorky, Maxim (1868-1936) Russia; novelist, dramatist, short story writer

Gregory, Lady (1852-1932) Ireland; playwright

Hafiz (Shems ed-Din Muhammed, fourteenth century A. D) Persia; greatest lyric poet

Hardy, Thomas (1840-1928) England; novelist, poet

PART 3: ADDITIONAL AIDS TO REVIEW AND STUDY

Hawthorne, Nathanial (1804-1864) America; novelist, short story writer

Heine, Heinrich (1797-1856) Germany; poet, prose sketches

Henry, O. (Sidney Porter, 1862-1910) America; short story writer

Homer (about 1000 B. C.) Greece; The *Iliad* and *Odyssey*

Horace (Quintus Horatius Flaccus, 65-8 B. C.) Italy; poet

Hugo, Victor-Marie (1802-1885) France; novelist, poet

Ibsen, Henrik (1828-1859) Norway; dramatist

Irving, Washington (1783-1859) America; biographer, historian, essayist

Jonson, Ben (1573-1637) England; comic, dramatist, poet

Keats, John (1795-1921) England; poet

Khayyam, Omar (about 1050-1123) Persia; poet

Kingsley, Charles (1819-1875) England; novelist

Kipling, Rudyard (1865-1936) India; author, poet

Lagerlof, Selma (1858-1940) Sweden; novelist

Lamb, Charles (1775-1839) England; essayist

Lanier, Sidney (1842-1881) America; poet

Lardner, Ring (1885-1933) America; short story writer

Leacock, Stephen (1869-1944) Canada; essayist, journalist

Lewis, Sinclair (1885-1951) America; novelist

Lincoln, Abraham (1809-1865) America; addresses, letters, state documents

Li T'ai Po (1701-1762) China; poet

Livy (Titus Livius, 59 B. C.-17 A. D.) Italy; historian

Longfellow, Henry Wadsworth (1807-1882) America; poet

Lowell, Amy (1874-1925) America; poet, biographer, critic

Ludwig, Emil (1881-1948) Germany; dramatist, biographer

Macaulay, Thoams Babington (1800-1859) England; essayist, historian

FAMOUS WRITERS

Materlinck, Maurice (1862-1949) Belgium; poet, dramatist

Mann, Thomas (1875-1955) Germany; Novelist, short story writer

Mare, Walter de la (1873-1956) England; novelist, poet

Masefield, John (1878-1967) England; poet

Masters, Edgar Lee (1869-1945) America; novelist, poet

Maupassant, Guy de (1850-1893) France; short stories

Maurois, Andre (Andre Herzog, 1885-1967) France; novelist, essayist

Millay, Edna St. Vincent (1892-1950) America; poet

Milton, John (1608-1674) England; poet

Moliere, (Jean Baptiste Poquelin, 1622-1673) France; satirical comedy

Montagu, Lady Mary Wortley (1689-1762) England; letters

Montaigne, Michel de (1533-1592) France; essayist

Montesquieu, Charles Louis de Secondat (1689-1755) France; letters, lawyer

Moore, Thomas (1779-1852) Ireland; poet, musician

Motley, John Lothrop (1814-1877) America; historian

O'Neill, Eugene Gladstone (1888-1953) America; dramatist

Ovid (Publius Ovidius Naso, 43 B. C.-17 A. D.) Italy; poet

Pepys, Samuel (1633-1703) England; Diarist

Petrarch (Francesco Petrarca, 1304-1374) Italy; Sonnets

Pindar (522-443 B. C.) Greece; Lyric poet

Plato (427-347 B. C.) Greece; *The Republic*

Pliny, The Younger, (62-114) Italy; *Letters*

Plutarch (46-120) Greece; biographer

Poe, Edgar Allen (1809-1849) America; critic, poet, short story writer

Pushkin, Alexander (1799-1837) Russia; poet

PART 3: ADDITIONAL AIDS TO REVIEW AND STUDY

Rabelais, Francois (1483-1553) France; satirist

Reese, Lizette Woodworth (1856-1935) America; poet

Rilke, Rainer Maria (1875-1926) Czechoslavakia; poet

Robinson, Edwin Arlington (1869-1935) America; Poet

Ronsard, Pieere De (1524-1585) France; poet

Rossetti Christina (1830-1894) England; poet

Rostand, Edmond (1868-1918) France; dramatist

Rydberg, Victor (1828-1895) Sweden; poet

Sand, George (1804-1876) France; novelist

Sandburg, Carl (1878-1967) America; poet

Santayana, George (1863-1952) America; author, philospher

Sappho (sixth century B. C.) Lesbos; love lyrics

Schiller, Johann Christoph Friedrich von (1759-1805) Germany; dramatist, poet

Schopenhauer, Arthur (1788-1860) Germany; *The World as Will and Idea*

Scott, Sir Walter (1771-1832) Scotland; novelist, poet

Sevigne, Madame de (1626-1696) France; *Letters*

Shakespeare, William (1564-1616) England; dramatist

Shelley, Percy Bysshe (1792-1822) England; poet

Sheridan, Richard Brinsley (1751-1816) England; dramatist

Simonides (556-468 B. C.) Greece; lyric poet

Stephens, James (1882-1950) Ireland; poet, story-teller

Stevenson, Robert Louis (1850-1894) Scotland; novels, short stories

Strachey, Lytton (1880-1932) England; biographer

Teasdale, Sara (1884-1933) America; love lyrics

Tennyson, Alfred, Lord (1809-1892) England; poet

FAMOUS WRITERS

Thackeray, William Makepeace (1811-1863) England; novelist

Thoreau, Henry David (1817-1862) America; poet, naturalist

Tolstoy, Count Leo Nikolaievich (1828-1910) Russia; novelist, poet, social reformer

Twain, Mark (Samuel L. Clemens, 1835-1910) America; humorist

Villon, Francois (1431-1464) France; ballad writer

Virgil (Publius Vergilius Maro, 70-19 B. C.) Italy; *Aenid*

Voltaire (1694-1778) France; dramatist, philospher, satirist

Walpole, Horace (1717-1797) England; novelist

Webster, Daniel (1782-1852) America; orator

Wells, Herbert George (1866-1946) England; essayist, novelist, historian

Whitman, Walt (1819-1892) America; poet–"free verse"

Wilde, Oscar (1858-1900) England; dramatist, short stories, poems

Wister, Owen (1860-1938) America; novelist

Wordsworth, William (1770-1850) England; poet

Wylie, Elinor (1887-1929) America; poet

PART 3: ADDITIONAL AIDS TO REVIEW AND STUDY

Topics for Review in Music

HOW TO LISTEN TO MUSIC

Mood
Rhythm
Tempo
Colors of sound
Voices: soprano; alto; tenor; bass
Melody
Various instruments and their identification

THE SYMPHONY

Role of the conductor
Type of composition: four movements; "absolute" or "pure" music; principles of organization as used in movements

INSTRUMENTS OF THE ORCHESTRA

Four families of instruments: strings; brasses; woodwinds; percussion
    The string family consists of: violins; violas; cellos; basses
    The brass family consists of: trumpets; french horns; trombones; tubas
    The woodwind family consists of: flutes; oboes; clarinets; bassoons
    The percussion family consists of: snare drums; bongo drums; tympani; bass drum; Accessories: cymbals, castanets, maracas, claves, triangles and whips

THE FOUR PROPERTIES OF MUSICAL SOUND

Pitch
Duration
Volume
Timbre (color)

THE HARP

THE PIANO

THE ORGAN

THE SAXOPHONE

THE GUITAR

"Country" style music
"Rock and Roll" music

MELODY

HARMONY

RHYTHM AND METER

TOPICS FOR REVIEW IN MUSIC

TEMPO

TIMBRE

THE TEXTURE OF MUSIC

Monophonic (single-voice-melody without harmonic accompaniment)
Polyphonic (many-voiced- -two or more melodic lines combined)
Homophonic (single-melody- -with chords)

BASIC CLASSIFICATION OF MUSIC

Absolute (without story: expresses human emotions)

EXAMPLES:

Bartok	*Concerto No. 3 For Piano And Orchestra*
Beethoven	*Symphony No. 5 In C Minor*
Brahms	*Symphony No. 1 In C Minor*
Haydn	*Symphony No. 94 In G Major*
Rachmaninoff	*Concerto No. 2 In C Minor For Piano And Orchestra*
Tchaikovsky	*Concerto In D Major For Violin And Orchestra*

Program (with a story or non-musical idea: has three basic classifications)
    Imitative- -imitates the sound of an object
        Descriptive- -describes an event, such as a storm, sunset, etc.
        Narrative- -tells an interesting story

EXAMPLES:

Copland	*A Lincoln Portrait*
Debussy	*Prelude To The Afternoon Of A Faun* (Symphonic Poem)
Gershwin	*An American In Paris*
Grofe	*Grand Canyon Suite* (Orchestral Suite)
Rimsky-Korsakov	*Scheherazade* (Orchestral Suite)
Rossini	*William Tell Overture*

MAJOR ERAS OF MUSICAL DEVELOPMENT

Renaissance (1400-1600):
growth of Polyphony;
beginning of Homophonic Texture;
Outstanding Renaissance Composers,

Obrecht (1453-1505), des Pres (1450-1521), di Lasso (1532-1594), Palestrina (1526-1594), Victoria (1540-1611)

Baroque (1600-1750):
        Compositions increased in length;
        Music more homophonic during early period, to polyphonic later.
        development of the opera;
        outstanding baroque composers:
        Monteverdi (1567-1643); Lully (1632-1687); Purcell (1659-1695); Bach (1685-1750); Handel (1685-1759)

PART 3: ADDITIONAL AIDS TO REVIEW AND STUDY

Classical (1750-1827)
- Period between the deaths of Bach and Beethoven
- Usually homophonic in texture; separated melody and accompaniment
- Great concern with form, emotional restraint, balance, proportion, formal design
- Outstanding example of classical technique: Mozart's *Symphony No. 40.*
- Beginning of use of strong emotion: Beethoven's *Fifth Symphony*
- Outstanding Classical Composers: Gluck (1714-1787); Haydn (1732-1809); Mozart (1756-1791); Beethoven (1770-1827);

Romantic (1827-1900)
- From death of Beethoven into the classical.
- Classical composers restrained emotionally; Romantic composers "went overboard" in expressing emotions.
- "Program music" was developed for the first time.
- Outstanding romantic composers: Schubert (1797-1828); Schumann (1810-1856); Chopin (1810-1849); Mendelssohn (1809-1847); Brahms (1833-1897); Liszt (1811-1886); Tchaikovsky (1850-1926)

Opera Composers: Wagner (1813-1883); Verdi (1813-1901); Rossini (1792-1868)

Modern (1900- -)
- Use of different styles and approaches: Neo-romanticism (continuing romanticism); Neo-classicism (modern music in classical style); Atonality (twelve tones of the chromatic scale)
- Experimentation with style and form
- Impressionism (France): Debussy (1862-1918), Ravel (1875-1937)

Strange and unusual patterns and harmonies, chords but few melodies with shifting rhythms are characteristic of this music. Emphasis upon the external.
Expressionism: leading exponent Arnold Schoenberg (1874-1951)
Emphasis upon the internal and the subconscious.
Neo-Classicism: Stravinsky (1882–); Prokofier (1891-1953); Hindemith (1895-1963)
Returned to the objectivity of the classical school. Composers attempted to simplify and clarify form.

BASIC PRINCIPLES OF MUSICAL ORGANIZATION

Form in Music
- One-part form: use of single musical idea; folk songs, Patriotic songs (*America the Beautiful*), Children's music, Special songs (*Anchors Aweigh*), Hymns (*Abide With Me*)
- Two-part form (binary): Use of two distinct musical ideas in the composition; can be diagrammed as an *A-B* structure; *A* and *B* may be repeated in the composition. (*America,* and *Brahm's Lullaby*)
- Three-part from (ternary): an *A-B-A* structure with *A* always used to make the third part.
- Used frequently in popular music: examples in works of Mozart, Beethoven, and others; example of old-time favorite- -*Drink to Me Only With Thine Eyes*
- Rondo form: Easily discovered, *A* structure constantly repeated; the design may use *A-B-A-C-A-D-A*, etc.

EXAMPLES:

Mozart	*Eine Kleine Nachtmusik* (second movement, *A-B-A-C-A*)
Haydn	*Symphony No. 97* (fourth movement, *A-B-A-C-A*)
Beethoven	*Piano Sonata No. 8* (the "Pathetique," *A-B-A-C-A*) .

TOPICS FOR REVIEW IN MUSIC

Theme and Variations: procedure, introduce a theme or main melody; in various ways use theme over and over again.

EXAMPLES:

Brahms	*Symphony No. 4* (fourth movement)
Haydn	*Symphony No. 94* ("Surprise")
Beethoven	*Symphony No. 3* ("Eroica")

During the Baroque period this concept of composition was used in two other types, the *passacaglia* and the *chaconne*.

Passacaglia - use four or eight measures of music in the bass in majestic, triple meter as the foundation for continuous variations in polyphonic arrangements.

Bach used this device of composition in his work, *Passacaglia in C minor for Organ.*

Chaconne - differs from the passacaglia in that the progression of chords becomes the basic idea rather than a melody. Harmony is more important than melody in this composition.

Sonata Allegro Form: organized around the *A-B-A* principle

The first and sometimes the last movement of a sonata, symphony, overture, concerto, or quartet is organized around three areas of emphasis:

A, the exposition, in which the first theme and second theme are often repeated, followed by a closing section called the "codetta."

B, the most important part of a movement, develops motives from one or both of the themes in part A. These are presented by different instruments of the orchestra, in different keys, or with variations of expression.

A, a type of recapitulation of the first and second themes, summarizes the music for the listener through the use of the "coda" at the end of the movement.

EXAMPLES: Schubert *Unfinished Symphony;* Mendelssohn *Violin Concerto;* Beethoven *Symphony No. 5*

TYPES OF MUSICAL COMPOSITIONS

The Symphony: composition for orchestra, usually four movements.

First movement — vital, demanding, dramatic in the sonata allegro form

Second movement — beginning of contrast, lyrical quality, slower than the first movement

Third movement —Mozart and Beethoven used the minuet form, Beethoven's use of the scherzo began with his *Third Symphony.*

Fourth movement — repeats some of the main themes, may be in these forms: rondo, theme and variations, sonata allegro form

PART 3: ADDITIONAL AIDS TO REVIEW AND STUDY

The Concerto: a composition for one or more instruments and orchestra, usually in symphonic form

Double concerto — uses two instruments; usually three movements

EXAMPLE: *Schumann Piano Concerto*

The Sonata: a composition for solo instrument, usually the piano, and orchestra, usually has four movements which follow the same arrangement for contrast as the symphony, which is a sonata for orchestra

EXAMPLE: Beethoven *"Moonlight" Sonata*

Sonata for four instruments (two violins, one viola, and one cello)

EXAMPLE: Beethoven, *String Quartet No. 16 in F, Op. 135.*

The Concerto Grosso: Uses a small group of players to contrast with a whole orchestra. The compositions use the "fugal" form and not "sonata form" of musical development.

THE OVERTURE: A one-movement composition in sonata form for orchestra. The organization lost its sonata form in the late Romantic period and now can use any form to become a type of program (non-musical idea) form of musical expression.

EXAMPLE: Tchaikovsky *Overture 1812*

THE SUITE: The suite is a collection of separate pieces. During the seventeenth and eighteenth centuries it was a collection of four dances of different tempo: The *Allemande*, slow; The *Courante*, simple rhythms; *Saraband*, slow, ceremonial; *The Gigue*, fast and lively

THE FUGUE

The main theme is repeated in various higher or lower keys as the subject seems to take flight from its original key.

EXAMPLE: Bach *C-minor Fugue*

THE CANON

The repetition of any melody in different pitch level and at different times.

EXAMPLE: "Row, Row, Row Your Boat" when it is sung as a *round*.

FREE FORMS OF COMPOSITION

   The Prelude — as composed by Bach it was to come before something else; now it may also be a separate piece in itself.

   The Nocturne — usually meditative evening pieces; Chopin

   The Ballade — a narrative piece; Chopin

TOPICS FOR REVIEW IN MUSIC

The Impromptu — an improvised piece of music of light, fanciful nature; style made famous by Schubert and Chopin.

EXAMPLES: Schubert *Impromptu, Op. 142;* Chopin *Impromptu, Op. 26*

The Symphonic poem: form of program music in a single movement for orchestra, usually with a descriptive title.

The Capriccio: used by Brahms for his capricious piano works.

The Intermezzo: intended as an interval between more serious or heavier works.

FORMS OF VOCAL MUSIC

Choir — group of religious singers

Chorus — soloists with male or female singers

Motet — usually a religious choral work

Madrigal — entertaining music for choral groups; sixteenth and seventeenth centuries

Oratorio — a dramatic vocal composition for chorus, orchestra, and soloists based upon religious themes

The Cantata — a lyrical choral form using either religious or secular theme shorter than the oratorio; Bach

The Chorale — Protestant hymns in four-part harmony, at first in unison; form made famous by Bach

The Passion — a religious work based upon the suffering and death of Jesus, a type of oratorio made famous by Bach using the narrative and recitative styles in his *St. John Passion* and *St. Matthew Passion*

The Mass — uses the Gregorian Chant; the main religious service of the Catholic Church

The Opera — vocal drama with most of the words sung rather than spoken by members of the cast; sung usually in the language in which the opera was written

EXAMPLES: Verdi *Aida;* Rossini *Barber of Seville;* Wagner *Tannhauser*

PART 3: ADDITIONAL AIDS TO REVIEW AND STUDY

TOPICS FOR REVIEW IN ART

Prehistoric Art in Europe
    Late Paleolithic period, greatest advance in Ice Age cave
    paintings
    Bison standing — Altamira cave, Spain
    Rock painting — Spain, men in new light as they pursue the fleeing herd
    Bronze age rock paintings show a decline in realism and abstract
    works become close to a pictorial language
    Had developed metal ornamental art styles before the Roman invasion in England

Egyptian art
    Architecture as a major art originated in Egypt
    Tombs
    Temple at Karnak
    Palette was a votive table dedicated to a god — early dynastic period
    Memphis tombs (2600 B.C.) man and wife relief
    Tomb of King Tutankhamen (New Empire period) golden mask, a studied portrait
    Ramesses II, black granite
    Large statues often represented royalty or priests. The soul was made in the form of a bird which
        descended from heaven
    Statues painted over stucco were white, black, yellow, dark red, or turquoise green even if of the hardest
        stone
    Characters made in cubical form to show dignity and everlasting rest
    Head of Rameses II was huge and of great power and dignity
    Funerary papyrus records the belief that the dead were judged by Osiris

Ancient Near Eastern Art
    Mesopotamia
    Created to glorify despotic rulers

Ancient Greek Art
    Alexander the Great brought Oriental art in contact with Greek art
    Greece became a Roman province (146 B.C.) Greek art influenced Roman art until the Christian era
    Greek art conceived or gods in the image of man
    Temples and statues were supported by state funds
    During a period of two hundred years (Greek art at its maturity) second half of the fifth century under
        Pericles and the fourth century (Great Period) Greek art reached its height
    No Greek paintings have survived
    The city-state of Athens demonstrated the impact of art upon human life
    Man, in Greek sculpture, shows the ideal of human dignity,

repose, poise, and without flaws	Praxiteles: satyr, copy
Marble maidens	Silanion: portrait of a boxer
Statues from the sanctuary of Apollo	Geometric-style vases
Centaurs	Black-figured style vase
The bronze Zeus	Black and red-figured style vases
The marble head of Zeus	Model of the Acropolis
Head of Youth, marble	Model of the Parthenon
Freestanding colossal statues,	
Athena Parthenos and Zeus at Olympia	

Etruscan Art
    Native style of terra cotta, bronze works, as well as tombs and temples

TOPICS FOR REVIEW IN ART

Roman Art
   Roman art combined Etruscan and Greek ideas in the building of temples
   View of the Colosseum
   Constantine legalized Christianity in A.D. 313. Roman art belongs to these five centuries:
      1. (27 B.C. – A.D. 68) Augustus and the Julian emperors, Tiberius to Nero Art, Statue of Augustus, Altar of Peace
      2. (A.D. 69-96) Flavian emperors, Vespasian, Titus, Domitian Art, Colosseum, Arch of Titus
      3. (A.D. 98-180) Trajan and Hadrian, Antoninus Pius, and Marcus Aurelius Art, Trajan Forum and Columns, Maisen Carrée, Pantheon
      4. (A.D. 211-377) Late Empire: Caracalla, Diocletian, and Constantine reliefs

Christian and Byzantine Art
   Basilica of St. Peters
   Statue of the Good Shepherd
   Churches, mosaic angels

Early Medieval and Romanesque Art: 100 B.C. – A.D. 1150
   Mausoleum of Theodoric
   Church of San Michele
   Worms Cathedral
   Romanesque lectern
   Medieval mural paintings

Gothic Art (1150-1400 A.D.)
   Art of France, Britain, and Germany
     Cathedral of Chartres, south facade
     Palaces and cathedrals
     Marble piers and Gothic sculpture reliefs
     Paintings by: Maitani, Duccio, Giotto, Martini

Renaissance Art (1400-1600)
   Hubert and Jan van Eyck: Ghent Altarpiece
   Signorelli: Fall of the Damned
   Mantegna: Calvary
   Gozzoli: Journey of the Magi
   Ghirlandail: Birth of the Virgin
   Botticelli: Madonna of the Magnificant
   Woodcuts, decorating printed books
   Works of Leonardo
   Raphael – Small Cowper Madonna, Portrait of Pope Julius II
   Michelangelo: Holy Family of the Doni and other works
   Titian
   Tintoretto
   del Sarto
   Donatello
   Calligraphic woodctus
   El Greco
   Brueghel
   Dürer
   Holbein the Younger
   Sansovino: Library of Saint Marks
   Carved arabesque
   Architecture: Palladio, John Thorpe
   Majolica pottery
   Renaissance silversmiths and their productions

Baroque and Rococo Art (1600-1800)
   Bernini
   Carracci
   Reni
   Etching – Piranesi
   Architecture, Palace at Würtzburg and others
   Wrought-iron works
   Vasquez, and Churiguera
   Velázquez
   Goya
   Rubens
   Van Dyck
   Rembrandt

PART 3: ADDITIONAL AIDS TO REVIEW AND STUDY

Reynolds
Gainsborough
Romney
Jones
Wren
Perrault
Lebrun

Clodion
Houdon
Poussin
Mellan
Watteau
Boucher
Furniture, book covers

Modern Art in Europe (1800-1950)

Ingres
Ericault
Corot
Millet
Daumier
Courbet
Turner
Morris
Beardsley
Friedrich
Jongkind
Manet
Degas
Renoir
Cézanne
Gauguin
Picasso
Marc
Barlach
Matisse
Rouault
Chagall

Mondrian
Miró
Debuffet
Hayter
Canova
Thorwaldsen
Rodin
Carpeaux
Lehmbruck
Brancusi
Arp (black and white abstract paper construction)
Maillol
Lipchitz
Giacometti
Laughans
Barry
Paxton
Eiffel
Garnier
Gaudi
Gropius
Le Corbusier

Art in the United States

Red Indian art (first in the United States)
Copley
Durand
Bingham
Whistler
Sargent
Ryder
Sloan
Hopper
Evergood
Stieglitz
O'Keefe
Sheeler
De Kooning
Kline
Pereira (abstractions based upon geometry)
Fels

Kohn
Tobey
Lissim
Pfeiffer
Herblock
Powers
Saint-Gaudens
Lachaise
Lipton
Gabo
Rozak
Borglum
Furniture
    Chippendale
Architecture
    Hamilton (Independence Hall)
    McBean (St. Paul's Chapel) New York

ENGLISH GRAMMAR AND USAGE

Thornton and Walter (Capitol, Washington, D.C.) Saarinen (staircase) (chair)
Renwich (Smithsonian)   Harrison and Abramowitz
Richardson   Kahn
Sullivan   Wright
Gilbert   Bronx-Whitestone (Suspension Bridge)

Two review books which contain 754 illustrations and can be purchased for $1.25 each plus 10 cents shipping charges. They are: MY700 Mentor Book *A Pictorial History of Western Art* by Christiansen and *The History of Western Art,* Christiansen can be obtained from: NEW AMERICAN LIBRARY, 1301 Avenue of the Americas, New York, New York 10019.

English Grammar and Usage

Practice Test 1

DIRECTIONS: There are five possible answers. Select the *one* best answer.

1. Which sentence is not punctuated correctly?

   (A) People who have money are lucky.
   (B) My uncle, a good mechanic, fixed my car.
   (C) Her new dress which was pink was lost on the train.
   (D) New York, which I haven't visited for two years, has many attractions.
   (E) The girls are ready, aren't they?

2. In which of these sentences should the italicized part be set off by commas?

   (A) A ticket was obtained by everyone *who waited in line.*
   (B) Boys *who are good dancers* are usually popular.
   (C) Girls *who work in the summer* will have spending money.
   (D) Mary *the girl we hired today* is the receptionist.
   (E) The people *who arrive late* will not be seated.

3. Which of these statements about the use of the comma is incorrect?

   (A) Restrictive statements are set off by commas.
   (B) Restrictive statements are not set off by commas.
   (C) Words in a series are set off by commas.
   (D) Non-restrictive expressions are set off by commas.
   (E) If non-restrictive expressions are left out, the meaning of the sentence is the same.

4. Which one of the following sentences is correct?

   (A) The bills were mailed on Friday December 30 1961.
   (B) Wednesday, February 12 1931 was the date of his birth.
   (C) We visited relatives in Detroit, Michigan during Christmas vacation.
   (D) He was born in Kansas City, Missouri, on Wednesday, September 15, 1915.
   (E) Address the letter to 15 Elm Street Atlanta, Georgia.

PART 3: ADDITIONAL AIDS TO REVIEW AND STUDY

5. Which sentence has a non-restrictive expression?

    (A) Children who eat candy have many cavities.
    (B) Our house, which is rather old, is on Oak Street.
    (C) The bowl that is broken lies on the floor.
    (D) Few pupils like to go through the door that leads to the principal's office.
    (E) The necklace that was on the dresser has disappeared.

6. Which sentence is correctly punctuated?

    (A) I cooked the meal while you were away.
    (B) I cooked the meal, while you were away.
    (C) Despite my suggestion he left early.
    (D) When the noise began the children screamed loudly.
    (E) Running after his mother he called for her to come back.

7. In which sentence is the semicolon used correctly?

    (A) One sister is talented, the other is not.
    (B) I want the first question; and you can have the second.
    (C) I went to college; but I stayed only one term.
    (D) My sister sings; my brother plays the quitar.
    (E) The girls like to swim; but the boys prefer tennis.

8. Which one of the following sentences is punctuated correctly?

    (A) Hurrah, we won the football game.
    (B) The floors are brown: the walls are white.
    (C) John likes school; but Joe does not.
    (D) My brother has pneumonia; he is in the hospital.
    (E) I wanted to go to Europe but, I did not have the money.

9. Select the one sentence which is punctuated incorrectly.

    (A) My Mother, is coming for a visit.
    (B) Ann injured her knee, however, it was not serious.
    (C) I like fruit; besides, it is good for me.
    (D) I didn't like the medicine; nevertheless, I took it.
    (E) The concert was great; therefore, we stayed for the reception.

10. In which sentence would you make a correction?

    (A) I invited Mother and my sister to the concert.
    (B) We are late, nevertheless, we should go.
    (C) The nurse said, "The doctor is out."
    (D) Harry said that she had called.
    (E) "She will be late," Ann replied.

VOCABULARY PRACTICE

11. Which sentence is punctuated incorrectly?

    (A) There are four of us here: John, George, Mary, and Sue.
    (B) "Will you, he asked, hurry with the medicine?"
    (C) "I love you," she said softly.
    (D) Betty said that she had seen him.
    (E) "Am I too late?" Mary asked.

    11. [A] [B] [C] [D] [E]

12. Which sentence would you correct?

    (A) "Who is there?" she asked in a frightened voice.
    (B) Did you say, "Mary is late"?
    (C) Mike said, "I heard your father say,'One o'clock."
    (D) She called, "Yes, I'm coming."
    (E) She said that she was lost.

    12. [A] [B] [C] [D] [E]

13. Which sentence is correct?

    (A) The teacher asked,"Why don't you look where you are going!"
    (B) Did you hear the speaker say, "It is late"?
    (C) Did she say, "Where is Sammy?"
    (D) "This" Father said "is too much for me!"
    (E) Tom said "I am feeling sick."

    13. [A] [B] [C] [D] [E]

14. Which sentence is punctuated incorrectly?

    (A) "We are moving to Chicago," Alice told us.
    (B) "Come quickly," she urged.
    (C) He yelled, "Eureka, we struck oil!"
    (D) When the package is marked "Special Delivery", it moves quickly.
    (E) "Tell me a story," said the child. " I am not sleepy."

    14. [A] [B] [C] [D] [E]

15. Which sentence is incorrect?

    (A) The following people attended the ball; Mary, Tom, Annette, and Kent.
    (B) When I left the house, it was snowing.
    (C) Don't tell me you never heard of the word "simile!"
    (D) She said, "I went; however, no one else was there."
    (E) "I will be away," Lynn said, "until Sunday."

    15. [A] [B] [C] [D] [E]

ANSWERS

1. C	4. C	7. D	10. B	13. B
2. D	5. B	8. D	11. B	14. D
3. A	6. A	9. A	12. C	15. A

PART 3: ADDITIONAL AIDS TO REVIEW AND STUDY

English Grammar and Usage

Practice Test 2

DIRECTIONS: Select the *best* answer from the five possible choices.

1. Which sentence is correct?

    (A) He shouted, "Where is the fire?"!
    (B) Why did you ask, "Where is Mary?"?
    (C) Gary, have you memorized "The Birches"?
    (D) He shouted "Help!"
    (E) Have you ever been in Detroit, mother?

    1. [A] [B] [C] [D] [E]

2. Which of these statements is correct?

    (A) The last syllable of any word can be carried over to the next line.
    (B) A hyphen is used to divide a word into syllables.
    (C) Bough can be divided at the end of the line.
    (D) The "y" in murky can be carried over to the next line.
    (E) Two letters can be carried over to the next line when a word is divided into syllables.

    2. [A] [B] [C] [D] [E]

3. Which sentence demonstrates the correct use of the apostrophe?

    (A) The girls' gave the book to the librarian.
    (B) Bob's and Bee's jackets were alike.
    (C) All of the ladie's hats were new.
    (D) I bought Lincolns' portrait.
    (E) I have an account at the Merchant's Bank.

    3. [A] [B] [C] [D] [E]

4. Which sentence is correct?

    (A) Theyr'e on their way to the school meeting.
    (B) The skys the limit!
    (C) The rules for voting (see list 1) are often violated.
    (D) This is her's.
    (E) The boys' hat is lost.

    4. [A] [B] [C] [D] [E]

5. Which sentence has an incorrect plural form of a noun?

    (A) Smog is a problem for the cities.
    (B) Fruit trees often grow in valleys.
    (C) The busses were full of passengers.
    (D) Ten lady's attended the meeting.
    (E) Two men's coats were taken at the theater.

    5. [A] [B] [C] [D] [E]

6. Which sentence is correct?

    (A) If I was you, I wouldn't go.

(B) It was him tapping on the table that aggravated me.
(C) Bobby and me cleaned the board.
(D) You take the car and us girls will take the taxi.
(E) I do not approve of their dating so young.

6. [A] [B] [C] [D] [E]

7. Which sentence is incorrect?

(A) Has everyone chose a partner?
(B) George drank all the root beer.
(C) He thought his chest would burst from the exertion.
(D) He dived into the pool with his clothes on.
(E) I had flown on an airplane before last week.

7. [A] [B] [C] [D] [E]

8. Which sentence is correct?

(A) If I had of known him better, I would not have loaned him my book.
(B) You had ought to dress more carefully.
(C) You hadn't ought to carry five subjects.
(D) Let me do the work myself.
(E) Leave him go.

8. [A] [B] [C] [D] [E]

9. Which sentence is incorrect?

(A) The trespasser will be persecuted.
(B) I shall go with you.
(C) I heard that you are leaving town.
(D) I will go to the meeting.
(E) The new laws will affect everyone.

9. [A] [B] [C] [D] [E]

10. Which sentence does *not* have awkward construction?

(A) If a teacher wants to get good results, you must establish a good learning climate.
(B) A college student must not only graduate, but also plans for a future career
(B) must be made.
(C) Running forward, Paul faced the crowd before he catches the ball and touches first base.
(D) As captain of the debating team he spoke well, and the trophy was saved for the school.
(E) A traveler must plan his trip carefully so that he can get the most mileage in the least time.

10. [A] [B] [C] [D] [E]

11. Which sentence is an example of a complex sentence?

(A) I do not know what made me do it.
(B) My friend made himself welcome by offering to help me.
(C) I had always wanted to meet him, and now he was here.
(D) The women and children were safe within the lifeboats.
(E) She sat very still on the fence, gazing at the apple orchard.

11. [A] [B] [C] [D] [E]

PART 3: ADDITIONAL AIDS TO REVIEW AND STUDY

12. Which line contains a misspelled word?

    (A) preceeding, siege, omission, usable
    (B) peacable, propeller, incidentally, until
    (C) irresistable, vengeance, incredable, permissable
    (D) perseverance, changeable, chauffeur, athlete
    (E) indispensable, exhaust, fascinate, intercede

    12. [A] [B] [C] [D] [E]

13. Which word contains an extra letter?

    (A) dilapidated   (D) outrageous
    (B) accommodate   (E) mischievious
    (C) rhythm

    13. [A] [B] [C] [D] [E]

14. Which word should be capitalized?

    (A) algebra   (D) negroes
    (B) sophomore   (E) arachnid
    (C) the Duke of Bedford

    14. [A] [B] [C] [D] [E]

15. Which line contains a misspelled word?

    (A) eligible, shriek, arguement, governor
    (B) comparative, despair, equivalent, committee
    (C) pervade, precedence, tragedy, unanimous
    (D) psychology, questionnaire, receivable, outrageous
    (E) privilege, proceed, grievous, gauge

    15. [A] [B] [C] [D] [E]

Answers

1. C	4. C	7. A	10. E	13. E
2. B	5. D	8. D	11. A	14. D
3. B	6. E	9. A	12. C	15. A

Part 4
Teaching Area Examinations

Sample Test Questions

Area Examinations

Art Education

Practice Test

DIRECTIONS: Select the one *best* answer which will complete the statement. Note the *five* possible choices.

1. The quality of an art experience refers to its

    (A) uniqueness
    (B) form
    (C) style
    (D) aesthetic significance
    (E) creativeness

    1. [A] [B] [C] [D] [E]

2. Artists may inadvertently borrow or imitate another artist's work. Picasso, for example did a series of paintings which were based upon

    (A) Mondrian's *Women*
    (B) Monet's *Scenes*
    (C) Delacroix's *Women of Algiers*
    (D) Pollock's *Abstracts*
    (E) Albers *Portrait of a Woman*

    2. [A] [B] [C] [D] [E]

3. Studies of creativity by Guilford, McKinnon, and others in their subjective analysis of the quality of an art experience include one of these elements:

    (A) aptitudes
    (B) timing
    (C) ordinariness
    (D) transcendence
    (E) structuring

    3. [A] [B] [C] [D] [E]

3. Art education is important for all children because it is a universal experience when individuals

    (A) learn to paint
    (B) design their homes
    (C) evaluate another's work
    (D) go to an art gallery
    (E) make daily art judgments

    4. [A] [B] [C] [D] [E]

ART EDUCATION

5. One of the basic educational functions of art is to

   (A) make every child an artist
   (B) aid in child growth and development
   (C) furnish busy work for gifted children
   (D) help every child have first hand experience
   (E) help children imitate great painters

6. Art contributes to the child's self-realization by

   (A) projecting the ego
   (B) encouraging exploratory attitudes
   (C) disciplining motor activity
   (D) following art patterns
   (E) working with group projects

7. Art education in the 20th century differs from art education in the curricula of the 19th century in that it

   (A) emphasizes art appreciation
   (B) is inartistic in nature
   (C) uses limited art media
   (D) uses limited techniques
   (E) provides sound aesthetic experience

8. Directed teaching is a term used by art educators when they refer to

   (A) art appreciation courses
   (B) art survey courses
   (C) finger painting lessons
   (D) project work
   (E) imitative procedures

9. Art education contributes to the child's problem-solving ability when it

   (A) exercises the creative imagination
   (B) follows a set pattern
   (C) utilizes early tracing techniques
   (D) helps children evaluate and express their ideas
   (E) uses sterotyped materials

10. The use of art as therapy for children should be

    (A) attempted by teachers in all grades
    (B) attempted only by trained personnel
    (C) used by the art supervisor
    (D) used with slow learners
    (E) helpful to children with emotional problems

PART 4: TEACHING AREA EXAMINATIONS

11. Guiding growth in observation involves all but *one* of these concepts:

    (A) seeing is an isolated function to the eye
    (B) telling someone what to see is not educating the eye
    (C) tactile, kinesthetic, and other senses are involved
    (D) situations drawn from life are incentives for looking
    (E) evaluation of what one sees involves meaning

12. The child who has participated in art courses should be better able to appreciate modern art because he

    (A) realizes the non-verbal nature of art
    (B) is an artist himself
    (C) has had an aesthetic experience
    (D) knows the use of various media
    (E) understands art

13. The teacher of art encourages expression which is highly personal yet

    (A) to the child it is merely making objects
    (B) sensations are the most important
    (C) the values go beyond subjective desires
    (D) feelings play a very small part in the creative act
    (E) imitative in form

14. All except *one* of these is a condition necessary to give form to experience:

    (A) a state of mind conducive to creation
    (B) the proper materials for expression of an idea
    (C) isolation or privacy
    (D) freedom from conventional methods
    (E) a model to study

15. The child's first artistic scribbles indicate that

    (A) form is most important
    (B) feeling is absent
    (C) motor coordination is good
    (D) feeling is present
    (E) children cannot react to experiences

16. Art first was placed in the curriculum in the 19th century as

    (A) finger painting
    (B) water coloring
    (C) ceramics
    (D) puppetry
    (E) freehand drawing

BIOLOGY AND GENERAL SCIENCE

17. The basic difficulty in developing an art program is to

    (A) develop a variety of experiences
    (B) establish a sequence of experiences
    (C) obtain sufficient interest by pupils
    (D) get teacher participation
    (E) achieve artistic productivity   17. [A][B][C][D][E]

18. For the timid child, or one who is slow in motor development, the medium which may be most helpful is

    (A) soap carving   (D) freehand drawing
    (B) paper sculpture   (E) painting with tempera
    (C) finger painting   18. [A][B][C][D][E]

19. Waste materials and inexpensive materials serve a purpose in art because

    (A) the child should learn to save
    (B) it heightens the child's awareness of things around him
    (C) schools can't afford art materials
    (D) he can use these materials at home
    (E) they are easily obtainable   19. [A][B][C][D][E]

20. Art has come to be considered as an integral part of education. If this concept is to be implemented effectively in the shcools, art must

    (A) be taught ony by art teachers
    (B) be taught by proper techniques
    (C) be a credit course in high school
    (D) be taught through a core of art activities
    (E) stress the individual development of the child   20. [A][B][C][D][E]

Answers

1. D	5. E	9. D	13. C	17. B
2. C	6. B	10. B	14. E	18. C
3. D	7. E	11. A	15. D	19. B
4. E	8. E	12. A	16. E	20. E

Biology and General Science

Practice Test

DIRECTIONS: Select the *best* answer from the five possible choices.

1. The word biology is derived from

    (A) Latin   (D) French
    (B) Greek   (E) Egyptian
    (C) Anglo-Saxon   1. [A][B][C][D][E]

PART 4: TEACHING AREA EXAMINATIONS

2. It was not until the work of William Harvey, the English doctor, that it was known that blood circulated in the human body. This occured in

   (A) the Middle Ages
   (B) the 15th century
   (C) the 16th century
   (D) the 17th century
   (E) the 19th century

3. Science is a vast accumulation of knowledge. The high school student should learn that science is

   (A) open-mindedness
   (B) curiosity
   (C) careful judgment
   (D) cause and effect
   (E) attitude and method

4. When teaching the topic of scientific method, certain principles are essential. One of these is fundamental to the others.

   (A) There are several scientific methods.
   (B) The method used depends upon the investigation.
   (C) The research method uses experimentation.
   (D) The most widely used method is the technical method.
   (E) The research method is used to prove or disprove an hypothesis.

5. Experimentation in biology must be controlled so as to

   (A) test only one variable factor at a time
   (B) study only living things
   (C) test only two variables at a time
   (D) permit observation of the experiment
   (E) prove the hypothesis in one experiment

6. Anton Van Leeuwenhoek opened up the whole world of biology when he

   (A) discovered the cell
   (B) examined plants and animals with a magnifying lens
   (C) used the first vaccination
   (D) discovered the virus
   (E) observed the interrelationship of living things

7. There are several specialized branches of biology. One of these is not a branch of biological studies.

   (A) Ichthyology
   (B) Herpetology
   (C) Psychology
   (D) Phycology
   (E) Ecology

8. The title of Father of Biology is given to Aristotle for his

   (A) dissections of many different kinds of animals
   (B) study of the stomach of cud-chewing animals
   (C) scientific writings

(D) study of the chick in the egg
(E) grouping and classifying of plants and animals

9. General science teachers can expect to find students indicating intelligence quotients from

   (A) 50 to 105
   (B) 60 to 115
   (C) 65 to 120
   (D) 70 to 110
   (E) 70 to 150

10. Which of the sciences appeals most to girls at the high school level?

    (A) General science   (D) Physics
    (B) Geology   (E) Astromomy
    (C) Biology

11. An unpredictable factor of considerable significance to high school science teachers is the

    (A) interest level of students
    (B) socio-economic background of students
    (C) range of experiences of students
    (D) age level of students
    (E) sex differences in ability

12. The teacher of elective sciences has fewer instructional problems that the teacher of general science because

    (A) students are in everal stages of development
    (B) students are younger
    (C) students' range of behavior is increased
    (D) students are more future goal-oriented
    (E) there is a wider age range in each class

13. The most acceptable way to utilize student objectives in the teaching of the sciences is to

    (A) base all learning tasks upon student needs
    (B) let pupil objectives parallel general educational objectives and relate to them
    (C) base progress upon examination scores
    (D) use only subject matter goals
    (E) let pupils establish the objectives for the course

14. A new student entered the biology class. Mr. *L* then had to change one of the lessons he had prepared. Why?

    (A) The new student changed the interests of the class.
    (B) Interests change as needs change.
    (C) Interests are subject to modification.

PART 4: TEACHING AREA EXAMINATIONS

(D) Students are motivated by felt needs.
(E) All of these.

15. Teachers will obtain more accurate learning from students when they use first-hand experiences if they

   (A) go along on the field trips
   (B) do all the demonstrations themselves
   (C) build a whole course on first-hand experiences
   (D) know that students vary in ability to interpret experiences
   (E) restrict the amount of material to be covered

16. Pictures in science books and manuals have serious limitations because

   (A) they are interpreted as three-dimensional images
   (B) perspective affects the interpretation
   (C) pictures are selective
   (D) only (A) and (B) are true
   (E) all of these are true

17. There are three levels of learning in general science. Some information is essential desirable, or just interesting. The great loss in the retention of information and the inability to transfer probably represents the unnecessary attempt to bring all science lessons to the

   (A) recall level
   (B) recognition level
   (C) mastery level
   (D) association level
   (E) retention level

18. Teachers of science often complain that students do not understand and demonstrate inductive reasoning processes without realizing that the

   (A) students have to gather the evidence
   (B) students cannot interpret the evidence
   (C) students dislike to think inductively
   (D) teachers too often give the students the answers
   (E) inductive reasoning is not practical

19. It is necessary to experiment to check inferences derived through deductive methods because

   (A) experimentation is always necessary
   (B) the basic generalizations may be incorrect
   (C) odd forms of reasoning may result
   (D) deduction involves going from the known to the unknown
   (E) there are always exceptions

20. When teaching scientific theories, the high school teacher should emphasize that

BUSINESS EDUCATION

(A) theories are not facts
(B) some theories are in dispute
(C) theories have limitations
(D) none of these
(E) all of these

20. [A] [B] [C] [D] [E]

Answers

1. B	5. A	9. E	13. B	17. C
2. D	6. B	10. C	14. E	18. D
3. E	7. C	11. C	15. D	19. B
4. B	8. E	12. D	16. E	20. E

Business Education

Practice Test

DIRECTIONS: Select the *best* answer from the five possible choices.

1. Which of these statements about the purposes of business education is false?

   (A) A proficiency standard of achievement needs to be used.
   (B) Business courses are a part of general education.
   (C) Standards must conform to prevailing business practices.
   (D) Pupils need to develop an occupational intelligence.
   (E) Shorthand and typewriting should be taught in the sophomore year.

   1. [A] [B] [C] [D] [E]

2. One of the major weaknesses of business education programs is that there is

   (A) sufficient practice on school time
   (B) a preponderance of "C" students in the courses
   (C) inadequate equipment and facilities
   (D) a gap between school standards
   (E) too much emphasis on occupational criteria

   2. [A] [B] [C] [D] [E]

3. Tests used in business subjects should meet all *except one* of these requirements:

   (A) Tests should check minimum proficiency.
   (B) Tests should be given frequently.
   (C) Tests should evaluate students' knowledge of theory mainly.
   (D) Tests should simulate office conditions whenever possible.
   (E) Scoring time should be short.

   3. [A] [B] [C] [D] [E]

4. When selecting a method of teaching, the business education teacher must consider all *except one* of the following basic principles:

   (A) Provisions must be made for manipulative skills
   (B) Time must be given to growth in occupational intelligence.
   (C) The ultimate goal is to help students live in a democratic society.

195

PART 4: TEACHING AREA EXAMINATIONS

(D) Business courses cannot be taught with planned objectives.
(E) Students must develop marketable competency.

4. [A] [B] [C] [D] [E]

5. A good lesson plan will include three major divisions. One of these will *not* apply:

(A) knowledge
(B) objectives
(C) materials
(D) procedure
(E) (A), (C), and (D)

5. [A] [B] [C] [D] [E]

6. The teaching of business subjects differs from the teaching of the social studies, for example, in that

(A) objectives are limited to student abilities
(B) different laws of learning apply
(C) the textbook is only a source book
(D) students are more interested in business subjects
(E) repetitive practice is more essential

6. [A] [B] [C] [D] [E]

7. Physical devices for accelerating learning have their place in the classroom. However, before purchasing several such devices the teacher should consider

(A) whether the device contributes to the objectives of the course
(B) the effectiveness of learning through teacher-made or standardized tests
(C) the self-learning and reduction of teacher assistance because of the visual aid
(D) only (A) and (B)
(E) all of these

7. [A] [B] [C] [D] [E]

8. Certain factors have contributed to the confusion between the objectives of business courses and the social studies. The factor which did not contribute to the confusion of objectives was:

(A) the need in the social studies for more economic content
(B) every member of society is concerned with phases of business
(C) all students should have consumer education
(D) social studies content is essential for occupational adjustment
(E) certain technical skills can best be taught through business education

8. [A] [B] [C] [D] [E]

9. Business education was given its first federal aid through the

(A) George-Deen Act (1936)
(B) Public Law No. 812 (1914)
(C) Morrill Act (1862)
(D) Nelson Amendment (1907)
(E) Smith-Hughes Vocational Act (1917)

9. [A] [B] [C] [D] [E]

10. A valuable source of information for the business teacher concerned with improved teaching practices would be found in

BUSINESS EDUCATION

    (A) state courses of study and syllabi
    (B) N.E.A. department publications
    (C) regional business organizations
    (D) state boards of education
    (E) all of these

11. The major weakness of the beginning business teacher usually involves

    (A) lack of provisions for motivation activities
    (B) providing for individual differences
    (C) testing and evaluation
    (D) utilization of supplementary materials
    (E) inability to use business equipment

12. There are fewer discipline problems among students in business courses than in English courses, for instance, because

    (A) there are more frequent tests
    (B) machines keep the pupils busy
    (C) business teachers teach students instead of books
    (D) of the practical application of knowledge
    (E) more audio-visual aids are used

13. Office procedures should be an essential part of business courses for high school students. Instructions in office procedures can follow three different plans. One of these does not apply:

    (A) Rotation   (D) Battery
    (B) Integrated   (E) (A), (B), (D)
    (C) Mastery

14. When teaching several different office procedures in the same class, the first thing the teacher should do is

    (A) distribute "job sheets"
    (B) give general directions to all at the same time
    (C) begin with the machine bookkeeping students
    (D) make a tentative assignment for filing
    (E) start the duplicating machines

15. Courses in distributive education require the use of a teaching technique which is not often employed in other business courses. This technique is

    (A) on-the-job training   (D) quantitative analysis
    (B) dramatization   (E) social adjustment
    (C) personal evaluation

16. Adequate skill in transcription is one of the requirements for competency in shorthand. Certain principles apply to the teaching of transcription. One of these would be the *least* adequate:

PART 4: TEACHING AREA EXAMINATIONS

    (A) skill in typewriting is unrelated to transcription
    (B) first steps in transcription should be easy
    (C) copy letters in student's own shorthand and read it back from his notes, teacher assisting
    (D) dictate letters in class which students have practiced
    (E) after dictation, give a transcription preview   16. [A] [B] [C] [D] [E]

17. Certain principles relate the on-the-job business experiences to the total learning situation. One of these has little effect on the outcome of such experiences:

    (A) time spent should provide a worth-while experience
    (B) daily time should lead to achievement
    (C) work experiences should follow a degree of competency
    (D) the pay scale of the employer
    (E) supervision by the business teacher   17. [A] [B] [C] [D] [E]

18. Students who have achieved certain skills may be motivated best through individual assignments under the plan

    (A) daily task assignment plan
    (B) simulated office plan
    (C) contract plan
    (D) small group plan
    (E) general class assignment plan   18. [A] [B] [C] [D] [E]

19. The first pre-requisite for the teacher who is ordering new office machines is to

    (A) discover pupil needs
    (B) work with the faculty curriculum committee
    (C) survey the business community
    (D) take the advice of previous business teachers
    (E) consult the parents   19. [A] [B] [C] [D] [E]

20. The effective teacher will utilize certain guiding principles. Four of the five statements will lead to in-service growth. Which statement would be *least* productive?

    (A) Experiences should be realistic.
    (B) Students' experiences should be continuous.
    (C) Typewriting lessons should stress correct motions first.
    (D) Certain skill classes require the measurement of work through production output.
    (E) All teachers can use the same methods in the same subject.   20. [A] [B] [C] [D] [E]

CHEMISTRY, PHYSICS, AND GENERAL SCIENCE

Answers

1. E	5. A	9. C	13. C	17. D
2. D	6. E	10. E	14. A	18. C
3. C	7. E	11. A	15. B	19. C
4. D	8. E	12. D	16. A	20. E

Chemistry, Physics, and General Science

Practice Test

DIRECTIONS: Select the *best* answer from the five possible choices.

1. A student understands a law when he can

    (A) recall it in class
    (B) recognize it on a matching test
    (C) define it
    (D) explain its use
    (E) use it to solve a new problem

2. Students in physics should use theories, but with the understanding that

    (A) they use them with open minds
    (B) theories cannot be proven by direct evidence
    (C) theories should be used with qualifications
    (D) theories are based upon certain assumptions
    (E) all of these

3. Motor skills in the use of equipment can be taught in the laboratory most easily through

    (A) teacher demonstrations
    (B) special lessons
    (C) imitation
    (D) project work
    (E) free trial and error

4. The basic weakness of the use of laboratory manuals lies in the

    (A) stereotyping of the laboratory program
    (B) lack of pupil interest
    (C) unimaginative assignments
    (D) lack of sequence
    (E) lack of relationship to the regular lesson

199

PART 4: TEACHING AREA EXAMINATIONS

5. The first attempt at establishing a sequence of major science concepts for the teaching of general science was developed in

   (A) the 1960's
   (B) 1942
   (C) 1959
   (D) 1932
   (E) 1918

   5. [A] [B] [C] [D] [E]

6. The teacher of general science courses needs to realize the critical position of this course in the total science program. All but *one* of these indicates its importance.

   (A) Most pupils are required to take it.
   (B) Many pupils will develop attitudes toward other science courses.
   (C) The subject matter is taken from many specialized sciences.
   (D) It has its own body of subject matter.
   (E) Some students take no other science courses.

   6. [A] [B] [C] [D] [E]

7. Students consider the most difficult science course to be

   (A) earth science
   (B) physics
   (C) chemistry
   (D) general science
   (E) biology

   7. [A] [B] [C] [D] [E]

8. Too few students elect high school physics because of its

   (A) college preparatory function
   (B) dullness
   (C) emphasis upon mathematics
   (D) lack of relationship to contemporary life
   (E) emphasis upon laws and principles

   8. [A] [B] [C] [D] [E]

9. The first specialized high schools for the teaching of science were established in

   (A) Denver
   (B) Chicago
   (C) Detroit
   (D) New York City
   (E) St. Louis

   9. [A] [B] [C] [D] [E]

10. Mass science instruction assumes that all the pupils in the class are at the same level of development or have the same needs. The most satisfactory modifications of group science instruction occur when

    (A) competition is used in science fairs
    (B) students establish course objectives
    (C) sub-leaders teach the class
    (D) science clubs meet on school time
    (E) independent work is encouraged in school and home

    10. [A] [B] [C] [D] [E]

CHEMISTRY, PHYSICS, AND GENERAL SCIENCE

11. The two factors which prevented the development of physics among the Romans was the lack of experimentation and the

    (A) use of Roman numerals
    (B) lack of interest
    (C) emphasis upon law
    (D) use of speculation
    (E) emphasis upon observation

12. All measurement in physics can be expressed in five types of units.

    (A) mass, length
    (B) volume, height and (C)
    (C) time, temperature, and electric charge
    (D) centimeter, gram, second and (A)
    (E) (A) and (C)

13. The idea that matter is made up of atoms has aided scientific understanding for many years. It was even referred to by such great thinkers as

    (A) Galileo
    (B) Plato
    (C) the Curies
    (D) Aristotle
    (E) Edison

14. The most flexible and most searching form of evaluation can be achieved through the use of the

    (A) essay test
    (B) oral test
    (C) true-false test
    (D) matching test
    (E) completion test

15. The ability to recognize incorrect statements is essential to the science student. Therefore, while penalties for guessing may increase a test's reliability, they will reduce its

    (A) usefulness
    (B) objectivity
    (C) scale of items
    (D) weight of items
    (E) validity

16. Laboratory work is an essential part of the teaching of science. After adequate instructions have been given, the teacher should *not*

    (A) allow students to learn for themselves
    (B) guide from the background
    (C) move freely from student to student as requested
    (D) interrupt the work frequently
    (E) leave the laboratory

PART 4: TEACHING AREA EXAMINATIONS

17. The rapid growth of the sciences took place with the

   (A) development of systems of measurement
   (B) development of theories
   (C) discovery of the speed of light
   (D) discovery of gravity
   (E) discovery of atomic energy

   17. [A] [B] [C] [D] [E]

18. Teachers with limited funds for science education should not limit their demonstrations for teaching purposes but should attempt to use cheaper materials which will serve the same purpose. Even baking soda and vinegar can be used to

   (A) show examples of elements
   (B) study solutions
   (C) study a suspension
   (D) study sublimation
   (E) study chemical reactions and energy

   18. [A] [B] [C] [D] [E]

19. Since organic chemistry is a very complex topic, organic compounds are not prepared in the school laboratory, instead

   (A) the subject is not taught
   (B) understanding is inadequate
   (C) students lack interest
   (D) models can be used
   (E) inorganic chemistry should be emphasized

   19. [A] [B] [C] [D] [E]

20. One of these statements is *not* indicative of the approach to high school chemistry.

   (A) Laboratory experiments with radioactive materials are limited.
   (B) Atomic energy is usually not introduced until the junior high school level, therefore much work needs to be done in chemistry classes with introductory concepts.
   (C) Different forms of energy would be taught in chemistry.
   (D) Students will have some background from their study of light as elementary science students.
   (E) The chemical bond theory will be new to most students.

   20. [A] [B] [C] [D] [E]

Answers

1.	E	5.	D	9.	D	13.	B	17.	A
2.	E	6.	C	10.	E	14.	B	18.	E
3.	D	7.	B	11.	A	15.	E	19.	D
4.	A	8.	A	12.	E	16.	D	20.	B

EARLY CHILDHOOD EDUCATION

Early Childhood Education

Practice Test

DIRECTIONS: Select the *best* answer from the five possible choices.

1. During the primary years, body development needs attention. The percentage of first graders who do not have adequate vision for reading and close work has been shown through research to be about

   (A) 20% to 30%
   (B) 35% to 45%
   (C) 50% to 60%
   (D) 75% to 90%
   (E) 60% to 80%

   1. A B C D E

2. The poor posture of young school children is primarily due to

   (A) the broadening of the chest and the lengthening of the legs
   (B) "late blooming"
   (C) organismic growth
   (D) weak leg and knee muscles
   (E) a lack of exercise

   2. A B C D E

3. As a child matures in the primary years

   (A) legs lengthen slowly
   (B) growth in height averages two to three inches per year
   (C) the heart grows slowly
   (D) girls are a year behind boys in skeletal growth
   (E) pulse and breathing rates increase

   3. A B C D E

4. The rate of a child's mental growth is usually called the "Intelligence Quotient." The I.Q. can be determined by

   (A) the E.A.
   (B) the C.A. times 100
   (C) the M.A. divided by 100
   (D) the M.A. divided by the C.A., times 100
   (E) the C.A. divided by the M.A., times 100

   4. A B C D E

5. In a group of thirty seven-year-old children, how many will have mental ages between six years three months and seven years nine months?

   (A) five
   (B) eight
   (C) ten
   (D) fifteen
   (E) twenty-three

   5. A B C D E

PART 4: TEACHING AREA EXAMINATIONS

6. Research indicates that the average first grader can understand more than

    (A) 6,000 words
    (B) 8,000 words
    (C) 10,000 words
    (D) 16,000 words
    (E) 20,000 words

7. Readiness is essential to learning. Which one of the following statements is *least* important to readiness?

    (A) It takes a mental age of six years and six months for reading instruction.
    (B) A child with an immature nervous system cannot sit still for periods of instruction.
    (C) Immaturity may effect eyestrain in close work.
    (D) Slow muscular development affects the ability to begin handwriting.
    (E) All first graders should be six years old.

8. Practice is essential to the learning process. Which statement about practice is the *most* significant to the planning of learning experiences?

    (A) Children mature at different rates.
    (B) Practice makes perfect.
    (C) Practice and maturation go together.
    (D) Practice speeds up maturation.
    (E) Repetition counteracts forgetting.

9. Play is a vital force in child development. If Miss *A* understands the need for play, she will not make the following statement:

    (A) Active play is the child's work.
    (B) The difference between play and work lies in the child's motivation.
    (C) Play should be organized by the teacher.
    (D) Play is a natural learning procedure.
    (E) Play is creative.

10. Learning to live with people is essential for primary grade children. Miss *G* explains the experiences her second graders have during the year which improve group living. Which one of these is of least importance?

    (A) Role playing
    (B) A study of community helpers
    (C) Construction projects
    (D) A field trip
    (E) Care of the room and equipment

EARLY CHILDHOOD EDUCATION

11. Construction work is valuable for the process rather than the end results. If Miss D believes this, she does not

    (A) let first graders build a playhouse
    (B) let third graders build a real window box
    (C) consider the needs of the group
    (D) have concern about utility
    (E) have concern with adult standards

12. Committee work is possible for first graders. The personnel on committees tends to change often because of

    (A) their short attention span
    (B) inability to get along with others
    (C) their fluctuating interests
    (D) lack of experience
    (E) their need to play

13. Learning to read is a complex act. One of these statements does *not* apply to reading.

    (A) Reading depends upon the sensation of light upon the pupil of the eye.
    (B) Poor nutrition affects the child's readiness.
    (C) A feeling of security is essential for success.
    (D) Learning relates to past experiences.
    (E) Social experiences aid in learning.

14. Children in the kindergarten show that their greatest intellectual asset is their

    (A) curiosity
    (B) need for play
    (C) sense judgments
    (D) memory
    (E) questioning attitude

15. A good learning climate in the kindergarten classroom is characterized by the basic ingredient for all learning experiences:

    (A) construction activities
    (B) variety of experiences
    (C) pupil conversation
    (D) teacher guidance
    (E) freedom from unnecessary tension

16. The language arts program at the kindergarten level should begin with

    (A) an experience chart
    (B) a good speaking vocabulary
    (C) songs
    (D) games
    (E) films

PART 4: TEACHING AREA EXAMINATIONS

17. When planning social studies activities, the kindergarten teacher will usually *not* use

    (A) field trips
    (B) units of work
    (C) experience charts
    (D) stories
    (E) dramatizations

18. The kindergarten movement was begun by

    (A) Pestalozzi
    (B) Dewey
    (C) Montesorri
    (D) Froebel
    (E) Schurz

19. The first public-school kindergarten was opened in

    (A) Boston
    (B) Milwaukee
    (C) Detroit
    (D) New York
    (E) St. Louis

20. The major change which has occurred gradually in the kindergarten curriculum is the

    (A) use of Montesorri cards
    (B) recitation in unison
    (C) formal directed lesson
    (D) child-development approach
    (E) use of adult standards

Answers

1. E	5. D	9. C	13. A	17. B
2. A	6. D	10. B	14. D	18. D
3. B	7. E	11. E	15. E	19. E
4. D	8. C	12. A	16. B	20. D

Education in the Elementary School (1-8)*

Practice Test

DIRECTIONS: Select the *best* answer from the five possible choices.

1. The purposes of spelling instruction include the

    (A) learning of about 4,000 words
    (B) learning of words that occur frequently in writing
    (C) learning the words that children use in writing
    (D) none of these
    (E) A, B, and C

---

*For complete preparation in this area, see Barron's *How to Prepare for the NTE Area Examination: Education in the Elementary School (1-8)*

EDUCATION IN THE ELEMENTARY SCHOOL

2. The teaching of modern languages through televised programs often runs into difficulty because

    (A) pupils can't keep up with the lessons
    (B) the lessons are uninteresting
    (C) the time allotted is inadequate
    (D) teachers dislike television
    (E) pupils dislike television

    2. [A] [B] [C] [D] [E]

3. The educationally disadvantaged child has a basic handicap which affects all learning. This is

    (A) aggressive behavior
    (B) a lack of personal pride
    (C) the inability to communicate with the teacher
    (D) a lack of friends
    (E) a state of anxiety

    3. [A] [B] [C] [D] [E]

4. The difficulty in changing over from manuscript writing to cursive writing is brought about by

    (A) an abrupt change in motor skill
    (B) a natural change from unjoined writing
    (C) little practice
    (D) the similarity between strokes and proportions
    (E) little change in handwriting movements

    4. [A] [B] [C] [D] [E]

5. The criticism of the continuance of manuscript writing beyond the third grade exists because

    (A) it seems babyish
    (B) cursive writing is the socially accepted form
    (C) cursive writing increases speed
    (D) cursive writing is more legible
    (E) print is seldom needed

    5. [A] [B] [C] [D] [E]

6. The first essential step in getting children ready for creative work consists of

    (A) several periods of specific instruction about rules
    (B) reading well written themes
    (C) listening to records
    (D) having the teacher read stories
    (E) enriched experience

    6. [A] [B] [C] [D] [E]

7. Language is complex. It involves

    (A) listening and speaking
    (B) speaking and writing
    (C) all forms of interaction — thought, feeling, expression
    (D) listening, speaking, writing
    (E) thinking, and speaking

    7. [A] [B] [C] [D] [E]

PART 4: TEACHING AREA EXAMINATIONS

8. Children are talking in longer sentences and using larger vocabularies. This gain has been made by

   (A) learning to read earlier
   (B) radio and television programs
   (C) early entrance into nursery schools
   (D) parents' leisure time
   (E) (B), (C), and (D)

   8. [A] [B] [C] [D] [E]

9. The last communication which the child develops is

   (A) reading
   (B) listening
   (C) speaking
   (D) singing
   (E) writing

   9. [A] [B] [C] [D] [E]

10. The interrelationship among language skills is indicated by recent studies which report a high positive relationship by grade six between

    (A) reading and spelling
    (B) reading and writing
    (C) spelling and oral language
    (D) handwriting and reading
    (E) health and language ability

    10. [A] [B] [C] [D] [E]

11. The evaluation of a dramatization by children is done after the performance rather than during the action

    (A) so as not to interrupt the creative process
    (B) to encourage the flow of language
    (C) to encourage the expression of feelings
    (D) none of these
    (E) all of these

    11. [A] [B] [C] [D] [E]

12. The language arts should be taught through other subject areas because

    (A) thinking and language are closely related
    (B) thinking is done in words
    (C) listening is developed in the social studies
    (D) there is no intrinsic content in the language arts
    (E) every experience improves language usage

    12. [A] [B] [C] [D] [E]

13. The incidence of left-handedness is

    (A) decreasing
    (B) increasing
    (C) of little consequence to the learner
    (D) ignored by the effective teacher
    (E) affecting five per cent of elementary age children

    13. [A] [B] [C] [D] [E]

14. Speed will be emphasized least by the handwriting teacher. Why?

    (A) The child is too young to write rapidly.
    (B) The child must have mastery over the formation of all letters.
    (C) Mastery of some of the letters will increase speed.
    (D) The child does not need to increase speed.
    (E) Spelling is not affected by speed of writing.   14.   A B C D E

15. Roberts uses the structural approach to syntax and his sentence patterns involve

    (A) four basic types   (D) no basic types
    (B) five basic types   (E) eight basic types
    (C) ten basic types   15.   A B C D E

16. Structural linguists classify the parts of speech into

    (A) two categories   (D) four categories
    (B) three categories   (E) eight categories
    (C) no categories   16.   A B C D E

17. Information on the special problems of creative children will be found in the writings of

    (A) Torrance   (D) Kambly
    (B) Skinner   (E) Fife
    (C) Dewey   17.   A B C D E

18. The major difficulty in the teaching of elementary school science arises from

    (A) the immaturity of the children
    (B) lack of good text materials
    (C) poor classroom facilities
    (D) disagreement on scope and sequence
    (E) lack of interest by the children   18.   A B C D E

19. Every phase of daily experience can be utilized to teach mathematics because mathematics is

    (A) a social study   (D) both (A) and (B)
    (B) a science   (E) all of these
    (C) a language art   19.   A B C D E

20. "Provisional tries" should be encouraged in mathematics instruction because

    (A) the student should learn to accept failure
    (B) anxiety is increased through failure
    (C) This is the essence of problem solving
    (D) the teacher cannot explain everything
    (E) pupils have many success experiences   20.   A B C D E

PART 4: TEACHING AREA EXAMINATIONS

Answers

1. E	5. B	9. E	13. B	17. A
2. A	6. E	10. B	14. B	18. D
3. C	7. C	11. E	15. C	19. E
4. A	8. E	12. D	16. D	20. C

English Language and Literature

Practice Test

DIRECTIONS: Select the *best* answer which will complete the statement. There are five possible choices.

1. There is general agreement that English content is irreplaceable in the curriculum. The debate concerns the best way to present the content. Education for life adjustment is opposed by

    (A) Harold Rugg
    (B) Thorndike
    (C) Arthur Bestor
    (D) Max Bernstein
    (E) B. F. Skinner

2. Despite the group-mindedness of the adolescent, individual development must be extended. Homework can serve this purpose if

    (A) the pupils enjoy it
    (B) it is relevant
    (C) it is not repetitious
    (D) parents do not object
    (E) there is time for feedback

3. English teachers tend to view core concepts as

    (A) introductory
    (B) terminal
    (C) too specialized
    (D) very essential at the high school level
    (E) necessary for synthesizing usage

4. The one factor essential to individual growth in English usage is

    (A) practice
    (B) drill on essentials
    (C) creative activity
    (D) pacing the work
    (E) immediate feedback

5. The student who has difficulty with comma placement can be assisted by

    (A) admonishment
    (B) immediate feedback
    (C) workbook practice lessons

210

ENGLISH LANGUAGE AND LITERATURE

   (D) reading aloud and listening for pauses
   (E) class discussion

6. Those who attack the teaching of formal grammar often quote research studies which show that

   (A) students dislike grammar
   (B) grammar is uninteresting
   (C) grammar is time consuming
   (D) usage is more important
   (E) grammar does not transfer

7. When teaching Shakespearean plays, audio-visual records and films should be used

   (A) as a pre-test
   (B) for orientation purposes
   (C) to arouse interest
   (D) after the plays have been studied in class
   (E) in place of class reading

8. The teaching of the narrative

   (A) is unsuitable for slow learners
   (B) should be based upon language and verbalization
   (C) is based upon reading ability
   (D) relates to students' emotionality
   (E) should be related to intelligence

9. A narrative, popular with students, like *Johnny Tremain* requires

   (A) little explication
   (B) teaching for understanding
   (C) considerable orientation
   (D) frequent quizzing
   (E) teacher-dominated discussion

10. Students who are assigned the reading of Victorian novels must be assisted in

    (A) taking their time in developing plot
    (B) hurrying to find the climax
    (C) understanding descriptive material
    (D) vocabulary study
    (E) getting historical background

11. The basic importance of the publications of the NCTE Commission on the English Curriculum (1952-1963) lies in its attempt to

    (A) find common areas of agreement between teachers at different levels
    (B) establish a program of life adjustment English

PART 4: TEACHING AREA EXAMINATIONS

    (C) revise the college preparatory program
    (D) use English as a terminal course
    (E) prepare vocational English materials

11. ⬚A⬚ ⬚B⬚ ⬚C⬚ ⬚D⬚ ⬚E⬚

12. The Commission on the English Curriculum had great influence after World War II due to its recommendation for

    (A) increased study of grammar
    (B) the linguistic approach to the language arts
    (C) the inclusion of literature at all levels
    (D) the emphasis upon inquiry and inductive teaching
    (E) a specific content for all students

12. ⬚A⬚ ⬚B⬚ ⬚C⬚ ⬚D⬚ ⬚E⬚

13. Bold new programs which break down the barriers of subjects and time have been implemented in new courses in many high schools. These courses have come to be known as

    (A) the spiral curriculum
    (B) the essentials program
    (C) the humanities courses
    (D) integrated courses
    (E) unit teaching

13. ⬚A⬚ ⬚B⬚ ⬚C⬚ ⬚D⬚ ⬚E⬚

14. Research in teaching and in-service English workshops have been sponsored during the 1960's. A series of kinescopes designed for English department meetings have been developed by

    (A) the Office of Education   (D) the NEA
    (B) the NCTE   (E) the CEEB
    (C) Project English

14. ⬚A⬚ ⬚B⬚ ⬚C⬚ ⬚D⬚ ⬚E⬚

15. Teachers of language generally agree that there are two main functions of language, its referential function, and its

    (A) emotive function
    (B) communicative function
    (C) creative function
    (D) intellectual function
    (E) denotative function

15. ⬚A⬚ ⬚B⬚ ⬚C⬚ ⬚D⬚ ⬚E⬚

16. The term "developmental reading" is generally applied to

    (A) remedial activities within the regular class
    (B) reading laboratories
    (C) the all-school reading improvement program
    (D) individual tutoring
    (E) "interest groups", regardless of age

16. ⬚A⬚ ⬚B⬚ ⬚C⬚ ⬚D⬚ ⬚E⬚

ENGLISH LANGUAGE AND LITERATURE

17. Some of the main causes for slow reading can be quite easily improved by practice in the classroom. Reading improves when students do all *except one* of the following:

    (A) use different speeds for different reading matter
    (B) learn to concentrate
    (C) practice daily to improve speed
    (D) analyze their mistakes
    (E) use the finger to move rapidly across the page

    17. [A] [B] [C] [D] [E]

18. Dr. Conant's report recommends that the total time spend on the study of English during the four secondary school years be devoted to composition at the rate of

    (A) one paragraph a day
    (B) one theme a day
    (C) one theme a week
    (D) one theme every two weeks
    (E) three themes a month

    18. [A] [B] [C] [D] [E]

19. The regional conferences and the NCTE recommend a class load for English teachers of not more than

    (A) four classes (20 pupils each)
    (B) five classes (30 pupils each)
    (C) 135 pupils
    (D) four classes (25 pupils each)
    (E) five classes (25 pupils each)

    19. [A] [B] [C] [D] [E]

20. The primary goal for English composition during the secondary school year is

    (A) expression of meaning and thought
    (B) grammar
    (C) usage
    (D) linguistic information
    (E) improvement through practice

    20. [A] [B] [C] [D] [E]

Answers

1. C	5. D	9. B	13. C	17. E
2. E	6. E	10. A	14. E	18. C
3. B	7. D	11. A	15. A	19. D
4. D	8. D	12. D	16. C	20. A

PART 4: TEACHING AREA EXAMINATIONS

Home Economics Education

Practice Test

DIRECTIONS: Select the *best* answer from the five possible choices.

1. Home economics education must of necessity be concerned with individual differences. Under teacher guidance, students with different abilities

    (A) will be obviously inadequate
    (B) will have difficulty choosing projects
    (C) can choose goals according to differences in interest
    (D) will have little contact with each other
    (E) will work in separate groups within the classroom

2. Experiences should be related to the objectives of the unit. In a class with wide individual differences

    (A) group activities should be maintained
    (B) individual work should take the place of group activity
    (C) students should not try to work together
    (D) students should serve as class chariman
    (E) students should evaluate each other's work

3. Goals foster achievement. Four of the five statements relate to the principles for goal development. Which one is *least* effective?

    (A) The teacher should establish tentative goals.
    (B) If pupils' needs differ, the teacher should use her own goals.
    (C) Pupils work better if they use their own goals.
    (D) Learning how to choose goals is difficult for some students.
    (E) Goals should not change during the culmination phase of work.

4. Evaluation instruments should be carefully chosen to meet class needs. One of them is *not* a characteristic of a good test.

    (A) Questions should be arranged in order of difficulty.
    (B) It should differentiate the inferior, average, and superior students.
    (C) A suitable variety of questions should be included as time allows.
    (D) It should be short enough so all students can finish.
    (E) It should be long enough to give an adequate sampling of material studied.

5. Sewing machine troubles bother beginners. If the teacher uses a pretest to determine the level of understanding some of these problems can be avoided. Which type of test would reveal deficiencies best to the teacher?

    (A) True-false items (20 questions)
    (B) Completion questions (10 blanks)
    (C) Matching questions relating machine troubles to causes

(D) Three essay questions relating to the problems of operating a sewing machine
(E) Individual sewing demonstrations by students

6. Food preparation classes would meet the needs of most pupils if

   (A) they chose the foods they wanted to prepare
   (B) all students prepared the same foods
   (C) preparation followed demonstrations by the teacher
   (D) they prepared favorite foods
   (E) both food and meal preparation were taught

7. Learning a particular skill varies with individual differences. Learning will be improved if the teacher realizes all *except* one of the following:

   (A) Comprehension and meaningful repetition are both necessary
   (B) The amount of repetition necessary is unrelated to the pupil's intelligence.
   (C) Association learning aids retention.
   (D) Transfer is aided if students understand the *why* of an activity.
   (E) Correct initial learning eliminates later unlearning.

8. Courses in sewing often show poor motivation because of one of these factors:

   (A) Intrinsic motivation is sustained by emphasing marks.
   (B) Creative capacities are utliized in projects.
   (C) Individual goals are established early in the course.
   (D) Reproof is seldom used with slow pupils.
   (E) Praise is used more often than criticism.

9. One of the greatest weaknesses in sustaining interest in a homemaking class for one or two periods is the

   (A) number of domonstrations which must be given
   (B) different abilities of students
   (C) lack of variety in class activity
   (D) different work rates of various students
   (E) time it takes to complete one task

10. Miss *X* has a handicapped student in the 9th grade foods class. For best results she should do all *except one* of the following:

    (A) discuss her handicap with the class
    (B) use ingenuity and tact in relating to the student
    (C) encourage the student to do all work, regardless of handicap
    (D) encourage the student to become self-reliant
    (E) treat the student as a normal individual

11. Students with mental and emotional handicaps can accomplish much in home economics courses if their needs are considered. One of these statements would *not* apply:

    (A) Adjust the curriculum to the needs of the students.

PART 4: TEACHING AREA EXAMINATIONS

    (B) Teach students good health habits.
    (C) Give these students a feeling of security.
    (D) Competition should be increased as a motivation factor.
    (E) The guidance counselor can help to determine the degree of difficulty.   11. [A][B][C][D][E]

12. Jane is a student in Miss *Y*'s sewing class. Jane is a capable girl, but she never completes an assignemnt. Her mother is coming to the school for a conference. How should Miss *Y* begin the conference?

    (A) Miss *Y* should ask the mother if she can sew.
    (B) Miss *Y* should ask the mother about her relationship to Jane in the home
    (C) She should find out what her mother thinks of home economics courses.
    (D) She should talk about Jane's strong points.
    (E) She should criticize Jane for her shortcomings.   12. [A][B][C][D][E]

13. After a discussion of the basic seven foods in the diet, Mrs. *G* assigns daily record keeping of all foods eaten by the students for a two-week. At the end of this time she discovers that few students are obtaining adequate diets. She is correct is assuming that

    (A) pupils always eat what they like
    (B) parents don't care about proper foold
    (C) there is little transfer between classroom and home
    (D) most mothers are poor meal-planners
    (E) students have not made adequate diet one of their goals   13. [A][B][C][D][E]

14. It is difficult to strengthen the home economics program in some school systems due to one of these:

    (A) Educators disagree on the formulation of objectives.
    (B) Research throws light on educational programs.
    (C) The best way to improve a program is to point out its shortcomings.
    (D) Progress is made when dissatisfaction is shown with existing programs.
    (E) Each school must formulate its own objectives in light of student needs.   14. [A][B][C][D][E]

15. Research shows that students who have had home economics instruction tend to score better on

    (A) food choices when they have had instruction than when not
    (B) meal preparation tests than students who have no management experiences
    (C) increased interest in home responsibilities than those without school experience
    (D) home diets than those without home economics courses
    (E) certain activities, depending on whether the department is vocational or not   15. [A][B][C][D][E]

16. The selection of individual home projects will be limited most by

    (A) regional courses of study
    (B) school requirements
    (C) individual deficiencies

(D) family socio-economic background
(E) the teacher's goals

16. [A] [B] [C] [D] [E]

17. In food preparation courses sufficient emphasis should be given to

(A) holiday treats
(B) teen-age entertaining
(C) the making of desserts
(D) meat selection and preparation
(E) gourmet foods

17. [A] [B] [C] [D] [E]

18. When designing home economics space and equipment, the following criteria should be considered. Which statement is *least* important?

(A) Organization should be similar to that of a well-managed home
(B) Floors should be easy to walk on and clean.
(C) Adequate storage space should be allotted.
(D) Adequate hot and cold water supplies should be available.
(E) Separate rooms should be available for each type of program taught.

18. [A] [B] [C] [D] [E]

19. Sewing rooms often fail in one of these aspects:

(A) Too many movable pieces of equipment
(B) Poor natural and artificial lighting
(C) A lack of a specialized laboratory
(D) Too many all-purpose rooms
(E) A living center with standards of good taste

19. [A] [B] [C] [D] [E]

20. Four of the five administrative practices would improve the effectiveness of the home economics program. Which one has questionable value?

(A) Descriptions of standards should be phrased in general terms.
(B) Each school should decide on programs and practices.
(C) School experimentation should be encouraged.
(D) Frequent self-evaluation should be encouraged.
(E) Provide an adequate, flexible budget for the home economics department.

20. [A] [B] [C] [D] [E]

Answers

1. C	5. C	9. C	13. E	17. D
2. A	6. E	10. A	14. A	18. E
3. B	7. B	11. D	15. B	19. B
4. D	8. A	12. D	16. D	20. A

PART 4: TEACHING AREA EXAMINATIONS

Industrial Arts Education

Practice Test

DIRECTIONS: Select the *best* answer which will complete statement. There are five possible choices.

1. One of the most important names in the industrial arts movement in America was:

    (A) John Ordway
    (B) George Treadwell
    (C) John Hartwick
    (D) Manual Morris
    (E) A. A. Ferster

    1. [A] [B] [C] [D] [E]

2. The sloyd system of instruction was introduced in America from

    (A) Russia
    (B) Italy
    (C) England
    (D) Sweden
    (E) France

    2. [A] [B] [C] [D] [E]

3. The term *manual arts* was first used in the U. S. around

    (A) 1930
    (B) 1850
    (C) 1865
    (D) 1915
    (E) 1893

    3. [A] [B] [C] [D] [E]

4. Early manual arts training emphasized

    (A) student interest
    (B) the project as the goal
    (C) industrial processes
    (D) the preservation of craft traditions
    (E) experimentation

    4. [A] [B] [C] [D] [E]

5. When the disciplinary nature of manual training declined it came to be called industrial arts. Now the emphasis was upon

    (A) individual crafts
    (B) project planning
    (C) design
    (D) tools, and occupations of industry
    (E) manufacturing processes

    5. [A] [B] [C] [D] [E]

6. Industrial arts education is assured of a place in the curriculum because of the current emphasis upon the need for

    (A) occupaptional information
    (B) technical education
    (C) general education
    (D) auto mechanics
    (E) space scientists

    6. [A] [B] [C] [D] [E]

INDUSTRIAL ARTS EDUCATION

7. Several types of laboratories are used in secondary schools. The one designed for a multiple-activity program is the

   (A) unit shop
   (B) machine shop
   (C) comprehensive general shop
   (D) general unit shop
   (E) general crafts shop

8. The laboratory which is designed for highly specialized industrial arts instruction is the

   (A) metals shop
   (B) unit shop
   (C) machine shop
   (D) comprehensive general shop
   (E) general area shop

9. Industrial arts education at the elementary level is *not* characterized by one of these:

   (A) creative activities
   (B) construction activities
   (C) unit teaching
   (D) standardized programs
   (E) independent activity

10. One of the major drawbacks of teaching industrial arts to elementary children in a central activity room is the

    (A) number of periods a day
    (B) need for advance scheduling
    (C) lack of teacher participation
    (D) lack of individual projects
    (E) need for supervision

11. The first responsibility which an industrial arts teacher of elementary school children has is to

    (A) provide the equipment
    (B) integrate the total experiences
    (C) follow the course outline
    (D) teach the children tool safety
    (E) teach the teachers to assist the children

12. Industrial arts equipment which will be used by elementary school children should be characterized by

    (A) simplicity
    (B) extra safety features
    (C) relative size and weight
    (D) a lack of power tools
    (E) the use of electricity

13. The primary purpose of industrial arts education at the junior high school level is the

    (A) teaching of particular skills
    (B) use of enrichment units

PART 4: TEACHING AREA EXAMINATIONS

    (C) exploratory or orientational activities
    (D) relationship to mathematics
    (E) emphasis upon creativity   13. [A][B][C][D][E]

14. Industrial arts students in grade 8, usually are introduced to

    (A) graphic arts or electricity   (D) basic machines and tools
    (B) woodworking   (E) drawing
    (C) metalworking   14. [A][B][C][D][E]

15. One of the most difficult assignments for the industrial arts instructor of junior high school students is the requirement that

    (A) girls take 6 weeks of shop
    (B) drafting be required at grade 9
    (C) individual projects be graded
    (D) competition be encouraged
    (E) the program meet the needs of all students   15. [A][B][C][D][E]

16. Present-day high school programs in industrial arts are characterized by

    (A) great similarity of program
    (B) emphasis upon special education
    (C) emphasis upon technical education
    (D) divergent purposes
    (E) poorly trained personnel   16. [A][B][C][D][E]

17. The college-bound student can benefit from industrial arts instruction if he is

    (A) a pre-engineering student
    (B) undecided about a vocation
    (C) good in mathematics
    (D) interested in drawing
    (E) in need of a fifth subject   17. [A][B][C][D][E]

18. The use of industrial arts as part of the program for the terminal student is recommended by

    (A) John Dewey   (D) all educators
    (B) James Conant   (E) the U. S. Office of Education
    (C) John Kilpatrick   18. [A][B][C][D][E]

19. When selecting the facilities for industrial arts education for senior high schools all *except one* of these guiding principles should be considered:

    (A) The shop wing or building should be a single-story.
    (B) Noise interference with other classrooms must be considered.
    (C) A first-aid kit should be located in each shop.
    (D) Power controls should be in a master panel near the instructor's desk.
    (E) The unit shop is the best facility.   19. [A][B][C][D][E]

MATHEMATICS

20. In the future, research in industrial arts education will probably develop processes and objectives for teaching the

(A) adults
(B) emotionally disturbed
(C) new technical skills
(D) blind and physically handicapped
(E) elementary school teacher

20. [A] [B] [C] [D] [E]

Answers

1. A	5. D	9. D	13. C	17. A
2. D	6. C	10. B	14. A	18. B
3. E	7. C	11. E	15. E	19. E
4. B	8. B	12. C	16. D	20. D

Mathematics

Practice Test

DIRECTIONS: Select the *best* answer from the five possible choices.

1. Teacher-made tests can be improved by four of the following. Which one makes *little* difference?

   (A) Directions for true-false items should inform the student whether a penalty for guessing will be used.
   (B) If answers are to be given to the nearest tenth, direction should specify it.
   (C) Problems should be arranged in order of difficulty.
   (D) Avoid the use of negative statements.
   (E) Avoid giving the student extraneous clues.

   1. [A] [B] [C] [D] [E]

2. Test interpretation, if the student's grade is the major purpose, falls short of an evaluation procedure. Evaluation involves the use of four of these. Which one is *least* essential?

   (A) Derived scores are used as relative measures.
   (B) When T-scores are used, a mean of 50 is always chosen.
   (C) The norm for one class is an average
   (D) Single test scores are compared with other singles scores.
   (E) A standard deviation is used compare individual scores in the same class.

   2. [A] [B] [C] [D] [E]

3. One basic concept of measurement used in evaluation is *objectivity*. Objectivity may be defined as

   (A) the relevance of information collected
   (B) the accuracy of the measurements
   (C) the results of an item analysis

221

PART 4: TEACHING AREA EXAMINATIONS

    (D) the stability of the test results
    (E) similar conclusions by several evaluators

4. Which statement is incorrect regarding test construction?

    (A) Problem-solving questions give the student little chance to guess.
    (B) True-false items require the student to select rather than produce an answer.
    (C) Essay items offer less opportunity for bluffing than other types.
    (D) Matching questions test the relationships among facts.
    (E) Completion items can be scored with objectivity.

5. The content of mathematics is constantly changing. The curriculum of high school mathematics is placing greater emphasis for scientific use on the inclusion of

    (A) probability theory
    (B) deductive reasoning
    (C) applied mathematics
    (D) general mathematics
    (E) algebra

6. The following are examples of approximate numbers. Which one is incorrect?

    (A) logarithms   (D) fractions
    (B) square root   (E) none of these
    (C) division

7. Mathematics in industry is characterized by the following use of certain kinds of numbers. One does *not* apply.

    (A) manufacturing requires a knowledge of inverse proportions
    (B) banking–the date of maturity
    (C) engineering–dividends
    (D) brokers–dividends
    (E) none of these

8. Which is the mistaken assumption teachers often make about errors made by students in mathematics courses?

    (A) Errors may be "provisional tries".
    (B) Errors are all of the same kind and all bad.
    (C) Errors may be the result of poor reading ability.
    (D) Errors may invlove faulty technique.
    (E) Some errors may be "good" errors.

9. The mathematics teacher has the instructional responsibility to begin with one of the following to increase student development:

    (A) Teach students to do as they are instructed.
    (B) Diagnose the consistency in errors made by students.
    (C) Work as few problems as possible for examples as students imitate these techniques.

MATHEMATICS

    (D) Assume that deficiencies will disappear automatically.
    (E) Encourage bright pupils to assist the slow ones with problem-solving techniques.   **9.** Ⓐ Ⓑ Ⓒ Ⓓ Ⓔ

10. Problem-solving ability can be improved through the use of four out of five of the following. Which one would be of *least* importance?

    (A) Problem solving is improved through estimating answers and comparing them with computational results.
    (B) Select another way of solving the problem.
    (C) Select the most efficient way to solve a problem.
    (D) Develop reasons for computational techniques.
    (E) Have pupils use the textbook to write their own problems.   **10.** Ⓐ Ⓑ Ⓒ Ⓓ Ⓔ

11. Maintaining pupil interest is difficult at the junior high school level. One of these techniques would be *less* effective than the others.

    (A) Develop problem-solving ability through oral discussion.
    (B) Build concepts through the use of students' ideas.
    (C) Spend most of the class period drilling on the essentials.
    (D) Use overhead projection to explain problems.
    (E) Encourage the making of inductive inferences.   **11.** Ⓐ Ⓑ Ⓒ Ⓓ Ⓔ

12. The third dimension of space is difficult for students to describe and quantify. The following ideas will assist the students in gaining perception. Which one should not be used?

    (A) The depth dimension of space can be thought of as a plane moving vertically to its surface.
    (B) A three-dimensional angle is a plane rotating about a line.
    (C) Our primary concern is with the measurement of surface area.
    (D) The intersecion of two walls and a ceiling is an example of a trihedral angle.
    (E) When one opens a hinged door, he is using a dihedral angle.   **12.** Ⓐ Ⓑ Ⓒ Ⓓ Ⓔ

13. The ratio referred to as "pi" is represented by an irrational number idea. This can best be taught to students by explaining that

    (A) there is not constant relaitonship between the circumference and the diameter of a circle.
    (B) the numberical value of the ratio cannot be computed exactly by our system of notation
    (C) its symbol is π
    (D) 3.1416 is an exact number
    (E) it is an approximate number   **13.** Ⓐ Ⓑ Ⓒ Ⓓ Ⓔ

14. Students have less difficulty in understanding time concepts than they do space concepts. When teaching the abstract perception of these concepts all *except one* of these would aid studnet understanding.

    (A) Time is a continuum which extends linearly and depthwise.

PART 4: TEACHING AREA EXAMINATIONS

    (B) Space measurement deals with both direction and linear distance.
    (C) Any event will serve as a referent point for the description of time.
    (D) Space problems involve the matter of angular measurement.
    (E) Space measurement involves the quantification of objects.

15. The metric system causes students of mathematics considerable trouble. All *except one* of these concepts would aid student understanding.

    (A) All units of measure are multiples of subdivisions of three basic units.
    (B) All measures of the metric system are given in fractional units.
    (C) All measures of weight are related to the gram.
    (D) Multiplication or division can be made by shifting the decimal point.
    (E) The advantage of the metric system lies in the interrelationship among measures of weight, length, and capacity.

16. Students who plan to have careers in science or technology should be encouraged to study mathematics for

    (A) 3 years   (D) 6 years
    (B) 4 years   (E) 2 years
    (C) 5 years

17. Certain principles assist in the development of curriculum for a particular subject or subject area. One of these would be *least* important.

    (A) All pupils should experience the same content.
    (B) Certain content should be available for students who want it.
    (C) Certain experiences should be of a remedial nature.
    (D) Individualized instruction should be possible.
    (E) The gifted should be able to specialize.

18. Mr. *Y* is organizing a mathematics club. Which of the following statements is he *least* likely to make when convincing others of the need for the club?

    (A) It will be a "knowing" club rather than a "doing" club.
    (B) It will be an extension of the curriculum.
    (C) Students have requested it.
    (D) Students need the social life.
    (E) Gifted students plan to work on special projects.

19. Advocates of the experience curriculum in mathematics are primarily concerned with the

    (A) passing interests of the child
    (B) pressure groups in the community
    (C) use of community resources
    (D) continuing interest and needs of students
    (E) broadening of students' horizons

MUSIC EDUCATION

20. Current teaching of mathematics is concerned with the concept of sets and the relationships among sets. Mr. *D* is explaining this to parents. What is his strongest point.

    (A) Things in nature are grouped in sets.
    (B) The idea of sets in not new.
    (C) Many language terms like group, flock, etc., have similar connotations to the word set.
    (D) A set of facts is interpreted in the scientific method.
    (E) It helps the pupil differentiate between what a thing is as well as what it is not.

Answers

1. D	5. A	9. B	13. B	17. A
2. D	6. E	10. E	14. A	18. D
3. E	7. E	11. C	15. B	19. D
4. C	8. B	12. C	16. D	20. E

Music Education

Practice Test

DIRECTIONS: Select the *best* answer from the five possible choices.

1. The main purpose of music eduaction in the secondary schools is

    (A) to educate the gifted
    (B) to teach the cultural contribution of music as an art
    (C) to teach music as a hobby
    (D) the development of music appreciation
    (E) the development os social relationships

2. The total student body should be exposed to music through

    (A) the mixed chorus
    (B) instrumental music
    (C) listening sessions
    (D) general music classes
    (E) musical theory courses

3. The junior high school instrumental music classes should be offered to all interested students. Class size should be

    (A) between 10 and 20 students
    (B) between 6 and 10 students
    (C) between 6 and 15 students
    (D) between 5 and 10 students
    (E) between 20 and 30 students

PART 4: TEACHING AREA EXAMINATIONS

4. Why is there difficulty in obtaining boys for choral work?

    (A) Peer-group discouragement
    (B) Athletic interests conflict
    (C) Uninteresting literature
    (D) Few male choral directors
    (E) Maturation level

    4. [A] [B] [C] [D] [E]

5. If music groups meet daily, pupils should

    (A) have full hour rehearsals
    (B) get a full credit
    (C) be performance groups
    (D) get one-half credit
    (E) get one-fourth credit

    5. [A] [B] [C] [D] [E]

6. Gifted pupils who have an interest in choral music may have their needs met through choral ensembles. How large should an essemble be?

    (A) not more than fifteen students
    (B) less than thirty students
    (C) more than thirty students
    (D) forty-five students
    (E) not more than fifty students

    6. [A] [B] [C] [D] [E]

7. When a music teacher attempts to select gifted students, the first thing which must be done is to

    (A) check pupil's past experiences
    (B) ask parent's permission
    (C) give an aptitude test
    (D) listen to the pupil play the piano
    (E) have choral tryouts

    7. [A] [B] [C] [D] [E]

8. The biggest problem that teachers of music at the junior high school level have is

    (A) scheduling
    (B) class management
    (C) finding interesting literature
    (D) keeping boys interested
    (E) developing performance groups

    8. [A] [B] [C] [D] [E]

9. What is the greatest disadvantage of block scheduling for music classes?

    (A) Short infrequent periods
    (B) Too large class size
    (C) Inability to develop performance ability
    (D) Lack of pupil interest
    (E) Lack of continuing, cumulative experiences

    9. [A] [B] [C] [D] [E]

MUSIC EDUCATION

10. The charging of fees for school music classes is generally discouraged by administrators in that

    (A) it is discriminatory
    (B) it is supported by regular funds
    (C) it is supported by special state aid
    (D) it is supported by local taxation
    (E) it is supported by performance fund-raising activities

11. One organization that has attempted to establish guiding principles for music festivals is the

    (A) NFA
    (B) North Central Association
    (C) Music Educators' Association
    (D) District Music Clubs
    (E) Associations of Professional Musicians

12. When planning public performances, the underlying purpose should be to

    (A) furnish a vehicle for the gifted
    (B) make them open to all students
    (C) plan programs only for special occasions
    (D) develop music taste (audience and performer)
    (E) demonstrate the teacher's ability

13. Every school music program needs to be evaluated. Where can the music teacher obtain information of criteria for evaluation?

    (A) the Music Educators Conference
    (B) Association of Secondary Principals
    (C) the Cooperative Study of Secondary School Standards
    (D) state music associations
    (E) the National Association of Music Educators

14. Music teachers often augment their income. Which of the following is considered to be an unethical practice?

    (A) Giving private music lessons
    (B) Directing church choirs
    (C) Directing summer programs
    (D) Working in summer camps
    (E) Selling musical instruments and supplies

15. The music teacher must be aware of the Copyright Law in regard to

    (A) the use of musical compositions
    (B) use of recordings in class
    (C) class use of sheet music
    (D) use of orchestrations
    (E) unauthorized use of compositions with visual projectors

PART 4: TEACHING AREA EXAMINATIONS

16. 19th century music education differed from contemporary approaches in that the school curriculum was limited to

    (A) instrumental study
    (B) piano lessons
    (C) vocal experiences
    (D) only band instruction
    (E) few performance opportunities

17. Prior to World War I, music received new impetus through the work of

    (A) the Eastern Music Supervisor's Conference
    (B) the Music Supervisiors National Conference
    (C) the Committee on Reorganization of Secondary Education
    (D) the Elementary School Principals Association
    (E) the Commissioner of Education

18. Those who emphasize instrumental music as the "universal" language are referring to its

    (A) lyric quality   (D) beauty of tone
    (B) diversity   (E) harmony
    (C) indefiniteness

19. Glee clubs for many years were delegated to second place as high school musical organizations in that

    (A) the quality of performance was poor
    (B) the band was more flashy
    (C) the chorus had all the good singers
    (D) no credit was given
    (E) it had a social emphasis

20. Theory courses for high school students should be planned around four of these principles. Which one does *not* necessarily apply?

    (A) Theory should be functional.
    (B) Creative composition work should be required.
    (C) Eye and ear training should be coordinated.
    (D) Music should be esthetically satisfying.
    (E) Musical terminology should be studied.

Answers

1. B	5. D	9. E	13. C	17. C
2. D	6. A	10. A	14. E	18. C
3. C	7. C	11. B	15. E	19. A
4. E	8. B	12. D	16. C	20. B

PHYSICAL EDUCATION

Physical Education

Practice Test

DIRECTIONS: Select the *best* answer from the five possible choices.

1. In ancient Greece, physical education was principally

    (A) used as general education
    (B) used for war preparation
    (C) a minor subject
    (D) for men only
    (E) used to teach discipline

2. The need for activity is basic to human development. However, the pattern of behavior demonstrated by the adolescent differs from that of the child because of

    (A) age
    (B) maturation
    (C) socialization
    (D) none of these
    (E) all of these

3. The child demonstrates his first rapid growth from

    (A) puberty to age 15
    (B) age 10 to 12
    (C) age 2 to 6
    (D) birth to 6
    (E) 6 months to 2 years

4. Differences in the maturation rate of American boys and girls must be considered by the physical education teacher when planning activities. Studies of children show that

    (A) American girls reach pubescence at age 12-14
    (B) American boys reach pubescence at 11-13
    (C) late-maturing girls show variation if the 6th and 7th grades
    (D) the early-maturing boy has a shrill voice
    (E) children in the same class will have little difference in height after grade 7

5. Coeducational team sports and competitive games are undesirable during pubescence because

    (A) boys do not like them
    (B) girls are self conscious
    (C) girls like the boys too much
    (D) girls tend to be taller and heavier than boys at this age
    (E) girls may be too easily injured

6. If sports were utilized in the school for student development according to Sheldon's somatotyping, basketball teams would be mostly composed of

    (A) mesormorphs
    (B) endomorphs
    (C) ectomorphs
    (D) none of these
    (E) either (A) or (B)

229

PART 4: TEACHING AREA EXAMINATIONS

7. When planning a program for individual differences, the physical education teacher is cautioned to

   (A) observe sexual differences
   (B) be aware that differences within a sex may be greater than between sexes
   (C) girls and boys should be pitted for endurance contests
   (D) girls have structual advantages for movement
   (E) masculinity and feminity can be evaluated by structure

   7. [A] [B] [C] [D] [E]

8. Many similarities and differences occur among the sexes. All *except one* of these statements are medically true:

   (A) Muscular strength is related to size.
   (B) The putuitary gland in women is larger than in men.
   (C) Women have a more rapid calcium metabolic rate than men.
   (D) It is not known which came first–function or structure.
   (E) Men have less endurance than women during exercise.

   8. [A] [B] [C] [D] [E]

9. One of these statements about physical fitness is not true. Select the *incorrect* statement.

   (A) One of the easiest to administer tests for heart recovery rate is the Harvard Step Test
   (B) There is little difference in endurance between the fit and unfit.
   (C) Physical fitness is an objective rather than a standard.
   (D) Physical fitness is a by-product of the physical education program
   (E) Fitness can be lost quickly without exercise.

   9. [A] [B] [C] [D] [E]

10. Fatigue has a number of causes. One of these is *not* a cause related to physical activity:

    (A) Fatigue can be induced by boredom.
    (B) Fatigue may become chronic.
    (C) Fatigue normally follows strenuous activity.
    (D) Fatigue is a natural condition (barring physiological changes).
    (E) Players often reach a state of complete exhaustion

    10. [A] [B] [C] [D] [E]

11. Physical education courses often emphasize posture improvement. When planning work with students who need assistance, the teacher should realize that

    (A) a diagnosis of need must first be made
    (B) great benefit is derived from general posture exercises
    (C) little change in body configuration is brought about by lordosis
    (D) mass exercises accomplish more than individual exercises
    (E) good results can be achieved from body mechanics courses

    11. [A] [B] [C] [D] [E]

12. The risk of injury is lessened when

    (A) good mechanical principles are used in movement patterns
    (B) distributed practice is used
    (C) a long warm-up period is used

PHYSICAL EDUCATION

    (D) speed is greater than skill
    (E) human behavior is controlled

13. The competitive nature of many physical education programs would make them weak in all *except* one of the following:

    (A) developing individual sports
    (B) encouraging leisure time physical activity
    (C) requiring individualism
    (D) developing team loyalty and school spirit
    (E) demonstrating non-conformity

14. The transfer of learning is of considerable concern to all teachers. Physical education skills will transfer if four of these conditions are met. Which one does *not* apply?

    (A) The more similar two conditions are, the more likely transfer will take place.
    (B) Student understanding of the skill aids transfer.
    (C) Skills transfer automatically during childhood.
    (D) Meaningful teaching helps students identify values.
    (E) Intelligence is related to transfer.

15. Eye-hand coordination shows rapid improvement for many children at the age of

    (A) 4 or 5   (D) 9 or 10
    (B) 5 or 6   (E) 14 or 15
    (C) 7 or 8

16. The physical education teacher has to use a variety of procedures to facilitate learning. The nature of the presentation should consider the following facts about skill learning. One of these statements is incorrect.

    (A) Skills should be taught by the unit idea of pattern.
    (B) Skill patterns should be taught by component parts.
    (C) Learning is based upon sensory perception of structure.
    (D) Demonstration is successful for most learners.
    (E) The learning curve usually shows a spurt of progress, then a leveling off of performance.

17. Practice has the following qualifications. Select the incorrect statement.

    (A) Hockey can be learned from the goalie position.
    (B) Drills assist all students in participation.
    (C) Practice periods are governed by the span of attention.
    (D) Short, frequent practice periods get the best results.
    (E) Mental practice is effective at advanced levels.

18. Physical education at the first grade level usually involves three types of activities. Which activity would *not* be appropriate for this age group?

(A) story plays
(B) hunting games
(C) active games
(D) dance activities
(E) relay races

18. [A] [B] [C] [D] [E]

19. Simple athletic games can be taught as early as the

(A) 1st grade
(B) 2nd grade
(C) 3rd grade
(D) 4th grade
(E) 5th grade

19. [A] [B] [C] [D] [E]

20. One of the main difficulties in planning a curriculum for physical education is

(A) scheduling the courses
(B) including health units
(C) including recreational skills
(D) using progression with minimum repetition
(E) individualizing instruction

20. [A] [B] [C] [D] [E]

Answers

1. B	5. D	9. B	13. D	17. A
2. E	6. C	10. E	14. C	18. E
3. D	7. B	11. A	15. C	19. C
4. C	8. C	12. A	16. A	20. D

Social Studies

Practice Test

DIRECTIONS: Select the *best* answer from the five possible choices.

1. While the cognitive objectives for the social studies have been strengthened, an erosion of affective objectives is occuring. All *except one* of these is a cause for the changing approach to affective objectives:

   (A) interests, and attitudes develop slowly
   (B) cognitive attainments can be more easily evaluated
   (C) certain cognitive behaviors may destroy certain affective behaviors
   (D) experiences do not always produce desired changes
   (E) indoctrination involves both cognitive and affective behaviors

   1. [A] [B] [C] [D] [E]

2. The role of citizenship training in the social studies curriculum was publicized through the American Heritage Foundation with its projects located at

   (A) Columbia University
   (B) Georgetown University
   (C) Tufts University

SOCIAL STUDIES

    (D) The University of Michigan
    (E) Detroit

2. [A] [B] [C] [D] [E]

3. Gordon Allport asserts that a person's political behavior is

    (A) completely imitative
    (B) largely affective in nature
    (C) indistinguishable from his personality as a whole
    (D) based on adolescent experiences
    (E) controlled by the family

3. [A] [B] [C] [D] [E]

4. The importance of structure in the continuity of learning is basic to the design of the the curriculum according to

    (A) Thorndike
    (B) Dewey
    (C) Wesley
    (D) Hartshorne
    (E) Bruner

4. [A] [B] [C] [D] [E]

5. The nature of intuitive thinking makes it possible for an individual to do all *except one* of these:

    (A) develop a step at a time approach
    (B) solve scientific problems
    (C) do without analytic thinking initially
    (D) utilize the complementary nature of intuitive and analytic thinking
    (E) achieve a solution without formal proof

5. [A] [B] [C] [D] [E]

6. The student of history learns how the historian decides what is fact and what is not. Historians disagree regarding facts because of their

    (A) methods
    (B) hypothesis
    (C) background
    (D) frame of reference
    (E) understanding of history

6. [A] [B] [C] [D] [E]

7. When serving individual differences, all *except one* of these statements would apply:

    (A) plan specific individual programs
    (B) use 15 to 20 minute modules
    (C) schedule classes four days a week
    (D) use the "back-to-back" arrangement
    (E) all teachers should give enrichment materials

7. [A] [B] [C] [D] [E]

PART 4: TEACHING AREA EXAMINATIONS

8. Inductive-teaching techniques require

    (A) standard froms of lesson plans
    (B) a body of facts and genralizations
    (C) the lecture method
    (D) general goals
    (E) planned teaching strategy

9. Major unit objectives which would be classified under *affective* learning would be one of the following:

    (A) knowledge of terminology
    (B) knowledge of methodology
    (C) preference for values
    (D) establishing any hypothesis
    (E) evaluating internal evidence

10. Teaching high school students about socialism has complex problems because

    (A) students assume they have accurate information
    (B) the school board will not approve
    (C) it is above their heads
    (D) this is only for adults
    (E) parents will disapprove

11. Students should be taught proper note-taking for all *except one* of the following reasons:

    (A) note-taking is a tool for social studies understanding
    (B) notes aid thinking and analysis
    (C) verbatim copying aids thinking
    (D) note-taking saves study time
    (E) students translate reading facts into their own words

12. The social scientist frequently uses the sample survey to gather evidence. One requirement of the sample survey which is fundamental is:

    (A) it has a research design
    (B) it must be random
    (C) it should be wrighted
    (D) it must be representative
    (E) conclusions must be drawn about the "population" as well as the sample

13. Essay testing is a controversial subject because of all *except one* of these:

    (A) teachers do not agree on its value
    (B) reading and writing support each other